ENDORSEMENTS

'Through building and leading Discovery, Adrian has demonstrated how disciplined leadership, innovation, and long-term optimism can create enduring value. This book brings together the principles that underpin that success'

Larry Fink, Chairman and Chief Executive Officer, BlackRock

'Building at scale requires understanding how time, goals, and optimism interact to create momentum. Adrian's *The Four Principles* offers both evidence and inspiration for leaders seeking to create outsized impact in their institutions and our society'

Ruth Porat, President and Chief Investment Officer, Alphabet and Google

'Most of us think we're making decisions based on logic but as Adrian deftly shows in this book, we're often not and we need to overcome our instincts.

What I like about this book is that it doesn't try to overwhelm you with ideas. It simplifies things in a way that actually makes you pause and rethink how you move through the world.

Adrian lays out a framework that feels practical and optimistic and at times even uncomfortably true.

It's not about being smarter or working harder. It's about seeing differently and realizing that a few decisions, made well, can change everything'

Trevor Noah, Comedian, Author, Political Commentator and TV Host

'*The Four Principles* takes the reader on a journey well beyond the significant industry transformation that Adrian has led. It's an examination of overcoming obstacles that applies not only to leaders, but to anyone interested in maximizing their human potential'

Jeff Williams, Former Chief Operating Officer, Apple

'This book's thought-provoking principles draw on extensive behavioural science and economic theory to set out a framework for success in the modern age. Important reading for those aspiring to leadership or seeking to make an impact on the world'

Lord William Hague, Chancellor, University of Oxford; Former UK Foreign Secretary

'Leading in the Ryder Cup has taught me that performance isn't linear – a few key moments, decisions and beliefs can determine everything. Adrian's Four Principles capture that reality with real clarity. Disciplined optimism shapes what you see, focused urgency drives when you act, declared goals align a team, and the ability to recognize the moments that matter most is what ultimately separates good from great. This book is a compelling framework for turning potential into meaningful, lasting impact'

Luke Donald, European Ryder Cup Captain; Former World No. 1 Golfer

'Leading modern institutions demands constantly navigating complexity, uncertainty and ambiguity. With this as context, I have seen first-hand how Adrian's disciplined focus and clear application of core principles has compounded over time to deliver sustained and significant success. *The Four Principles* distils decades of leadership and insight into a practical framework that explains what matters – and why. Thoughtfully, grounded in science, experience and rigorous thinking, it offers a valuable guide and practical framework for effective leadership and lasting positive impact'

Sir Mark Tucker, Chairman, AIA Group

'Adrian has demonstrated the impact of the Four Principles in an extraordinary way through his successful business – which is built on the Principles, and through his broader leadership in society at large. A terrific book by a terrific leader. I learned a huge amount from reading it'

Dominic Barton, Former Global Managing Director, McKinsey & Company; Chairman, Rio Tinto

'Adrian's visionary leadership and scientific rigour have reshaped an entire industry, exemplifying how business can drive meaningful social good while achieving global excellence – a story that deserves to be widely heard'

Colm Kelleher, Chairman, UBS

'We're all working with a brain that wasn't built for the modern world. *The Four Principles* shows, with both rigour and clarity, how our built-in biases quietly limit what we see, decide, and achieve – and, more importantly, how we can overcome them to make a much bigger difference than we thought possible. Precise, timely, and genuinely hopeful'

Matthew Walker, Professor of Neuroscience and Psychology, University of California, Berkeley, Best-selling Author of *Why We Sleep*

'I still enjoy the immense privilege of serving or advising on boards chaired and driven by Adrian. For well over a decade, I have witnessed first-hand every principle and its underpinning that are espoused in *The Four Principles*. That Adrian has committed these nostrums to paper and generations of future leaders is characteristically generous. That he understands that genuine leadership is a synthesis of art and science is his towering legacy'

Lord Sebastian Coe, President, World Athletics,
Olympic Gold Medallist

'Adrian, founder and CEO of Discovery Group and architect of the globally recognized Vitality model, brings decades of experience and entrepreneurial wisdom to *The Four Principles: Multiply Your Impact in Life and Leadership* – a concise, powerful playbook for enhancing your opportunity to achieve extraordinary results in business and in life.

Gore's central argument is that exceptional impact is not the exclusive province of rare talent, but of people who consistently apply the right principles with discipline and focus. (Pareto Tail is perhaps the book's most provocative insight: a handful of pivotal decisions account for a disproportionate share of all outcomes, meaning that strategic optimization – not effort or talent alone – is the true differentiator between those who plateau and those who leave a lasting legacy.) Grounded in real-world experience, *The Four Principles* is an indispensable guide for all of us as leaders and individuals who want to make the most of our time on earth'

Margery Kraus, Founder and Executive Chair, APCO

'Many talented people can get lost in their potential. This book provides a framework for turning that potential into impact. While all Four Principles are rules to compose a life by, the Pareto Tail is the differentiator that reminds each of us that we compose our lives every single day by just a few big and small decisions that can reshape our own lives but also the lives of others. Having run operations all around the world, the multiplier effect of these principles is that they transcend culture, geography and all walks of life'

Jean Baderschneider, Chair and Founding CEO, Global Fund to End Modern Slavery, Non-Executive Director, Fortescue Limited

'Great ideas are often born on the periphery. The first mRNA vaccine came from a Turkish immigrant in Germany; the first global AI powerhouse from a Londoner of Greek-Singaporean origin. In 1992, amidst South Africa's greatest moment of uncertainty, Adrian Gore applied that same "outsider" courage to healthcare – founding an insurer that would become a partner in human longevity. Read this book to delight in his story. Read it to realize your own potential'

Sebastian Mallaby, Journalist, Economist and Author of *The Infinity Machine: Demis Hassabis, DeepMind and the Quest for Superintelligence*

THE FOUR PRINCIPLES

MULTIPLY YOUR IMPACT IN LIFE AND LEADERSHIP

Adrian Gore is the founder and CEO of The Discovery Group, a global financial services organization that serves over 50 million customers across 37 countries (including VitalityHealth in the UK). He is the architect of the revolutionary Vitality Shared-Value model, a system that fundamentally links better health outcomes to economic rewards and is taught as a case study at Harvard Business School. Gore built the company from the ground up in South Africa during a period of intense political and social upheaval, demonstrating the courage and optimism required to pursue disruptive ideas against a backdrop of uncertainty.

David Cohen (writer-collaborator) is an award-winning author and journalist. Based in London, he is the co-founder of the *Evening Standard* Dispossessed Fund, which has raised over £65 million for charities tackling poverty, inequality and social exclusion. His first book, *Chasing the Red, White and Blue* (2001), won the Jenny Crwys-Williams Prize for Book of the Year and his second book, *People Who Have Stolen from Me* (2004), was a number one bestseller in South Africa. In the UK, he has won journalism awards for his investigative and campaigning work on the *London Evening Standard*, including the Paul Foot Award, the Cudlipp Award, the Edgar Wallace Award and several British Press Society of Editors awards. He has also been published in *The Guardian*, *The New York Times* and *The Independent*. He is a former investment banker and a Harkness Fellow, and, like Adrian, a keen runner.

ADRIAN GORE

THE FOUR PRINCIPLES

MULTIPLY YOUR IMPACT IN LIFE AND LEADERSHIP

MACMILLAN BUSINESS

First published 2026 by Macmillan Business
an imprint of Pan Macmillan
The Smithson, 6 Briset Street, London EC1M 5NR
EU representative: Macmillan Publishers Ireland Ltd, 1st Floor,
The Liffey Trust Centre, 117–126 Sheriff Street Upper,
Dublin 1 D01 YC43
Associated companies throughout the world

ISBN 978-1-0350-7647-5 HB
ISBN 978-1-0350-7648-2 TPB

1 3 5 7 9 8 6 4 2

A CIP catalogue record for this book is available from the British Library.

Typeset in Adobe Caslon Pro by Palimpsest Book Production Ltd, Falkirk, Stirlingshire
Printed and bound in the UK using 100% Renewable Electricity by CPI Group (UK) Ltd

MIX
Paper | Supporting
responsible forestry
FSC www.fsc.org FSC® C116313

For my wife Lauren, and my children, Sarah, Rebecca, Jake and Gabriel. For you – and inspired by you – you have given me more than I can ever give back.

CONTENTS

INTRODUCTION

There are Four Principles that I consider fundamental to maximize our human potential. When combined, their impact creates a powerful multiplying effect on our life and work. That is why I am writing this book. First, let me tell you how I got to this point.

My story begins in the insurance industry, which may sound staid and institutional, but bear with me.

It was 1987 and I remember it like it was yesterday. I was twenty-two years old and had just joined Liberty Life – then the Goldman Sachs of South Africa. I had started in the newly formed product development department after my friend and fellow student Barry Swartzberg convinced me of the opportunity.

Soon after, Herschel Mayers, my manager, invited Barry and me to lunch at a local steakhouse. Both of us were still studying to qualify as actuaries, a gruelling seven-year process that applies mathematics to finance and insurance to assess risk. It attracted the brightest talent, and we were precociously ambitious go-getters setting out to conquer the world.

'Why,' Herschel asked, 'do ideas for new products have to start at the top? Why don't you guys come up with some of your own?'

In his question, I sensed both exasperation and encouragement.

In those days, the best graduates sought jobs in big business, and in my world, nobody was bigger than Liberty. Sir Donald Gordon, its legendary founder, was a God-like figure. But Liberty was also rigidly hierarchical. I reported to my manager, who reported up the chain to a director, and things were done in a particular way – 'the Liberty way' – that had not changed in years. So, although Barry and I thought we were 'masters of the universe', and although product development was the department where the real action was, we were also very clearly at the bottom of the pile.

Nevertheless, when I left the office that day, my mind was ticking. I had been given permission to influence the organization – and that feeling of agency was exhilarating.

After a few years of working on improving different products, I came up with an idea that I knew was a potential game-changer.

In the late eighties, South Africa's insurance industry was dominated by not-for-profit mutual insurers that offered both life insurance and health insurance, the latter through generous 'medical aid schemes' that provided near-complete coverage for healthcare expenses, but only for a small, privileged group: the white, employed, higher-income population. With medical costs fully reimbursed, healthcare consumption of this group had surged, leading to incredibly high rates of medical inflation, placing significant financial strain on the system. I knew that with government reforms on the horizon and an urgent need to address deep health disparities, the model would no longer be sustainable.

I conceived of a completely new kind of health insurance product, which we called 'Medical Lifestyle', designed as a complementary top-up to the existing not-for-profit sickness funds that were the primary form of health insurance at that time. It focused on covering major, high-cost health events while leaving routine, day-to-day care to the established medical aid schemes.

The product was innovative because it applied sophisticated actuarial principles to a sector that had been run on the basic pooling of funds with poor financial controls. Also, its focus on providing comprehensive coverage for major medical expenses ensured that it didn't run out of benefits when people were very sick, which existing products tended to do – forcing sick people to self-fund large gaps in coverage. The financial structures and actuarial techniques required to achieve this took years of sustained work and would have a transforming effect on the industry.

As we approached the launch date, there was increasing excitement and anticipation. Liberty had planned a massive rollout across the country to be spearheaded from Johannesburg. Thousands of financial advisers and intermediaries were expected to attend – it was going to be a real point of inflection. Names and careers were made by those who appeared at these launches and by how they performed.

Picking my moment, I said to Herschel, 'I want to present this.'

'No,' he said. 'That's my role.'

Given the company's hierarchical structure, his response was standard for such an audacious request. But I already had experience in resisting the hierarchy. At Liberty, new actuaries were rotated through various departments – a routine and rational approach to ensuring broad exposure. However, when it came time for me to move to a three-month stint in underwriting, I had flatly refused. I knew in my gut that product development was not only interesting but also a quicker route to the top. They were not used to such resistance.

Eventually, tiring of my stubborn attitude, they sent people to physically pick up and relocate my desk to underwriting. I still refused to budge and insisted: 'I'm staying in product development.'

Seeing I was unshakeable, they relented and moved my desk back.

Buoyed by this memory, I approached Herschel again. 'Look, I developed the product. I'm asking you – let me present it.' This time, he agreed. It was a magnanimous gesture, and it spoke volumes about his leadership style, friendship and belief in me.

That launch, in front of 5,000 key influencers, was my breakthrough. The product became highly successful, and it positioned me in a completely different realm, giving me a profile within Liberty way beyond my station.

At twenty-six, I was the young protégé in Liberty's hottest team. The company was writing massive amounts of new health insurance business. The company's share price was incredibly buoyant. My future within Liberty was golden and assured.

That was when I decided to leave the company and build an insurance company of my own.

I knew that I wanted to build something from the ground up. I had experienced the remarkable impact an institution of Liberty's scale could have on society, and in an emerging new South Africa, I wanted to build a different health insurance company – not just a product range, but a brilliant institution that would have a substantial impact on our country and hopefully beyond. I was driven by an uncanny sense of urgency, a feeling that I needed to act now. This sense of urgency, as you will see, is an important part of my story and this book.

To fully grasp the craziness of this idea, you need to understand the times we lived in, and that no major insurer had launched in decades.

It was 1992, a moment of dramatic political, economic and social transformation in South Africa, as the country transitioned from apartheid to democracy. Nelson Mandela had already been released after twenty-seven years of imprisonment, but we were still two years from democratic elections and the country's direction was far from certain. In March 1992, then-president F. W. de Klerk held a referendum in which white South Africans voted in favour of continuing negotiations to end apartheid. There was a huge amount of political violence and instability across the country, with brutal clashes between supporters of the Zulu nationalist

Inkatha Freedom Party (IFP) and Mandela's African National Congress (ANC), creating an atmosphere of fear and uncertainty.

Our TV screens were full of deeply upsetting scenes of bloody pitched battles between the two sides. One of the worst was the Boipatong massacre, which took place in June 1992, sixty-five kilometres from my home. Armed IFP supporters attacked and killed forty-five people in the township of Boipatong, including women and children, injuring many more. The apartheid South African police force stood by and let it happen – and stories swirled that they had in fact facilitated the violence. During that period, crime and economically motivated criminal violence soared nationwide.

To many people, the idea that I would want to start a new company during such a period of instability and uncertainty, seemed completely bizarre. To add to the peril, there were no actual health insurance companies, only life insurers and medical aid schemes, and, as I have mentioned, no major new insurer had launched in decades.

But times of danger are also times of opportunity. In such moments, people are fearful, assets are underpriced and the competition is distracted.

Besides, I was not consumed by the generalized anxiety and fear around me. I saw a profoundly attractive business opportunity to create a new type of health insurance model that I believed people would want – one that would disrupt the tired, traditional model. I was infused with self-belief and an optimism that I could make a success of the opportunity I had identified – and an urgency to get started as soon as possible. And what's more, I thought we would have a relatively free run at it.

The immediate challenges were to get regulatory approval and to raise the necessary capital. Regulatory approval was a tough process due to the institutional nature of the business and the capital required was significant.

I had heard through a friend who worked at Rand Merchant Bank that the bank owned a dormant life insurance license called Magnum Life, and that they were looking for ideas on what to do with it. I thought that if we could use Magnum Life as our launch vehicle, and get Rand Merchant Bank to fund us, we could kill two birds with one stone.

When I met their co-founder and CEO, Laurie Dippenaar, I had no traditional business plan to speak of – no projections, no capital plan, no defined product idea.

My pitch to Laurie was instead all about the emerging environment post-apartheid, what would happen to the demand for healthcare, and how it would need to be funded. And – crucially – the opportunity to build a pure health insurance company based on sound values and hiring the best people.

Underlying my vision for the new business was a powerful sense of purpose. I have always been struck by what Walt Disney said when asked about Disney's purpose: 'To make people happy.' Maybe I was channelling Walt, but I, too, wrote down our purpose: 'To make people healthier.'

I was incredibly lucky to have approached Laurie. He immediately got and shared my vision and commitment to build a company of unique purpose and quality.

Rand Merchant Bank went on to invest an initial R10 million – then the equivalent of just over £2 million, and today, adjusting for inflation, close to £5 million – and this funding, along with their strategic and back-office support, gave me lift-off.

When I launched, my day-one message to myself was: 'Find some products.' Ironically, I had a deep conviction about the business opportunity, but no specific products in mind. I still have that original piece of paper – now framed up in my office – to remind me of how it all began.

I recruited Barry Swartzberg, my former colleague at Liberty, who would become my co-founder at Discovery. The two of us set out to change the world of health insurance, starting in South Africa.

It was, certainly to others, an act of pure and outrageous optimism.

Yet to me, it wasn't that outrageous at all. It was, instead, the most rational strategy. My optimism had given me a tactical advantage – the ability to see clearly, take risks, and not be paralyzed by the prevailing headwinds of fear that left protagonists distracted and unable to act.

By the time of publishing in 2026, Discovery has grown from a company with one employee and no products into a global insurance and financial services group, serving over 50 million customers in 37 countries, employing more than 15,000 people, and with revenue exceeding £3 billion.

We did this by reimagining health insurance – from simply paying for people's medical expenses to actively incentivizing people to be healthy – and calling it Vitality. It began with discounted access to gyms and morphed into a globally applicable and differentiated economic model for insurance based on behavioural science. At the time, the shift from passive insurer to active partner in a customer's wellbeing was unique.

The Vitality model proved popular and repeatable, enabling our expansion into health and life insurance globally. We also applied it to disrupt other financial sectors – including banking and motor insurance. This led to groundbreaking partnerships – such as our collaboration with Apple, which allows customers to get free Apple Watches, earned through exercise.

It also became an exemplar of what is now known as the Shared-Value model – and I have had the privilege, as a guest instructor, of watching Michael Porter teach the Vitality case study at Harvard Business School as an example of how to create simultaneous value for companies, customers and society. It came at just the right time – as capitalism was seeking to create a broader base of winners than just shareholders. And behind it all was some very smart theory – requiring the coalescing of actuarial science, medicine, technology, data science and behavioural science.

As the company globalized, we had to navigate the challenge of integrating our model into some of the most sophisticated healthcare systems in the world, underscored by demanding regulatory environments and geopolitical dynamics and change.

Through this, our business grew and thrived.

That leads me to the impetus for this book. The success of Discovery is due to the talent and hard work of many brilliant people. Throughout the evolution of Discovery, and my personal journey, I have observed the incredible ability of certain people to do amazing things – to grow, keep learning, keep succeeding. A business growing organically at the pace we have challenges people to grow at the same rate. Some people can, others cannot, and I became obsessed with trying to understand this.

I can trace this obsession back to a seemingly unimportant conference I attended in Palm Beach, Florida, five years after the launch of Discovery. It was a gathering of global entrepreneurs that covered many topics, but the session that changed my thinking was one led by a publication, *Investor's Business Daily*, on what they called 'Attributes of Success'. They presented research into what makes people impactful, showing that although successful entrepreneurs came in all shapes, sizes, ethnicities, levels of education and intelligence, they all shared just a few common attributes.

That session lit a fire in me because, as I said, I have always been fixated on the performance and impact of people, and because we have built our organization on a commitment, as stated in our values, to 'liberate the best in our people'. In short, a belief that each of us has the potential to achieve things way beyond what we could ever have imagined or expected.

My insight at that conference was that if just a few attributes drive success and impact, there is the possibility to understand them and help people to develop them at scale. My journey over the next three decades gave me the opportunity to observe whether the hypothesis at that conference was, in fact, correct.

First, scaling our organization from a start-up through organic growth to over 15,000 people globally has exposed me to – and given me the opportunity to work with – the smartest people from different backgrounds, cultures and geographies. Second, I have had the opportunity to work with, observe and learn from some of the best business leaders in the world, and discover what makes them effective. Finally, but critically, we have built our business from within South Africa, a country with a hugely troubled history of apartheid, a multifaceted journey into democracy, and a country with tremendous promise but with unique challenges of inequality, poverty, crime, corruption and joblessness. Leading in this context has required motivating people through incredibly intense periods of hope followed by despair and finding ways we could lean in and help build, not undermine, our country.

The central question I have sought to ask is this: why do people, regardless of their underlying ability, have such dramatic and vastly different levels of impact in their lives, as leaders, in building and scaling businesses, and in affecting society?

The answer cannot be based on talent and ability alone, but rather on how it is applied. For any given set of talents, impact is achieved through four dimensions. First, the scale of our ambitions and the motivation to achieve them; second, within this context, our ability to identify opportunities and to execute on them; and third, how much time we have to do this. The fourth dimension is a consequence of the other three: the decisions and actions we actually take. This is how the rubber hits the road and it determines the actual impact we will have in life and leadership.

The problem is that each of these dimensions requires optimization – we lack the necessary motivation and drive, we are bombarded by challenges and opportunities seem scarce, and time seems to pass by too quickly.

Central to overcoming these challenges and maximizing our impact is understanding that we are genetically miscoded for the context and dynamics in which we live.

We evolved on the savannah, where survival hinged on responding to immediate, physical threats and managing scarce resources. But today, in the wake of the agricultural, industrial and now digital revolutions, the challenges we face have shifted dramatically. Scarcity has given way to overconsumption and waste. Physical dangers have been replaced by systemic ones: risks to the orderly functioning of increasingly complex systems, including healthcare, education, governance and the economy.

Additionally, we have moved from simple, linear clan environments – where actions and consequences were proportional and tightly linked in time and space, so if you hunted more, you ate more – to a fast-moving, interconnected world. Yet evolution hasn't kept pace. After two million years as hunter-gatherers, the last 12,000 years – though radically transformative – have been too brief for our brains to catch up. This is profoundly problematic: the instincts that once kept us alive – our negativity bias and linear thinking – now often mislead us. What feels rational is frequently maladaptive, undermining our ability to succeed, achieve happiness and make an impact.

Our cognitive operating system needs a reset.

This is where the Four Principles come in – each of them describing the central tactics needed within each dimension of impact to remedy our miscoding. In brief, the Four Principles are as follows:

The First Principle: Disciplined Optimism

We are coded to seek out negative signals and think pessimism is sophisticated and rational, but it isn't. It is disciplined optimism that enables us to counter these natural instincts to see positive signals as well, to identify opportunities we would ordinarily miss, and to execute on them in the complex networked world in which we live.

The Second Principle: Focused Urgency

Life is much shorter than we think because of the way time is experienced – we have just 20 per cent of our life to make an impact and leave a legacy, and we need to pursue the important, with focus and urgency.

The Third Principle: Declared Goals

When we set goals and declare them to make them visible, either personally or publicly, we create something to lose. This has a multiplicative impact on our motivation because potential loss motivates more than potential gain. That's why setting goals isn't childlike or mundane – but crucial for impact.

The Fourth Principle: The Pareto Tail

Only a few decisions and actions determine the impact of our lives. This is because our lives are governed by the Pareto principle, also known as the 80:20 rule, which explains how a small number of causes generate a disproportionately large share of the effects, and in which actions in the 'Pareto tail' determine our impact.

They are principles because of their key properties. Each of the Four Principles is:

- *Fundamental* – because they underpin the common attributes of successful people and lead to profoundly different life outcomes if pursued. Importantly, success is not necessarily defined as achieving material wealth, but rather by what a person seeks to achieve: financial, societal, charitable, physical, political.

- *Counter-intuitive* – because they fly in the face of what we perceive as common sense. They also appear simplistic, but they are not, so while we think we understand them, we do the opposite. Thanks to our miscoding, tactics that appear basic are the opposite, and vice versa. This is exciting, both intellectually and practically. Once revealed, their truth and relevance are difficult to unsee.

- *Demonstrably exponential in impact* – they are grounded in various fields of science, and scientific laws and theories, particularly prospect theory and loss aversion, and network theory – as descriptive frameworks to explain our negativity and linear thinking biases and the cost thereof. This gives weight to each Principle, lifting them above fluffy, subjective opinion. It also enables a proper evaluation of the multiplicative nature of each Principle on an individual's impact, and the exponential combined effect of all Four Principles.

Putting numbers to ideas imposes discipline. It requires first articulating a theoretical model of how a phenomenon works, then testing whether the evidence coheres around that framework. Once established, the model helps us understand dynamics, make better predictions and bring greater objectivity to decision-making.

This is more than a technique – it is a worldview that underpins how we run our business and complements intuitive decision-making in life. For each Principle in this book, we propose a theoretical framework and match it with empirical evidence. The examples show that the supporting evidence is extensive and robust enough to estimate the approximate quantitative impact of applying each Principle. This allows us to derive a multiplier that illustrates both the validity and the order of magnitude of the effect – while keeping in mind statistician George Box's famous forecasting caveat: 'All models are wrong, but some are useful.'[1]

Accordingly, at the end of each chapter we highlight the approximate numerical impact of applying that Principle, with a brief explanation. What matters most is not the exact size of the effect, but the realization that these Principles can be transformative – and that their impact is multiplicative. Disciplined Optimism can increase impact by roughly six times, Focused Urgency by two times, and Declared Goals by two times. Applied together, their combined effect is substantial. This helps explain why many people operate far below their potential, and why focusing on a few high-leverage principles can produce Pareto-like outcomes in our lives.

For readers who want more depth and are technically inclined, each chapter links to an appendix covering the underlying mathematics and science. This material is optional and not in any way required to grasp the core ideas.

What is hugely exciting, and what motivated me to write this book, is that the Four Principles are teachable and learnable – and can be passed on to others.

I deal with each Principle in a separate chapter in a specifically chosen sequence: Disciplined Optimism, Focused Urgency and Declared Goals, with the Pareto tail sitting at the end as the powerful phenomenon that flows from the application of the other three Principles. Importantly, the concepts themselves are well established, but I have applied them in a new way that demonstrates their impact in life and leadership.

These ideas about leadership were reinforced by one of the most inspiring encounters of my career – with Nelson Mandela. I went to visit him at his home in Houghton, Johannesburg, in the mid-nineties, when he was still president. It was a meeting with no fixed agenda, but it came at a time when Discovery was beginning to scale rapidly, and I was hoping to present our credentials to him and ask him about his vision for our country. He had turned our nation around post-1994 and had galvanized people to come together in an extraordinary way, and I wanted to understand something about his magic in achieving that and to ask him about the power of forgiving after the incredible sacrifices he had made.

What I took away from that meeting and have never forgotten, was a vision for how I could give, how I could contribute. That was part of the brilliance of Mandela, turning the spotlight back on whoever he was speaking with, asking them to ask more of themselves. He mainly spoke about leadership, and as a young leader of a new business, this resonated with me. He impressed on me that a leader's greatest responsibility – and most powerful tool – is to provide hope.

I have a deep conviction that if we can live more consciously by the Four Principles, we can unlock our potential. This isn't just about personal gain. In a networked world – where leaders govern systems and systems are interdependent – applying the Four Principles can have real, scaled significance for our families, our companies, our communities and even our countries. Therein lies hope.

THE FIRST PRINCIPLE: DISCIPLINED OPTIMISM

We are coded to seek out negative signals and think pessimism is sophisticated and rational, but it isn't. It is disciplined optimism that enables us to counter these natural instincts to see positive signals as well, to identify opportunities we would ordinarily miss, and to execute on them in the complex networked world in which we live.

Imagine a private business calling up the mayor of London or New York and saying: 'We want to help fix the city's pothole problem. And don't worry, we will fund it – it won't cost the taxpayer a penny.'

We made that call.

In Johannesburg, a city of around six million people where our business was born and where we still have our global headquarters, our roads had become riddled with potholes – and we decided to pitch in to be part of the solution.

Why would a private business spend millions to fix a public good?

Almost every major city has a pothole problem. The UK is estimated to have several million potholes in its cities, despite filling 1.4 million of them in 2023 and 1.9 million in 2024;[1] and with compensation claims to councils more than doubling since

2022.[2] British Chancellor Rachel Reeves announced an additional £500 million in her 2024 October budget to address the issue, bringing the total pledged to £1.6 billion – an amount that road safety experts still derided as a 'drop in the ocean' compared to the billions needed.[3]

In New York state, Governor Kathy Hochul declared a 'war on potholes' when elected in 2022, pledging $1 billion towards a problem that contributes close to $9 billion in annual vehicle repair bills for New Yorkers.[4]

Potholes don't just damage vehicles – they also cost lives. It is estimated that, on average, around ninety people a year are killed or seriously injured in accidents involving potholes in England and Wales. In India, potholes cause the deaths of approximately 1,800 people a year.

So, potholes are a drain on financial resources and a serious safety hazard. But it is their third impact that really interests me.

When the number of unfilled potholes passes a tipping point, they become a potent symbol of urban decline. Reeves, for example, called them, 'A visible reminder of our failure to invest as a nation.' Sometimes a pothole is more than just a pothole.

In Johannesburg, the sheer volume of potholes created a deep sense of malaise about the state of our infrastructure that had a profoundly negative impact on residents' morale.

I had my own weekly exposure to the pothole problem.

Every Sunday morning, I meet with six or seven long-time friends at a coffee shop for a catch-up and a chat. We've been doing this since we met at university forty years ago. Essentially, it is a group of old pals who get together to chew the fat and ruminate over the issues of the day.

Back in 2020, the deteriorating state of the roads had become a regular topic of conversation. Every week, someone would have a new and more dramatic pothole story to share – how it had caused them an inopportune puncture, how they had seen cars swerving dangerously to avoid one, how a pothole had even caused an accident. I knew what they were describing was real – a close friend had been hospitalized after hitting one. I also knew that pothole claims were soaring, costing our motor insurance business and the broader South African motor insurance industry millions each year.

At the same time, their stories irked me.

This was because I sensed that when they spoke about potholes, they were really talking about something else: the perceived deteriorating state of our city and country. To them, potholes were symbols – shorthand for what they saw as broader, irreversible decay. Their assumption was that the potholes could not be fixed and this married up with their assumption that the city's problems were similarly intractable.

One Sunday early in 2021, after another enervating round of pothole complaints, the thought occurred to me: what if Discovery got involved and changed the narrative by seeking to do something extraordinarily bold – fixing every pothole?

I had a deep conviction that doing so would fix more than just the road problem – shifting energy and perception – and potentially leading to a new frame for how people viewed their city and country.

It was more an emotional than a rational response to the problem, and I took this idea back to our leadership team at Discovery. A small group began to investigate: how many potholes are there? What causes them? Why is the city council struggling to keep up? What are other cities doing? What advances have been made in pothole-fixing technology? And critically, how much will it cost to fill every pothole in Johannesburg?

As context, Johannesburg is a vibrant metropolis that was founded in 1886, following the discovery of gold. It is one of the world's youngest major cities and is the country's economic and financial capital, boasting the largest stock exchange in Africa. With over six million trees, Johannesburg is also home to perhaps the world's largest man-made urban forest; has one of the largest hospitals in the southern hemisphere (the Chris Hani Baragwanath Hospital); and is near the Cradle of Humankind, a UNESCO World Heritage Site and a place of significant paleontological importance.

Once our team had secured some answers, we arranged a meeting with the then-mayor to discuss the issue. Keep in mind that in South Africa, roads are a public good and subject to regulations regarding their use and maintenance. Making changes to roads requires special dispensation from the relevant authorities.

The mayor told us he wished he could do more and talked about the multiple pressures on his budget – and that they were hundreds of millions of rand short of what was needed to fix the city's potholes. We said we knew it was a daunting task and that the expense would be substantial, but our assessment was that we could make inroads into helping him solve the problem for a lot less. We listened to the constraints he faced and offered to help pitch in at our own expense. The mayor readily agreed and we rolled up our sleeves, and, as I will describe later in this chapter, the public-private partnership that followed would go on to achieve remarkable things.

It was not the first time, nor would it be the last, that we would take on civic responsibility beyond the normal scope of our business. In 2021, we took a leadership role in helping South Africa respond to the Covid pandemic. More recently, we have been involved in supporting the government in tackling the country's electricity crisis.

Our actions are driven by our commitment to the Shared-Value model: the idea that business must generate benefit not only for shareholders but also for customers and wider society. This model, as I explain in the Fourth Principle, is part of the DNA of Discovery. But suffice it to say – if the city is healthier because there are fewer potholes, then our business is healthier because there are fewer motor insurance claims, and our customers are healthier and wealthier because there are fewer accidents.

We also believe that the private sector has a critical role to play in partnering with the public sector to tackle challenging public issues, especially in low- and middle-income countries like South Africa, where there are high levels of inequality and a mismatch in capacity, resources and skills between the public and private sectors.

These models help shape our ethics, our thinking and our actions – and, by and large, they are well received.

But beneath it all runs a core belief that motivates and drives my actions – and one for which I am often criticized.

I am widely known in South Africa, and to some extent abroad, for publicly espousing the need to seek out positive signals even, and perhaps especially, in difficult times, and when most other business leaders are openly negative and pessimistic. At dinners or international summits, I am often introduced as 'the CEO with the optimist's narrative'.

The South African context is important here. As mentioned in the introduction, South Africa's apartheid past, its high levels of poverty, inequality and unemployment, and the consequences of these forces, creates an environment where the narrative is volatile and substantially worse than reality. This creates a powerful laboratory for assessing principles and tactics for successful leadership and impact – especially with regards to attitudinal issues. Because of this, I draw substantially on my South African experiences in this chapter.

I am sometimes even called naive, but this is *the* central point – being optimistic is not naive; on the contrary, it is sophisticated and central to success and impact. The fact is we are coded to seek out negative signals, and this impedes our ability to get a balanced set of facts on which to make rational decisions, to act appropriately and to get the optimal results.

The root cause of our miscoding can be found in evolutionary biology. It argues that we are hard-wired for negativity as a core survival instinct – and that seeking out negative signals is our natural default. In fact, we are here today courtesy of our ancestors' ability to seek out negative signals – those whose genetic make-up made them less effective at doing this died off, leaving more 'pessimistic' survivors to continue the ancestral line.

We are the offspring of those early pessimists, and we continue to seek out negative cues in a modern world without even being aware of this bias. But this impedes our ability to see the full picture objectively, which can only be gleaned if we balance this negative instinct by making a conscious effort to seek out positive signals.

This leads to the First Principle: **Disciplined Optimism**. We have a default tendency to seek out negative signals and tend to think pessimism is sophisticated, but it isn't – it is concealing and limiting. It is the disciplined ability to resist our natural and primitive urges to be pessimistic that is a mark of true sophistication, and a fundamental requirement to thrive and be successful in today's interconnected world.

In this context, optimism can be defined as an outlook or attitude towards the future that is often grounded in hope and confidence in positive outcomes, not a naive sense of being happy. Seeking positive signals in an active, mindful way – the focus of this chapter – is an effective tactic to achieve a more balanced and constructive view of reality. Negativity towards the outside world, on the other hand, is the default practice of humans, not just of pessimists. The act of seeking out negative signals is the tactic that reinforces that worldview.

Why We Are Miscoded for Negativity

In 1979, Nobel laureate Daniel Kahneman and Amos Tversky introduced prospect theory as an alternative to traditional utility theory.[5] Their research found that losses loom larger than gains. They called this phenomenon 'loss aversion' – and, as we describe in full in the Third Principle, it provides the psychological and mathematical foundation for how negative information has a stronger grip on us than positive information.

Kahneman and Tversky did not explain why we are hard-wired to be loss averse. Their model was descriptive – it focused on how people behave, not why that behaviour evolved.

To explore the 'why', we can turn to evolutionary psychology, which suggests that loss aversion may have evolved as an adaptive survival mechanism.

Life on the savannah, where our human ancestors began life, was short, harsh and brutal. Take the famous 'Iceman' Ötzi, who appears to have been killed in a clash between hunting parties, or Lucy, an early human ancestor, whose remains suggest a fatal fall from a great height.

To overlook negative stimuli – such as predators, fatal infectious diseases or potentially deadly physical threats – carried a far greater risk to our survival than missing out on positive stimuli, such as opportunities or rewards. American social psychologist Roy Baumeister and his colleagues explain the cognitive tendency for negativity as follows: 'Throughout our evolutionary history, organisms that were better attuned to bad things would have been more likely to survive threats and, consequently, would have increased the probability of passing along their genes. Survival requires urgent attention to possible bad outcomes, but it is less urgent with regard to good ones. Hence, it would be adaptive to be psychologically designed to respond to bad more strongly than good.'[6]

Consider also the social dynamics of early human life. Baumeister and Mark Leary argue in a landmark 1995 paper that humans have a fundamental evolutionary drive to maintain their inclusion in social groups.[7] Being excluded from a tribe or community often led to isolation, vulnerability and death. The pain of being cast out was far more intense than the pleasure of gaining social status. In these high-stakes environments, avoiding loss – especially social loss – was often more critical than achieving gain.

Over time, as American social neuroscientists John Cacioppo and Gary Berntson argued, this bias may have been reinforced by natural selection: because the consequences of an injurious or fatal assault are more difficult to reverse than a missed opportunity, humans may have developed a propensity to react more strongly to negative rather than positive stimuli.[8]

This evolutionary coding has since been evidenced by further research across multiple domains that shows we attend to negative stimuli more quickly, remember bad events more vividly, and exhibit stronger physiological responses to negative input. Let's take each measure in turn:

- *Attention:* In visual bias tasks, people detect an angry face in a group of happy faces faster than a happy face in a group of angry faces.[9] This suggests that negative cues 'pop out' and capture our attention more readily than positive ones.

- *Memory:* Research shows that negative words are recalled more strongly than positive ones, and negative events are remembered with greater intensity and duration.[10] When asked to rate life events, people tend to give disproportionate weight to negative experiences. A single harsh criticism at work, for instance, outweighs a compliment of equal magnitude – indicating that our cognitive systems give extra emphasis to bad outcomes.

- *Physiology:* Autonomic responses – such as elevated heart rate, blood pressure, skin conductance or stress hormone levels – are consistently higher in response to negative stimuli than to positive ones.[11]

Consider the implications of this.

We are biologically wired to focus on threats, which means pessimism often outweighs optimism in how we interpret the world. This negativity bias distorts our perception of reality, darkens our expectations of the future, and fosters an inaccurate and self-defeating worldview. Its most damaging effect is that it blinds us to the positive signals and opportunities around us – including those that may be directly in front of us.

Why Seeking Out Positive Signals Is Sophisticated and Fundamental to Impact

The British philosopher John Stuart Mill recognized this veneration of pessimism over 150 years ago when he wrote: 'I have observed that not the man who hopes when others despair, but the man who despairs when others hope, is admired by a large class of persons as a sage.'[12]

Here's the message: pessimism is kneejerk, lazy and primitive. In contrast, actively seeking out positive signals and engaging in solutions is, in my view, the truly sophisticated way to tackle problems.

There are several reasons for this. First, seeking out positive signals requires conscious effort to override our default coding – demanding mindful awareness of the gap between our evolutionary instincts and the realities of the modern world.

Second, because nobody wants to be judged as naive, seeking out positive signals requires courage: a willingness to challenge the prevailing gloomy narrative.

There's an inherent contradiction in how we interpret our evolutionary wiring. Our ancestors developed two powerful survival instincts: one that tuned us to detect negative signals to protect us from threats, and another that pushed us towards instant gratification when resources like food were scarce. Yet today, we judge these instincts very differently. We admire people who resist the pull of instant gratification – such as avoiding unhealthy but tempting foods – but we rarely praise those who counter the equally strong instinct to focus on the negative.

This is well illustrated by the Stanford marshmallow experiment, a psychological study conducted by Walter Mischel in the late 1960s that explored a child's ability to delay gratification by offering them a choice between one marshmallow as an immediate reward or two marshmallows if they waited.[13] To delay gratification meant overcoming an evolutionary instinct to take the food now, because food may not be available later – a classic survivalist reflex. The experiment became famous for suggesting a correlation between delayed gratification and later life success.

This ability to resist our evolutionary coding in this case is correctly seen as sophistication because it requires discipline and gets better results. It is interesting and vexing that resisting the tendency to focus only on negative signals – and instead focusing on positive signals as well – is seen as naive.

I argue that resisting negative signals is even more sophisticated: it demands that we exercise control over subconscious cognitive responses, as opposed to conscious physical ones – eat now or later; sleep now or later.

The bottom line is that resisting primitive coding – in whatever form – requires disciplined self-mastery.

Why does it matter that our strongly held declinist narratives are wrong, and why does it matter that we should challenge them?

Because when we fail to see the world as it truly is, we risk making the wrong decisions. In short, we miss out on a host of opportunities – individually and collectively.

When pursuing impact in life and leadership, it is fundamental to be able to decide on what to pursue, and to be able to execute on that choice.

Pursuing the correct opportunity is a key skill – what business to start, what job to take, what country to live in, and so on. But this is the issue – our natural coding means that as we go through life, we are presented with hundreds of opportunities, choices and decisions to be made, but our natural coding leads us to seek out negative cues, and we tragically miss the positive opportunities that are in front of us. The central question is how many prospects around us do we actually miss?

The quantitative argument behind optimism's impact starts with human psychology: we naturally weigh negative information more heavily than positive. The work done on loss aversion by Kahneman and Tversky sheds light on the scale of this. In prospect theory, they derive a powerful curve – as depicted in the graph – illustrating how we perceive gains versus losses of equal proportions.

Prospect Theory

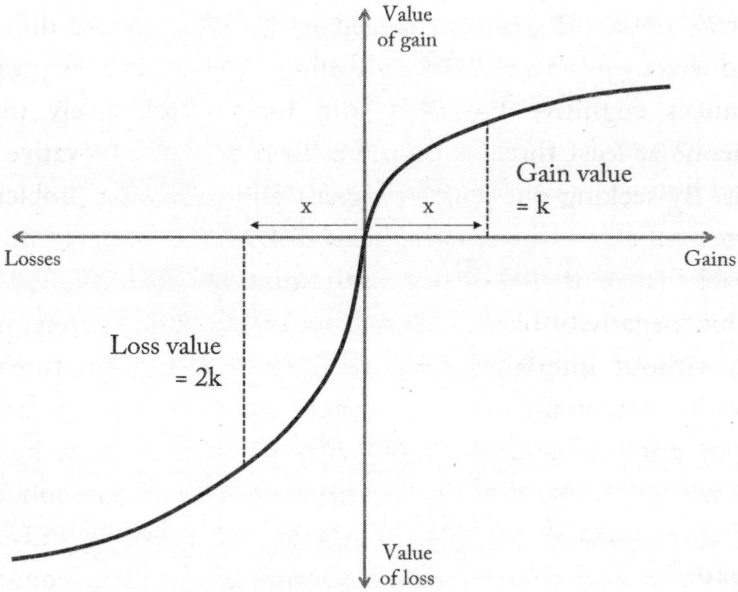

Their research shows that losses are felt roughly twice as strongly as gains of the same size – which is why the loss curve is about twice as steep as the gain curve.

In addition, an important meta-study by Baumeister and colleagues, explored the extent of negative biases – and found conclusively that negative attitudes are about twice as prevalent as positive ones, and so to influence our attitudes, positive information needs to work doubly as hard.[14]

Beyond loss aversion, the above is supported by psychologist Barbara Fredrickson and other researchers who have found that positive emotions broaden thinking.[15] Their broaden-and-build theory describes how positive emotions widen our perceptual field and thinking. In practical terms, an optimist is more likely to notice novel ideas or silver linings where a pessimist sees none.

Laboratory evidence supports this: in one study, volunteers put into a mild positive mood solved a creative problem at a much higher rate (approximately 75 per cent solved it) than those in a neutral mood (20 per cent solved it).[16] This dramatic difference – induced by just a small upbeat feeling – quantifies how positivity enhances cognitive flexibility and insight, effectively making someone at least three times more likely to find innovative solutions. By seeking out positive signals and reframing problems as opportunities, an optimist can thus discover far more avenues for impact than a neutral or negatively minded person.

This 'negativity bias', to which we're inherently prone, means that without intervention, we're likely to focus on threats or setbacks, potentially missing chances for advancement. Imagine encountering a hundred stimuli, fifty positive and fifty negative. You will readily notice all fifty negative signals, but only about half of the positive ones. The remaining twenty-five positive cues simply slip past your awareness. Optimism works by countering this bias and tuning our attention towards positive possibilities. By counteracting our built-in sensitivity to losses, optimism helps us register the positive signals we would otherwise overlook. In effect, it can double your ability to spot opportunities – including those that might be sitting right in front of you.

Consider my experience when starting out in my career. As I explained in the introduction, in a South Africa emerging from apartheid to democracy, there were so many signals and threats, from high crime rates inherited from the apartheid era and widely (if inaccurately) perceived as a 'post-apartheid crime wave',[17] to potential political instability. During this period, it was difficult to focus on the positive even though considerable societal change brings substantial opportunities.

Most people responded to the negative signals. There was an important positive signal that I responded to: the reality that healthcare would need to change and the opportunity that it presented.

The clear and strong conclusion is that optimism enables us to identify opportunities that we wouldn't ordinarily see without it. I am not suggesting we ignore bad news or negative signals – only that we are already evolutionarily attuned to those signals and need to be sophisticated and strong-minded enough to seek out positive signals as well in order to reach a balanced position, and to identify opportunities where they are present. In a complex system, this seeking out the positive to create balance is crucial.

Seeking Out Positive Signals: Identifying Opportunities and Executing on Them in a Networked World

The power of optimism is not only in enabling us to identify opportunities, but crucially, in facilitating their execution. This is a direct consequence of the deeply networked nature of the modern world.

In the world of our ancestors – a world of wild animals, physical threats, deadly infectious diseases, food scarcity, death in childbirth and average life expectancy below forty – the negative instinct was the correct one. It kept us risk-averse, vigilant and alive. In today's highly interdependent environments, however, we face entirely different threats that are largely systemic in nature – arising from failing healthcare and education systems, crumbling city infrastructures, attacks on governance, financial crises, as well as climate change, pandemics, global conflict, artificial intelligence and cyberattacks. These are complex systems. To influence or lead in these systems requires a different approach to how we evolved.

These challenges require leadership and collaboration generated by seeking out positive cues. Importantly, getting a system to work and fostering cooperation entails motivating strangers who are dispersed across time and space, not living in the same place and in the same clan. Negative feedback loops rarely drive change or progress. Systemic challenges require an affirming framework – one that sets a vision, defines goals and creates positive feedback loops.

This is the key strength and importance of optimism. A positive attitude and pro-social behaviour tend to spread through social contacts, multiplying impact.[18] Long-term studies have shown that happiness and optimism are contagious across connections. For example, a 2008 study in *The British Medical Journal* of thousands of individuals over twenty years, found that if someone becomes happier, the chance of their close contacts (friends, spouses, neighbours) becoming happier significantly rises – by about 8 per cent for spouses, 25 per cent for friends, and 34 per cent for adjacent neighbours.[19] In other words, one person's optimism measurably improves others' emotional state, which can create clusters of positivity in a community.

This matters because when people feel positive and trusting, they share information and cooperate more readily. Information and ideas flow faster in a positive network, and opportunities that one person spots can quickly propagate to others.[20]

There's also a collaborative ripple effect: research on cooperative behaviour found that one act of kindness or generosity can inspire others to pay it forward, cascading through multiple degrees of separation. In a controlled experiment, a single altruistic contribution to a group resulted in others contributing three times as much collectively in subsequent rounds – effectively tripling the impact of that initial positive act through chain-reaction cooperation.[21]

Take modern-day organizations. Starting a business involves an intricate process of managing many stakeholders and networks – shareholders, regulators, employees, customers, and more. Organizations are also decentralized, interconnected and information-rich. In terms of leading an organization, influence and outcomes are shaped laterally and emergently, not just top down. Seeking out negative signals erodes nodes in the network (people, teams, platforms) by creating noise and distrust, and undermining coordination. Seeking out positive signals, in contrast, strengthens nodes by building trust, cooperation, faster learning and innovation. It changes the attitude – which in turn changes the narrative.

This last point is especially important. As leaders, how we frame the narrative is crucial – but I argue that attitude is even more important.

People tend to assume that attitude follows facts. In complex systems, however, attitude often precedes outcomes – and in doing so, shapes the facts themselves.

Systems analysts tell us that in these systems, the most effective place to intervene – the true leverage point – is not in tweaking the rules, setting new targets or changing the parameters. Rather, the most powerful lever is to shift the mindset or paradigm through which we engage with the system in the first place.

Donella Meadows, the influential American systems thinker, developed a hierarchy of leverage points – places to intervene in a system ranked by effectiveness. Near the top of her list? 'The mindset or paradigm out of which the system arises.'[22]

She wrote: 'Paradigms are the sources of systems. From them, come system goals and information flows, feedback, stocks, flows and everything else about systems . . . You could say paradigms are harder to change than anything else about a system and therefore this item should be lowest on the list, but there's nothing necessarily physical or expensive or even slow in the process of paradigm change. In a single individual it can happen in a millisecond. All it takes is a new way of seeing.'

And how do you change paradigms? Meadows continued: 'You insert people with the new paradigm in places of public visibility and power. You don't waste time with reactionaries; rather you work with active change agents and with the vast middle ground of people who are open-minded.'

It is those open-minded people, the active change agents, who hold the key. In essence, she was talking about people who have been disciplined and sophisticated enough to resist their default negativity bias and embrace the possibility of positive change.

Bringing all this together, it becomes clear that the First Principle, Disciplined Optimism, is fundamental to impact in life and leadership. Seeking out positive signals enables us to identify opportunities, and then seeding the networks required to execute on them with optimism maximizes the chance for success.

By combining these effects, we demonstrate that optimism can serve as an impact multiplier. Personally, a deliberate positive mindset can make you about two times more likely to spot and pursue opportunities (offsetting the 2:1 negative bias). Socially, this optimism multiplies information and positive behaviour and encourages a network of people to achieve better outcomes together, giving a combined effect of at least threefold across observed studies of diffusion and collaboration.

Multiplying these factors, an optimistic approach could increase the results of your efforts by roughly $2 \times 3 = 6$ times compared to a pessimistic approach. In summary, optimism works through reasoning (by widening one's own perspective to find value where others see loss) and through evidence (by leveraging well-documented psychological and network effects). This not only improves one's chances of success but also spreads benefits to others, significantly magnifying the overall impact.

Using Positivity to Frame and Tackle South Africa's Electricity Crisis

Seeking out positive signals and creating positive feedback loops is complicated, incredibly powerful and fundamental in large interconnected systems. An excellent example of this is the tackling of South Africa's electricity crisis that lasted from 2008 to mid-2024.

This problem involved a uniquely complex network: business, government, thousands of people, competing ideologies, gaps in trust, nationwide utilities and public expectations. It illustrates not only how seeking out positive signals across a network enables solutions to be identified but also how positive signalling drives the efficiency and effectiveness of a network.

The story I am about to recount has never been fully told.

To grasp its significance, we need to understand both the size of the grid and the scale of the country's electricity crisis.

South Africa's grid is massive. This is not just due to the size of the population but is also because of its large and energy-intensive mining sector. In 2025, South Africa produced over 200 terawatt-hours of electricity – more than Israel, New Zealand, Ireland and Portugal combined[23] – placing it among the world's top 25 electricity producers.

The scale of the power produced and consumed is important to comprehend because it sets up the magnitude of the crisis that arose – and that needed to be fixed.

In Europe, it had been the Russia–Ukraine war that began in February 2022 that plunged the region into an energy crisis after Russia cut 80 billion cubic metres of pipeline gas supplies to Europe. But in South Africa, chronic power shortages had been around on and off since 2007 due to chronic underinvestment in the grid and serious mismanagement.

Our electricity crisis entered a critical phase in 2022 when the country's energy grid experienced a calamitous collapse, resulting in up to half of the generating capacity being lost. The list of problems included crumbling infrastructure, lack of investment in ageing coal-fired power plants (which comprised three-quarters of the country's generating capacity), widespread corruption, lack of skills, mismanagement and sabotage.

Eskom – the state-owned utility responsible for providing the nation's electricity – responded to the shortage of supply by introducing planned blackouts, known as load-shedding, to save power and to keep the grid operational. The scale of the load-shedding was communicated to the public by defining it in escalating stages, from 1 to 8. Stage 1 meant two hours of power outages per day; Stage 4 meant six hours; Stage 6 meant eight to ten hours; and Stage 8, at least twelve hours a day. Eskom sought to avoid Stage 8 but typically oscillated between Stages 4 and 6.

This cost the country R27 billion – £1.2 billion – a month.[24] What is more, the failing infrastructure became a potent symbol of inept governance and national decline.

There is nothing so dispiriting as driving through a city at night where the streets are dark, the traffic lights are down, and houses along the route are blacked out. Sitting down for dinner at home, or in a restaurant, only to have the power fail and everything go pitch black is profoundly depressing. There was a real fear that the grid would shut down completely and that anarchy would result. Unsurprisingly, this crisis became the number one topic of conversation – the whole country was worried and deeply pessimistic.

A widespread belief took hold that the problem was too big to fix and that the levels of load-shedding would only get worse. Among my friends and colleagues, and in the country at large, there was a creeping dread that this shocking state of affairs was the thin end of the wedge. Our UK and South African risk committees – along with the governance committees of other blue-chip companies – prompted us to prepare for a total grid collapse. It felt apocalyptic.

There had been several initiatives aimed at arresting the situation. Importantly, in July 2022 the president announced his Energy

Action Plan and set up a National Energy Crisis Committee in his office to implement it. They focused on cutting red tape and coordinating the government's response to the crisis. In addition, the licensing cap for private generation was removed; additional power was imported; and a team of independent experts started to work closely with Eskom to improve plant performance.

In March 2023, a full year before South Africa turned the corner on the electricity crisis, I published an opinion piece on *News24*, South Africa's biggest online news site, that attracted the attention of President Cyril Ramaphosa. The piece was entitled 'My view on SA remains unchanged: We need action, not despair'.[25]

The article spoke about how tough times were and that there was widespread despondency. I proposed that the solution was to focus on our potential – and that doing so required seeking out positive signals and taking deliberate action, rather than succumbing to fatalistic pessimism.

The private sector was agile, and business, with its considerable skills and resources, could be constructively engaged. My piece ended with a plea: 'Business is ready. We need to work together with government urgently to get this done – and we can.'

Off the back of that article, the president reached out and asked me to help rally the business community more purposefully – to scale up the assistance being provided and to give additional impetus to what was already underway to address the crisis.

It was a great response from the president, but immediately I realized I had created a risk of being hoist by my own petard because we faced major obstacles in collaborating effectively with government.

After the Covid pandemic, during which business and government had successfully partnered to address the crisis and procure and distribute vaccines, there had been several joint meetings to address other emergent issues, but we had not made any substantive headway.

There had also been many efforts to address the energy crisis specifically, with multiple stakeholders involved, but for various reasons these hadn't gained sufficient momentum. There was dysfunction and distrust between government and the private sector – and within the different elements of the business community. The focus was always on what we couldn't do and why we couldn't do it.

There was a lot of tension, partly because the issues we were covering seemed to be too broad to get traction, and partly because further liberalization of the energy sector was needed to empower private suppliers. For many years, there had been a cap on how much power the private sector could generate. In July 2022, the president announced that the cap would be removed altogether. This was a hugely important signal that the government was liberalizing the sector. However, as with any government, they didn't want to create an impression that private business was the saviour. We needed a new approach – and so before we even started, we had to stake out areas of common ground based on shared values.

Martin Kingston (executive chairman of Rothschild & Co South Africa), Cas Coovadia (then CEO of Business Unity South Africa) and I had worked tightly together on behalf of business with the government during Covid, and we met again to work out how the learnings from the pandemic could be applied to the energy crisis.

We all agreed that the same governance structures that had been deployed to tackle Covid – in the form of Business for South Africa (B4SA) – would work well. B4SA was the implementation arm of Business Unity South Africa (BUSA), the apex business body in South Africa, of which I was vice president. The steering committee was chaired by Martin, who brought strategic insight and deep relationships within the public and private sector, and who had played a pivotal role in organized business for years.

We went back to the president and agreed to formalize the

Government-Business Partnership that would focus on three key areas that needed urgent attention and would turn the flywheel of economic growth: energy; railways, ports and roads; and crime and corruption.

During the country's Covid vaccine rollout, we had set up a Joint Strategic Oversight Committee (JSOC), a joint government and business committee, to manage the programme and provide strategic direction. We agreed to use the same structure and the JSOC became the fulcrum through which we would report back to the president every eight weeks on the progress we had made, the problems we were having, and the governmental blockages we were facing – and he would seek to unblock them.

But there was one further thing we needed, I believed, to side-step the inevitable debates among the business community and get us underway – and that was a definitive positive framework that we could all agree on as a bedrock.

The context was that the CEOs of many of the country's top businesses were in a state of despair. Mike Brown, CEO of Nedbank, articulated the dominant view when he said that 'The shortage of electricity supply – and hence very high levels of load-shedding – is currently the most material constraint on GDP growth.'[26] And yet it was these very CEOs and their companies that we needed to step up to offer their resources, funding and expertise to help the government tackle the energy crisis.

We couldn't rally CEOs around negativity. Instead, we needed to lift our gaze from the dire present to the possibilities of the future.

I worked with the B4SA steering committee to devise a pledge to emphasize our joint interests and act as a clarion call to put aside the prevailing sense of despair – and to pursue a common agenda with hope, agency and positivity.

We instigated a drive to seek widespread endorsement. The

pledge was overwhelmingly supported. Published on 27 July 2023, and signed by 115 CEOs (with a further forty signatories added soon thereafter), the pledge stated:

> As South African business leaders, we firmly believe in the immense potential of our country. We are committed to building it and have come together to address the current challenges with the aim of achieving sustainable, inclusive economic growth. Through strategic partnerships and focused interventions, we have the power to make a significant and positive impact on our nation, creating hope for all South Africans. We are resolutely committed to being a force for good.

This pledge was an instrument that aimed to create a shift from current despair to potential – a mechanism to elicit positive signals.

The following year, the Government-Business Partnership codified this future focus and created a framework of 'Investment, Growth, Jobs, Confidence' – a 'virtuous cycle' with clear measures in each of the categories. Understanding the causal links between these elements showed how the cycle could reinforce itself. Three per cent growth was necessary to begin to turn the national flywheel, and we committed to that as our collective ambition. The pledge and the virtuous cycle worked well together to shift negative signals to positive ones, and to create an effect in the network that would get it galvanized and active.

Some might disregard these mechanisms as mere symbolic gestures, full of platitudes and of little consequence, but in my view, they are among the most important things we, as a business community, have ever done.

This is why.

First, both the pledge and the GDP target created a framework to pull people and organizations into the process at scale. The heft and diversity of the companies behind the pledge was unprecedented. They ranged across all sectors of the economy – the value of the listed entities exceeded R11 trillion (£478 billion), and they employed more than 1.2 million people.

Second, it shifted the narrative from negativity to active optimism. At the time, experts across the board were predicting doom and gloom – that blackouts were set to continue, and that the power crisis would take 'at least another five years' to phase out.[27] However, our newly framed pledge of intent started to shift this. CEOs started to become invested in the process and believed that they could fix it. We then followed it up with milestones and timeframes to measure progress, and hard targets and clear metrics to measure success (such as megawatts for energy, and megatons for logistics).

The cumulative results were staggering.

By the end of 2024, there had been a 76 per cent reduction in load-shedding compared to the prior year. In 2025, the situation improved even further, with load-shedding down by 98 per cent by the end of the third quarter. While there are still intermittent power outages, the dark days of widespread daily power outages appear to be behind us. In May 2024, Eskom declared the crisis had been 'fixed' and that 'the chances of having load-shedding again are small'.[28] Even our typically cautious media waxed lyrical, opining: 'Load-shedding has now, miraculously and wonderfully, been largely fixed.'[29]

How did this happen?

I am not seeking to make any grandiose claims here. A lot of people in the public and private sector will rightly take credit for turning around the electricity crisis. Many factors played a part. In addition to those listed above, at the end of 2023, Eskom had appointed a new leadership team. The new CEO was respected and well-liked by Eskom's management and staff, as well as key private sector players, which was crucial for improving morale. At least six of Eskom's fourteen giant coal-fired power plants that were malfunctioning had their management overhauled and effective maintenance plans put in place. Some power plants that were offline and out of commission were brought back on stream. As encouraged by the policy changes of July 2022, the private sector started to develop innovative solar and wind-powered energy initiatives and many households and businesses installed rooftop solar. This helped significantly to ease reliance on the national grid.

Overall, it was an enormous team effort. But indulge me – I believe that disciplined optimism and actively seeking out positive signals also played a key role in driving forward these many positive developments.

Once our business leaders had committed to the Government-Business Partnership, the support made available by them in terms of skilled resources and funding was massive, hugely scaling the support that was already in place behind the scenes. Over 350 highly qualified individuals – the best in the business, including top engineers – were assigned from several dozen businesses to assist pro bono. They spent an estimated 12,000 hours engaging with Eskom managers and other stakeholders. We know this because we kept track. In addition, businesses and philanthropies provided more than R100 million (£4.5 million) in direct funding and donated many millions in technical, legal and project management resources.

I believe that our pledge was a useful mechanism in helping turn the corner on load-shedding. It demonstrated business's goodwill and credentials, and this in turn helped Eskom and the government to reorientate. It aligned multiple stakeholders towards a common goal and inspired the collaboration that made possible what was previously so insurmountable.

Cas Coovadia called the pledge 'an important collaboration' that had to overcome 'many obstacles', including the 'narrative of decline and hopelessness' that 'hindered our path to prosperity'.

We see the essential elements of the disciplined optimism playbook at work, both with the pledge and the 3 per cent GDP growth target. In late 2024 and 2025, when GDP growth projections were paltry, agreeing to a bold ambition inspired us all to reach higher. In both instances, it was about disciplined optimism in looking for green shoots, slim threads and areas of aligned interests to resist the prevailing negative narrative.

I am convinced that it changed the energy in the room. It was subliminal. This, together with other factors, resulted in us turning around load-shedding in a year, far sooner than anyone had imagined. We did it as a team.

The example of a partnership to fix a nationwide technical challenge is seminal because it illustrates the power of seeking out the positive within a uniquely complex system.

At Davos 2025, President Ramaphosa talked about South Africa being 'a shining example' of what 'collaboration between government and business can achieve'. He said: 'We can showcase to the world what collaboration does. I am proud to say that by working together we have seen tremendous progress in several areas – including innovations to tackle energy security and infrastructure gaps.' He framed what we achieved as a scalable case study for international best practice of public and private collaboration.

Independent advisers who saw the process unfold from the inside also believe the pledge was a critical antidote to the pervading cynicism. As I have said, few CEOs like to stick their head up above the parapet and take risks they don't have to – and this allowed them cover because they could be part of a larger collective. They could also hold two views at once: they could be critical to their shareholders about the government and the outrageous cost of load-shedding, and they could be positive about the need to pitch in and help rebuild. The pledge allowed them to own the process.

Why was that important?

Because, as cognitive psychologist Martin Seligman has argued in his research on 'learned helplessness' – a condition in which individuals become passive and give up in the face of repeated and uncontrollable stressful events – the perception of control is central to resilience.[30] The more people believe they have control over a situation, the more optimistic and proactive they tend to be. This sense of control – or lack thereof – explains why people often feel pessimistic about the trajectory of countries, over which they feel powerless to effect change.[31] The pledge and the 3 per cent GDP ambition gave many CEOs something tangible to commit to, creating a positive feedback loop by giving them a vested interest in things going well.

And when the energy changes, everyone wants to be part of it. We saw this: things that were stuck suddenly got unstuck. Suddenly there was hope.

It was just as Nelson Mandela had told me at his house in Johannesburg when he looked me in the eye and said: 'A great leader creates hope in the people that he leads.'

How do you create hope? Not through seeking out negative signals, which sucks people down. Not by unthinking negativity, which leads to passivity. Rather, by choosing to seek out the positive and rolling up your sleeves and getting involved to make change happen. You must find the vision, frame it positively and take people along with you. It is not easy, but leaders who do that can have a massive impact on the world.

Earlier I said that in today's networked world, we face threats that are systemic in nature – arising from failing systems, crumbling infrastructures, as well as pandemics – and that these challenges require leadership and collaboration, and positive feedback loops generated by seeking out positive cues.

This example exemplifies how seeking out positive signals to change a system can work. In this case, seeking out positive signals was vital because it initiated a proactive mindset; reframed challenges from positions of cynicism to ones of cooperation and problem-solving; encouraged action; triggered reinforcing dynamics; and enabled systems-thinking that looked beyond the present moment.

In short, it changed the attitude, which in turn changed the narrative.

By the time this book is published, there may well be a new crisis in South Africa to address – quite possibly a scarcity of water, exacerbated by ageing infrastructure and lack of maintenance.

I would hope that we would have applied the same disciplined optimism framework to drive public-private engagement to fix the problem. We should feel confident that when we change the attitude, a new narrative is possible. When we don't, persistent and pervasive despair takes hold.

How Negativity Bias Leads to Declinism

The belief that our world (or country) is on an irreversible downhill trajectory – in contradiction to the available facts – is known as declinism.

While the exact origin of the term is unclear, declinism is widely associated with the German historian and philosopher Oswald Spengler, whose seminal work *The Decline of the West* – published in two volumes in 1918 and 1922 – explored the cyclical rise and fall of civilizations.[32] Spengler saw civilizations as akin to living organisms with a fixed lifespan whose decline was inevitable. His work profoundly influenced twentieth-century discourse on societal decline and laid the intellectual groundwork for the concept we now recognize as declinism.

Later thinkers would add another layer to the concept – the sentimental longing for an idealized past. Idealization of the past is a powerful overlay because it makes the present and future seem less good by comparison, and so the present and future need to 'work harder' just to keep up.

Analysed closely, declinism therefore tends to involve two factors: pessimism about the future, and nostalgia for a 'better' past.

Proof that declinism is an empirical real-world phenomenon was set out by cognitive psychologist Steven Pinker in his 2018 book *Enlightenment Now: The Case for Reason, Science, Humanism and Progress*. Drawing on multiple national surveys, Pinker showed that majorities in fourteen countries believed the world was getting worse. These included the UK, US, Germany, France and Australia – as well as surprising countries that consistently top global happiness rankings, such as Denmark, Norway, Sweden and Finland.

These declinist views persisted, he pointed out, despite robust statistical evidence to the contrary. As Pinker wrote, they are not just a little wrong, but 'wrong, wrong, flat-earth wrong'.

The only major country where a majority expressed optimism in Pinker's study was China, where the media is centrally controlled and messaging tends to emphasize growth and collective success. Also, over the past four decades, China has undergone a dramatic transformation, with hundreds of millions lifted out of poverty and major cities modernized beyond recognition. For China, there is no idealized past to which the present can be compared – just a difficult history characterized by economic struggle juxtaposed to the more recent economic upliftment for many.

Apart from China, this widespread declinism is further evidenced by contemporary polling.

A recent 2025 poll, called 'What Worries the World', asked

20,000 adults in thirty countries if they felt their country was on the right or wrong track – and nearly two-thirds felt their countries were heading in the wrong direction.[33]

So, these declinist views are consistent and clear. What's interesting is that, in contrast, the empirical data is also consistent and clear: in most areas of life, the world today is significantly better than it was in the past.

Life, on average, used to be shorter. We were sicker, less educated, much poorer, with less leisure time – and more likely to suffer violence.

Specifically, global life expectancy has risen from around thirty years in the eighteenth century to over seventy years today. Many infectious diseases have been dramatically reduced or, in some cases like smallpox, completely eradicated.

Over the past 200 years – despite the world population rising from 1 billion to more than 8 billion – the data shows:[34]

- Extreme poverty has dropped from 70 per cent to 9 per cent (though in parts of sub-Saharan Africa, it has persisted or worsened).
- Child mortality under five has fallen from 43 per cent to 4 per cent.
- Basic education has risen from 17 per cent to 86 per cent.
- Literacy has increased from 12 per cent to 87 per cent.

These markers of human progress show improvement whether measured over 200, 100, 50 or even just 20 years. Democracy, too, has expanded – rising from around 28 per cent of the global population in the 1950s to 45 per cent today.

Of course, as I have said, the future will look worse by comparison if we look back on history with rose-tinted spectacles. But what is the theory as to why we do so?

An argument that is used to explain both our idealization of the past and our pessimism about the future is that we often struggle to distinguish between relative and absolute changes. British historian David Edgerton says that mistaking relative for absolute decline is a common error that has led, for instance, to a misreading of British history as a story of inevitable decline. In his book *The Rise and Fall of the British Nation*, and in several articles, he argues that the UK declinist narrative is a myth perpetuated by confusing absolute and relative decline. He wrote: 'The long-term British relative decline, which has undoubtedly happened, and continues, has been mostly due to the success of other countries, not British failure.'[35]

In other words, things are not necessarily worse than they used to be – but they can feel that way because Britain's global influence has diminished, largely due to the rise of countries like America and China, and trading blocs such as the European Union. So, although the UK economy has grown in real terms, its share of the global economy has shrunk. Consider a startling statistic: in 2000, when Tony Blair was PM, the UK's nominal economy was roughly equal to the nominal GDP of both India and China combined, whereas today it has fallen to less than one-fifth of that composite total. This relative decline tends to be mistaken for absolute decline. Charges of declinism, says Edgerton, stem from a poor historical understanding of the facts and are a 'symptom of a nation unable to come to grips with its place in the world'.

Why is this important? Because, as Edgerton points out, 'understanding that real place . . . is central to any possibility of transformative politics'.

In other words, to find the right solution to a problem, you need an accurate understanding of the facts of your situation. Realizing that a country's decline – in Edgerton's example, Britain's – is relative, a result largely of the very successful growth of many other countries during a period of rapid globalization, reframes our understanding of a country's strengths and weaknesses and points toward more effective solutions.

The complexity of the modern environment – and the anxiety it causes – may exacerbate this negativity bias. For example, trying to understand the global economy in today's interconnected world can be overwhelming. In addition, the plethora of media and social media may lead to cognitive overload, making it harder for people to process information and contributing to a more negative outlook. If people can't see the big picture or understand how their actions contribute to the overall system, they are more likely to disengage. In this context, it is easy to understand why feelings of pessimism are so widespread. The amplification of rage and negative views by social media algorithms no doubt further contributes to this pattern.

But here's the nub of the problem: we have not just become habitually negative about the world around us – we have also somehow come to believe that being so is a savvy, rational and sophisticated response. Pessimism cloaks itself in intellectual credibility. We need to see this for what it is – and to counter it.

Ironically, research shows that people tend to be over-optimistic about their own abilities and health – such as how smart they are, how well they drive and how long they will live – but over-pessimistic about the outside world. This contrast between their optimism concerning their personal lives, within which they feel they have a measure of control, and their overly pessimistic view of the outside world, where they generally lack control, is known as the optimism paradox.

Fix the Streets to Fix Declinism: Filling 300,000 Potholes

In criminology, the 'broken windows' theory is the idea that visible signs of decay create an environment likely to lead to further decline. The concept gained traction in the 1990s when New York City police commissioner William Bratton argued that broken windows were not merely cosmetic issues but visual markers of lawlessness and key drivers of crime. Deal with the broken windows, Bratton said, and you reduce antisocial behaviour and more serious crime.

It made headlines because, until then, most people viewed broken windows as insignificant. This theory flipped that thinking on its head. While today some view the broken windows theory as an over-simplification of how to address crime, the broader insight – that seemingly small, visible problems can have a disproportionately large impact on society's collective psyche – still holds sway.

Fixing the potholes in Johannesburg, I came to realize, was much like fixing the broken windows of New York City. A lot more was at stake than just the potholes themselves.

Of course, as motor insurers, we had something to gain, too. From our South African motor insurance business, we knew that pothole-related vehicle repair costs were substantial – even though comprehensive national data was limited.

Just how substantial could those costs be for our industry?

The American Automobile Association reported that US drivers collectively spent $26.5 billion in 2021 on vehicle repairs attributed to pothole damage, with an average repair cost of $600 per incident. That implies around 44 million pothole-related repairs in a single year – a staggering figure. With 230 million licensed drivers in the US driving 283 million licensed vehicles, it suggests roughly one in five drivers suffered such a repair that year. Could that be right? Surprisingly, yes – in 2023, the AAA found that two in ten drivers have sustained vehicle damage significant enough to require repair after hitting a pothole.

In South Africa, extrapolating our data, we estimate that costs related to pothole damage exceed R2 billion annually (around £90 million).

The potential upside for the South African motor insurance industry in tackling the problem was indeed significant.

So, following our discussions with the mayor, our team at Discovery took up the challenge. One of the first issues we tackled was the speed with which new potholes were forming. The problem, we discovered, was that most potholes patched by the city did not stay fixed for long. A key reason was the city's ageing repair equipment.

We realized that to make a real difference – and ensure our repairs would last – we needed state-of-the-art technology, trained staff and a digital tool to help us prioritize the most urgent repairs.

So, we partnered with a company that owned a small fleet of vehicles and specialist pothole-filling equipment, and we developed an app for the public to report potholes and identify the most severe ones requiring urgent action. Then, in May 2021, we launched Discovery Pothole Patrol to operate in partnership with the city council.

In the first four years of the initiative, our public-private collaboration with the Johannesburg Roads Agency and city council saw us use over 11,800 tonnes of asphalt to fill over 300,000 potholes. That's 75,000 potholes a year, 1,442 a week, over 200 a day – a pretty decent rate of repair. Crucially, thanks to our state-of-the-art technology, less than 0.2 per cent of repaired potholes require further attention – meaning that around 99.8 per cent of the potholes that we fix stay fixed.

When we launched, I wanted to see the fledgling operation for myself, so one evening I donned a hard hat and overalls and went out with the team. I watched them use high-pressure and thermal processes to fill and compress the potholes, stamping them down flush with the road. It was quite something to observe, horribly cratered roads restored to beautiful, smooth surfaces. The speed and quality of their work were especially impressive.

What struck me most, though, was the excited reaction from the public. Drivers passing by hooted and shouted, 'Well done!' It was quite a scene. Their joy at seeing potholes being filled was palpable. I think it reflected something deeper: the emotional relief that comes when people witness visible signs of progress – tangible evidence that decline is being reversed.

To put it in mathematical terms, if the shape of the curve reflects the rate of improvement in tackling potholes, the public sensed that although our position on the curve was low, the slope of the curve was steepened by our involvement – and that slope, instantly grasped, allowed them to visualize the progress we would make as we moved up the curve; hence their excitement.

The impact of our intervention was indeed immediate and dramatic. In the first seven months of our operation, the number of potholes in Johannesburg declined by over 25 per cent. The improvement was even more striking when compared to the wider Gauteng region, where pothole incidence continued to worsen, soaring by nearly 50 per cent. Gauteng, South Africa's smallest yet most populous province, is home to 16 million people, a quarter of the country's population, and holds the highest concentration of wealth – so what happens there really matters.

The public responded with enthusiasm. Tens of thousands of people – well beyond our customer base – downloaded our app to report over 90,000 potholes to our Pothole Patrol helpline.

We have invested substantially in the project, but the net cost to us is far lower. Why? Because better roads mean fewer accidents and thus fewer motor insurance claims. The savings from the reduced claims relating to pothole damage is more than a quarter of what we spend fixing potholes. That means that if just four insurers work together, we would save more than it costs us to fix the entire city – and most importantly, it would make Johannesburg safer for all drivers.

It is a powerful example of how investing in public infrastructure can create shared value, delivering tangible benefits to both business and society.

There have been indirect benefits to our public reputation too. Local radio stations have praised the initiative, while international broadcasters, including those from Germany and France, travelled to South Africa to cover our work and laud our efforts. That fascinated me. The fact that a private business stepping in to fix a public problem made the evening news in Europe suggested that we were onto something with broader significance beyond South Africa – and perhaps beyond the issue itself.

In 2024, we doubled down, launching the Pothole Patrol Training Academy to build expertise in road construction and repairs, offering trainees a twelve-month course with an official qualification. Our current fleet and our team managing pothole call-ins and carrying out repairs will be further strengthened by these new recruits.

Importantly, we have seen renewed energy and optimism from the Johannesburg Roads Agency because of the joint success we are having. Despondency and despair have given way to determination and a shared sense that – together – we can turn the tide on Johannesburg's potholes.

It started with us resisting the popular declinist narrative, seeking out positive signals, and in this case, with setting the goal of eliminating all potholes to shift sentiment about the environment, followed by tactical decisions – to reach out to the city authorities, to forge a partnership, to focus on possibilities rather than hurdles and to step up to help do something about it.

But it is not just about seeking out positive signals and leaning in. It is that when we choose to do so, we create a platform – a vehicle – for others to lean in as well. We create a shared endeavour. What we do together will always exceed what any of us can do alone. The whole becomes greater than the sum of the parts.

And because no one wants to collaborate if the atmosphere is shrouded in negativity and the cause is perceived as lost, leadership plays a decisive role. Leadership that is rooted in disciplined optimism unlocks new possibilities for partnership. The attitude of the leader creates the opportunity – and that opportunity changes what's possible on the ground.

Attitude shifts the mindset, which in turn sets in motion a chain of events that alters the fundamentals. Suddenly, a problem that once seemed insurmountable is being effectively tackled.

But it is a battle that must be fought – and won – over and over.

I say this because, despite our pothole initiative being widely appreciated, you might wonder if it had an impact on people's attitudes. Take my friends at our Sunday breakfast club. Did our success with the potholes change their outlook?

Yes – and no.

Yes, they stopped grumbling about the potholes. But no, the mindset remained the same, and they moved seamlessly to the next problem of the day. Once again, their conversations were infused with negativity and an unwavering confidence that the new problem would never be successfully tackled. Once more, in their view, we were on a one-way ticket to disaster.

Fuelled by the media, which focuses relentlessly on the latest negative news and crises, while under-reporting long-term progress, this sentiment – I suspect – reflects a broader mood in society.

Positive outcomes have a short shelf life. Before long, people revert to their declinist default position. This makes the role of leadership – in having the discipline to hold the line and in defining a positive vision and driving change towards it – all the more vital.

Why It Is So Hard to Prove a Pessimist Wrong

Pessimists are fiendishly hard to prove wrong. That is because they are cognitive shapeshifters who keep moving the goalposts. If you succeed where they predicted failure, they quickly pivot – much like my friends – to the next seemingly intractable problem. You have solved one issue, but what about the next?

This mental sleight of hand is a well-documented concept in cognitive psychology known as 'motivated reasoning' – where individuals filter new information through a lens that confirms their pre-existing beliefs.[36] In the case of pessimists, it means continuously shifting the goalposts to preserve their outlook, creating an impenetrable cognitive shield that protects their world-view from disruption. At the extreme, it leads to 'cognitive immunization', a mental strategy whereby disconfirming evidence is swiftly reinterpreted or dismissed to preserve existing beliefs. In this scenario, pessimism becomes intellectually self-reinforcing.

By constantly recalibrating the criteria for what 'success' means, pessimists maximize their odds of eventual vindication and getting to say, 'I told you so.' If things go wrong, they claim foresight. If things go right, they dismiss it as a one-off, a fluke, or label it temporary – then move on.

It is a mindset also closely aligned with what researchers refer to as 'nocebo framing'. The nocebo effect (from the Latin 'I shall harm') is a form of reasoning where a negative predisposition drives how facts are framed or interpreted. It is the opposite of the placebo, which produces positive outcomes from positive expectations – such as a sugar pill making you feel better because you believe it to be medicine. In contrast, the nocebo generates negative outcomes from negative expectations irrespective of the evidence.

In summary, taking the negative view is a low-effort, high-defence position: intellectually easy to maintain, emotionally satisfying, impervious to contradiction – an unshakeable, closed stance that resists change. When things do go right, pessimists keep recalibrating and move on to the next evidence of decline – and when things go wrong, they call it.

Seeking out positive signals, by contrast, is risky and exposing. It means sticking your neck out and getting involved. It takes guts because it exposes you to failure and invites judgement, and even ridicule. You may be called naive or told that your optimism is dumb.

I often wonder why people are so wedded to the negative narrative. Yes, cognitive psychology – negativity bias, confirmation bias and nocebo framing – might mean we are wired for seeking out the negative. But why – when faced with clear facts showing that a problem is being solved or that things are improving – do perfectly rational people still default to negativity?

We have already looked at how negativity bias colours individual cognition and psychology. But what additional forces might be at play?

This question can be approached from two angles: the role of the media and the discourse of politics. Both exhibit a negativity bias – and crucially, they reinforce each other, making it even harder for people to assess and respond to events objectively.

The Role of the Media in Reinforcing the Negative

The media has arguably the most critical role to play in the functioning of a society, in questioning, highlighting and speaking truth to power. We are all safer with a vigilant and independent media.

However, people often comment on the negative nature of the news. What they miss, ironically, is that they are only interested in the negative, and the media reflects this.

The role of the media in amplifying declinism has been explored by Swedish physician and statistician, Hans Rosling, who used data and graphs to show how key metrics of wellbeing have overwhelmingly improved over time – despite the media's portrayal to the contrary. In his 2018 book, *Factfulness: Ten Reasons We're Wrong About the World – and Why Things Are Better Than You Think*, he highlighted the huge gap between actual human development and public perception, blaming this pessimism largely on the media's relentless focus on bad news.[37]

This idea is rooted in the same evolutionary psychology we discussed earlier – namely that readers are hardwired to be more attentive to danger. In this context, bad news about disasters, crises or scandals grabs their attention more profoundly because it may signal a need to take urgent action. As media outlets compete for clicks and advertising revenue, they plug into this instinct and are more likely to run stories about failure and impending catastrophe.

Most media bosses will tell you that bad news sells more readily than good – encapsulated by the old newsroom adage: 'If it bleeds, it leads.'

Take the reporting of plane crashes with fatalities versus that of successful emergency landings. There was one crash involving fatalities in every 5.8 million flights in 2024, while in the United States, where the safety record is remarkable, there were no fatal accidents in commercial passenger aviation from 2009 to 2024. Yet, plane crashes are reported far more frequently and with greater amplification than their positive and more frequent counterparts – emergency landings which save all passengers, estimated to be around 1 in 1 million flights.

Historically, newsroom bias was shaped by editors in daily conference. Today, the negativity filter is increasingly embedded in algorithms that decide what stories to serve up. Social media algorithms have learned that virality is most easily achieved by amplifying and circulating rage and other very negative views and emotions, and social media thus plays a massive role in confirming existing beliefs and making declinism even harder to counter. This tendency to seek out and better remember information that conforms to existing beliefs is known as confirmation bias.

Pessimists also benefit from the 'availability heuristic' – the tendency for people to judge the likelihood of events based on how easily examples come to mind. Because bad news is more widely reported than good, it is more readily available in memory, reinforcing a sense that things are getting worse.

But is data even enough to change minds? In an age where news is delivered by apps and social media platforms like LinkedIn, Facebook, X, Instagram and TikTok, the question becomes: what data gets seen? And how do people know what's true?

Media outlets often cherry-pick facts to suit their worldview, and social media algorithms create echo chambers that reinforce it.

So, facts alone are no longer enough.

Indeed, it is worse than that. Research by Tali Sharot, a behavioural scientist at University College London and MIT, finds that people often believe information based simply upon how often they hear it. Sharot calls it the 'illusory truth effect' – 'if you hear something repeatedly, you're more likely to believe it regardless of whether it is true or false'.[38]

In a 1977 study, participants were given sixty statements (some true, some false), of which twenty were repeated. What they found, said Sharot, was that repeated statements were more likely to be believed, simply because they were heard more than once, irrespective of whether they were true or false.

Cognitively, this is likely, Sharot added, because when you hear something repeatedly, 'your brain processes it less and less', so you question it less and accept it more. Also, the brain remembers what it has heard before but not necessarily where it has heard it, so the importance of source credibility diminishes over time. On social media, this effect is compounded because people are more likely to share what they already believe – creating a loop of repetition and reinforcement.

I see this all the time in South Africa, where half-truths and falsehoods about the state of the nation or the economy are treated as gospel – simply because they are repeated so often, with little scrutiny of their source.

The Role of Politics in Reinforcing the Negative

The second obstacle to having a clear-eyed perspective is politics. In the partisan world of political rhetoric, decline is often weaponized as a tool to unseat incumbents and to gain power.

Robert Ralston at the University of Birmingham writes that declinism most often comes from 'opposition brokers' who form a 'coalition' that is 'well positioned to lay blame for the nation's decline on the incumbent government and the opposition establishment'.[39]

This impulse is often reflected in President Trump's rallying cry to 'Make America Great Again'. Trademarked in 2012, and deployed during his 2016 and 2024 presidential campaigns, the MAGA slogan drew on a pre-existing declinist narrative. When President Trump ran as the incumbent in 2020, the slogan morphed into the non-declinist pitch to 'Keep America Great' – and he did not win re-election. Upon winning a second term in 2024, his inaugural address again returned to the declinist theme: 'From this moment on, America's decline is over. The golden age of America begins right now. I was saved by God to make America great again.'[40]

President Trump is not unique. Ronald Reagan used 'Let's make America great again' in his successful 1980 campaign against Jimmy Carter, highlighting inflation, economic woes and a perceived decline in national confidence. Bill Clinton also used the phrase – 'Together, we can make America great again' – in his 1992 campaign when he defeated the incumbent George H. W. Bush.

In truth, declinism is a staple of opposition politics. Parties seeking political power typically point out how bad things have become under the current regime and position themselves as 'the change agents' who will restore prosperity – regardless of the facts.

This tactic is not limited to politics. New business and religious leaders often bill themselves as a 'new broom to sweep clean'. They, too, promise to reverse the decline caused by their predecessor, be it the loss of market dominance or moral decay.

There is a paradox here: declinism gets you into power, but optimism makes you effective and keeps you there. Leaders often campaign on pessimism – and then govern on optimism. In both cases, we need to interrogate the facts.

It can be tempting to dismiss declinism as a quirk of evolutionary biology and psychology, amplified by media and politics. But left unchecked, it can foster widespread fatalism and passivity – undermining our ability to tackle societal problems.

From the electricity and pothole stories, we saw that sentiment can shape outcomes. And if that's true, then we need leaders who are willing to challenge false narratives – and make the case for positive change.

Yes, there are personal risks to rolling up your sleeves and getting involved. But sometimes, doing nothing poses much greater risk. We faced this challenge in the Government-Business Partnership established in 2023 to focus on accelerating crucial reforms and operational improvements to lift confidence levels and drive economic growth.

Optimism Drives Sentiment, Which Drives Progress and Economic Growth of Countries

An important question is whether optimism, and the narrative stemming from it, can influence a country's future and prospects. This is a crucial issue. In my work with business leadership and government, I've been embroiled in a debate about the narrative of our country. The seemingly rational view is that the narrative will improve when we improve the fundamentals. But that is not correct. Research shows that the story a country tells about itself can influence whether it grows or stagnates.

A 2023 paper from the University of Chicago makes the case directly. Titled 'Sentiment, Productivity, and Economic Growth', the paper found a clear correlation between sentiment and future economic growth – particularly in low- and middle-income countries. Optimism, it argues, plays a major role in macroeconomic momentum in the Global South.[41] Overall, sentiment explains up to 20–40 per cent of business-cycle and growth variation in developing economies, showing it is a significant economic driver rather than mere noise.

Their paper built on previous research that also showed correlation between sentiment and growth, but it went further by exploring why that might be the case. In developed markets, asset prices and fundamentals are widely publicized and well understood, so sentiment has limited long-term effect. But in developing economies, where there are fewer analysts and think tanks to provide trenchant analysis, sentiment and fundamentals are harder to separate – which gives narrative more influence over the economy itself.

For instance, an investor in New York may have little direct insight into South Africa's fundamentals and is more likely to rely on editorials, headlines and anecdotes – which can create persistent and hard-to-shift biases. As the paper puts it, bouts of optimism and pessimism have a direct effect on future fundamentals through a self-fulfilling feedback loop.

In this way, seeking out positive signals can trigger 'immediate and lasting economic growth' – even 'a large increase in economic growth' – while seeking out negative ones can pull us in the opposite direction.

The prevailing belief, as I have said, is that we must first fix things before sentiment improves. But as this chapter – and research – shows, sentiment is itself causal.

Seeking out positive signals can and does drive economic growth, while seeking out negative signals does the opposite.

South Africa has always suffered from a narrative that is substantially worse than its reality. Its history of apartheid and the high levels of joblessness, inequality and poverty that persist create a unique and complicated narrative. From an economic point of view, the country is internationally categorized as 'about to fail, not sustainable'.

Yet it is a country with an enormous amount going for it.

It is the most industrialized economy in Africa by far, with a sophisticated private sector and capital markets that hold over 70 per cent of the pension fund assets of the entire African continent. People who think South Africa is small and insignificant are surprised by the actual data: consider that the economy of one of our provinces, such as Gauteng, exceeds that of entire countries, such as Kenya. Other persistent tropes include the idea that education has deteriorated, and that the growth of the black middle class has stalled. Yet again, the actual data paints a different picture. Since 1993, the black middle class has grown sixteen-fold to over 5.6 million, and average years of schooling have increased from 8.4 to 10.5. Households with access to electricity have risen from 57 per cent to 94 per cent. I could go on.

Why does this matter?

When we misrepresent a country as small, risky or irrelevant, we risk scaring off international investors and increasing the country's isolation from the global economy. The impact of negative opinions is not linear – they feed on each other and become self-perpetuating.

Applications

When to Start a Business – Often Better in Difficult Times

It may seem nerve-wracking and counter-intuitive, but the best time to start a business, invest in the stock market, or launch a new product – from a rational perspective – is when times are tough and people struggle to see light at the end of the tunnel.

The consequences of our coding are that in difficult times, our bias is more pronounced, manifesting in assets being underpriced and competitors being more distracted and less willing to invest. It also means there are potentially new problems to solve with fewer competitors, and the ability for leadership impact to be magnified.

The logical implication of this is that if you do have the ability and capital, this is an ideal time to start up or invest. The only scenario in which this doesn't hold true is if you correctly anticipate an impending 'Armageddon'. It is axiomatic then, from a mathematical and risk assessment point of view, to hold your nerve and invest when markets are low. This strategy often results in businesses emerging at scale when times improve.

Take Netflix, which expanded its streaming service during the global recession of 2008, making streaming an attractive alternative to cable TV and movie rentals; and telehealth – the use of technology to deliver healthcare services remotely – which took off massively during Covid.

Lastly, the challenging environment forces businesses to be more adaptable and resilient, which in turn shapes a stronger organizational culture that can differentiate businesses in the long term.

Being able to resist the fear, cut through the doom and gloom, and think clearly in uncertain times confers clear benefits to those who seek out positive signals. They do well because they see opportunity where others do not, and because they see the potential of the future where others fixate on the difficult present.

As I described in the Introduction, this was the context in which we started Discovery in 1992, a time of massive political and economic upheaval in South Africa, and when many were predicting disaster.

It was, as I said, an act of pure optimism at a time when many people were consumed with fear – a fear that leads to contraction rather than expansion, and to irrational rather than rational responses.

Of course, the Discovery story is far from unique. Many of the world's largest and most successful companies were launched during economic crises. This list includes Microsoft, Airbnb, WhatsApp, Slack, Uber, Instagram, Square and Pinterest in America and Canada,[42] with JD Sports an example of a UK success story that began in tough times.

Microsoft was founded by Bill Gates and Paul Allen in 1975 during the oil embargo recession. Airbnb was started in 2008 at the start of the financial crisis and was valued at $88 billion upon IPO in 2020. WhatsApp was founded by two ex-Yahoo employees in 2009 in the thick of the global financial crisis – it is now owned by Meta and is widely believed by analysts to be worth well over $100 billion. The same recessionary years of 2009 and 2010 saw the birth of four more unicorns: Uber, Slack (the enterprise messaging app), Instagram and Pinterest – now worth an estimated $190 billion, $26 billion, $100 to $150 billion, and $18 billion, respectively. In the UK, JD Sports was founded during the 1981 recession and went on to become a highly successful company, worth several billion pounds today.

Products launched during times of economic hardship also do better. A 2023 study published in the *Harvard Business Review* revealed that new products launched during recessions outperform those launched during booms.[43] Researchers analysed 8,981 product launches in the UK across twenty consumer goods categories over the years 1995 to 2012, as well as 1,071 product launches in the US auto industry between 1946 and 2008.

Most surprising to the authors was the uniformity of the results. Whether the launches were for essential products or discretionary items, big-ticket items like motor vehicles or low-cost goods like detergent, products launched during a recession survived longer: 14 per cent longer in the case of consumer products and 19 per cent longer in the case of motor vehicles, when compared to similar products launched during economic expansions. Sales and market share penetration were higher as well.

These results were unexpected. M. Berk Talay, lead author of the study and a professor at the University of Massachusetts Lowell, had anticipated a clear difference between necessities (such as toilet paper and food) and discretionary products (such as hair dye). He said: 'I thought discretionary product launches would be more likely to fail, because nonessential purchases tend to decline in tough economies. But the effects are consistent across products and categories. A recession might be an ideal time to launch your product no matter what it is.'

Even more surprising was the finding that products launched in the depth of a recession fared better than those launched at the start. This is especially counter-intuitive, as early in a recession people still have savings to allow them to continue consuming – but over time, these are depleted. As demand drops, more companies fail, layoffs increase and demand plummets further. Yet the research showed that late recession launches had the greatest success. One explanation is that consumers tend to adapt to recessions and defer certain purchases – but can defer them for only so long.

Reasons for the success of recession-era product launches mirror the logic behind business launches in downturns: less competition and less noise to crowd them out. With established companies scaling back on advertising, it becomes easier to gain media coverage and consumer attention.

Similarly, businesses that continue to invest in R&D and in the professional development of staff – while others are cutting back – can open clear blue water between themselves and the competition, more so during recessions than in boom times.

The Launch of Discovery Bank – A Test of My Optimistic Resolve

I once heard a sports psychologist speak about how great golfers focus on the hole, not the lake they have to hit over – that is, they pay attention to the positive outcome they want to achieve, rather than the fear or risk of the obstacle in the way. I have often reflected on what I do, and if my attention lies on the opportunity or the hazard, especially in difficult times. I like to think that by and large, I tend to see the hole and not the lake. When calibrating big business decisions, I tend to focus on the upside rather than the downside – while staying acutely aware of the risks.

But sometimes, even my innate optimism gets tested to the limit, as was the case when we launched our banking business.

The launch of Discovery Bank in 2019 is a strong example of launching a start-up in difficult times. In fact, it is a classic case of taking a well-developed business model and making a deliberate decision to invest considerably in it to build a new business.

The context was not dissimilar to when we had started Discovery twenty-seven years before. The environment was precarious: we were in the midst of an economic downturn primarily due to worsening financial conditions, Jacob Zuma's presidency was causing deep uncertainty about the country's future, and xenophobic attacks and crime were rife, manifesting in profound social anxiety and economic uncertainty.

By now we were well-established in health and life insurance, both in South Africa and globally, but entering the banking space was a substantial tactical move in terms of investment and risk. And while we had planned for the recession from a business perspective, everything else that could go wrong, did.

A crucial step in the start-up of the bank was the acquisition of FirstRand's shareholding in the existing Discovery Credit Card business – a joint venture we had formed with FirstRand Bank a decade prior. We would inherit more than 250,000 existing Discovery Card customers – effectively making them our inaugural Discovery Bank clients and allowing us to hit the ground running. But then Covid hit, and the economy plummeted to depths nobody had anticipated. Additionally, a bank that had agreed to provide us with a crucial line of credit to fund the transfer of the Discovery Card business in-house pulled out at the last moment, citing Covid as the reason.

The approach we took was premised on 'no shortcuts'. We decided to build a substantial bank despite it requiring considerable capital – again an act of optimism given the environment. It was projected to absorb close to R15 billion (£650 million) and take nearly eight years of sustained development before reaching profitability.

Added to this, we faced the considerable challenge of launching something at scale that would be good enough to disrupt the competition. The South African banking sector has a reputation for being strong and sophisticated, so the competitive space we were entering was already of a high level.

At the time, I tried not to fixate on the plethora of negative scenarios landing on my desk – 'the lake' – instead focusing on the uniqueness and soundness of our idea that had prompted us to launch in the first place.

Discovery Bank would be a full-service digital retail bank – and, crucially, the world's first behavioural bank: designed to incentivize positive financial habits among clients. It was a natural extension of Vitality and the Shared-Value model we had developed so successfully in health and life insurance. Clients could earn points and get rewards for being financially responsible – for spending less than they earn, for saving regularly, paying off mortgages early and for investing for the long term. Incentives to customers for managing their money well included flexing interest rates up for savers and down for borrowers, and considerable cashback in the form of Discovery Miles, and flight discounts. The quality and design of our technology and the extremely smooth and satisfying client interface was also a big factor giving us a competitive advantage. Society would benefit, too – when individuals improve their financial health, they reduce dependence on social systems and contribute to national savings and investment.

Our planning had been meticulous: we had stress-tested our models and carefully plotted the path forward. And once the plan was set, I focused on the fundamentals: the solid assumptions they were grounded on, the long-term vision and the success it pointed to.

A critical success factor was to get customers to move to Discovery Bank and use it as their primary bank. Bear in mind that globally, there had been a considerable number of digital bank start-ups (neobanks) that had failed to get real revenue traction and scale because their offering was niche, and while they attracted a large number of customers, they weren't using these banks for their primary services. Furthermore, data showed that customers seldom change their primary bank accounts, with loyalty and inertia being powerful forces in this regard. Ironically, I still used the same bank account for my own salary that I started with all those years back at Liberty Life. Would this primary bank challenge be surmountable?

Despite my long journey in building Discovery, there was only one night that I woke up in a cold sweat, and it was around this issue. I was deeply concerned about the sheer number of new clients we'd need to bring in each week to stay on track – and alarmed by how far behind we were falling.

What came to mind was our earlier attempt to enter the US health insurance market, and why we had failed. In 2000, the US economy was experiencing a period of robust growth and low unemployment, fuelled by strong productivity and the dot-com boom. It was then that we entered the US with the launch of Destiny Health. A gutsy move – we were at that stage a small South African health insurer, and the boldness of what it would take to build a new health insurance company in the US was symptomatic of a young and maybe overconfident founding team.

The US private health insurance market was the largest in the world and highly sophisticated, but it resembled the South African private health insurance market in some ways. At the time, our strategy was to export Discovery's health technology and IP, combined with an experienced US team, to tap into the competitive and opportunity-rich US market. The idea of consumer-driven healthcare was just beginning to gain momentum in the US, and this – along with rising medical inflation and criticism of traditional health insurance 'managed care' products – provided a unique opportunity for market entry.

Or so we thought.

In 2003, Destiny Health established joint ventures with Tufts Health Plan (Massachusetts) and Guardian Life (the fourth largest US mutual life insurer) to market Destiny's plan throughout the country. Our behavioural insurance products resonated with the public, and we made considerable progress from our base in Chicago.

But there was a fatal flaw in our strategy. We had a team from McKinsey providing strategic guidance – and I remember the senior partner making a seemingly off-the-cuff comment that worried them deeply, but was lost on me at that moment: check the provider (hospital and doctor) discounts you are getting through the network you are using, and ensure it is competitive with Blue Cross of Illinois. It turned out that in those heady days of managed care, the battle for discounts between the large insurers and the 'rental networks' was a central issue. The few basis points we were off in the pricing we were getting, when compared to our largest competitor, made it impossible to get to the price necessary to win market share, and despite the incredible product offering, energy and brilliance of the team, we slowly – then rapidly – moved to an exit.

The economic environment was hugely favourable – and ironically it was this factor that had created the focus and competitive forces that led to our failure.

We finally exited in 2008 after losing about $100 million.

Was the network discount issue in the US analogous to the primary bank account issue in South Africa? In other words, despite all the planning and building, could this one key issue be fatal?

It was this experience that made me sit bolt upright in my bed, and for the first time in over two decades, I thought we may not make it. Simply put, if customers wouldn't move, we would not succeed.

It was then that I had to hold my nerve and remember the solid fundamentals that underpinned our endeavour – as well as steel myself to make difficult changes. We needed to far better integrate the bank's financial services with its behavioural incentives, and to scale it to viability. In my view, the changes that were necessary were so dramatic that they required a bold new leader. Hylton Kallner, at that time the CEO of Discovery South Africa, was tasked with scaling up the ambition, improving cultural alignment with the rest of the organization and leading the bank into its next phase.

Today, the optimism that I found in that clutch moment – my refusal to succumb to a default negative position fuelled by fear and instead keep a clear head to focus on the fundamentals – has been vindicated. In mid-2024, Discovery Bank reached a major milestone: one million clients – two years ahead of schedule – and is on target to double that within five years. It achieved operational profit break-even ahead of schedule at the end of 2024 and is on track to be a dominant force in the South African banking landscape. All the hypotheses upon which the bank has been built are playing out ahead of expectation: the Shared-Value model is performing better than expected, the attraction of clients in the middle- to upper-market segments has exceeded expectation, and the revenue per client is close to the highest in the market, despite the bank being a digital bank.

It seems clear to me now that starting businesses in difficult times – and the ability to focus on the hole and not the lake – is a powerful strategy because, as I said, assets are underpriced and opportunities are vast, but to do so requires drawing on the First Principle: Disciplined Optimism.

Success Is a Better Teacher than Failure

Conventional wisdom says that we learn more from failure than success, and our culture tends to support this, often romanticizing failure as a noble precursor to accomplishment. Business literature encourages us to 'fail forward' or 'fail better' – phrases that have become as ubiquitous as they are clichéd.

I don't agree with this. The following example can explain why.

We know that globally, around 70 to 80 per cent of business start-ups fail within ten years – in fact, wherever you go, the chances of failure of a start-up are overwhelmingly greater than the probability of succeeding. Taking the global data, if eighty in a hundred fail that means there are twenty recipes for success and eighty for failure. If you succeed, you have discovered one of the twenty routes to success, whereas if you fail, you have experienced one of the eighty routes to failure. In other words, in the case of a start-up business, experience of success is four times more valuable than the experience of failure. Success will always be more instructive than failure when the probability of success is less than that of failure – which is virtually always the case in endeavours of impact and scale. They are never easy.

We are further told that failure breeds resilience. Winston Churchill famously said, 'Success is going from failure to failure without losing enthusiasm.' While that made sense in the bleak early days of the Second World War, when successes on the battlefield were rare, overall failure is overrated as a staging post on the path to success.

To be clear: I am not saying we can't learn from failure, or that bouncing back from it isn't hugely commendable and character-building. Importantly also, the courage to fail emboldens people to try, and this is the bedrock of entrepreneurship and ultimately economic growth. But don't be fooled – at an individual level, success is a better teacher.

At Discovery, we have learned from both success and failure, but our most profound lessons have come from learning what went right.

In 2008, as I mentioned earlier, we exited the US health insurance market after eight years of trying to gain traction. Despite our efforts, we couldn't attract enough members to create the scale to compete with incumbent giants. It was a very painful and instructive failure. And yes, we learned lessons that helped propel us onto the global stage. Today, instead of competing head-on, we partner with global insurers.

But what has been the biggest cause of our progress? Is it learning from our failure in the US? Or is it the insights drawn from our success in incentivizing healthier behaviour and turning that into a scalable global model known as Vitality?

Both have been important. But in my view, the lessons from success have been more transformative.

The reasons why we learn more from success than failure lie in our psychology. Emotionally, failure is difficult to absorb. It feels bad. And when something feels bad, we tune out and don't absorb the learnings as deeply.

Behavioural science shows that people tend to avoid personal bad news. For example, in the US, a 2004 study among young men aged 15–22 in San Francisco reported that 34 per cent of those who tested HIV-positive, and 54 per cent of those who tested HIV-negative, did not return for their results.[44]

Cognitively, failure yields less useful information than success.

Whereas success reveals patterns and principles that can be replicated, failure tends to be less instructional – it tells us what not to do but rarely illuminates what we should do.

Research by American motivational psychologists Lauren Eskreis-Winkler and Ayelet Fishbach, who aim to better understand the nature of success by studying failure, found that failure undermines learning. In their 2019 paper, 'Not Learning from Failure – The Greatest Failure of All', they reported on five studies with over 1,600 participants, who were asked a series of binary choice questions.[45] For example: how much money do US companies lose annually due to poor customer service? They were given only two possible answers to choose from: $60 billion or $90 billion. They were then given the correct answers to all questions and retested. Given that there were only two possible answers in each case, participants ought to have been able to remember the right one. But those who got the answer correct the first time did better on retesting than those who got it wrong the first time. Why?

'Our society celebrates failure as a teachable moment', they wrote. 'Yet in five studies, failure did the opposite: it undermined learning. Why does failure undermine learning? Failure is ego threatening, which causes people to tune out.'

In the field of medicine, a fascinating study from Harvard Business School – 'Learning from My Success and from Others' Failure' – tracked seventy-one cardiothoracic surgeons over ten years and 6,500 operations. The research, by K. C. Diwas and colleagues, found that surgeons learned more from their own successes than from their own failures – and more from others' mistakes than others' successes.[46] Why? Because others' failures don't trigger the same ego threat, so we tune in more readily.

Ironically, while failure demands resilience, it doesn't always build it. Success does. It reminds us that winning and progress are possible.

Of course, there are times when failure is immensely instructive.

Plane crashes happen so rarely that when they do, they present rich opportunities for learning. If you are flying a space shuttle, you are only as strong as your weakest link and studying these allows you to avoid the same catastrophic outcome twice. In a manufacturing setup, where you are creating a product through a sequential, linear process, learning from failure is critical because a failure in one part of the process can sink the whole product.

But in networked systems, where processes are not linear, and where the chances of failure are greater than the chances of success – it is success that teaches best.

Performance Appraisals – Use Optimism to See Potential in Others

Personally, I have reservations about performance appraisals, because typically they are about seeking the weaknesses in people as a genuine attempt to help people improve on them. But they follow the same bias in that they miss the positives and the positives are more powerful. I don't want anyone telling me my weaknesses – so why would I think it helps others if I point out theirs? If we want our people to thrive, surely performance reviews should focus on strengths and build people up, not highlight flaws and break them down.

Yet many corporations still fixate on weaknesses. At the extreme end of this are the so-called 'rank and yank' policies made famous by former General Electric CEO Jack Welch. He would conduct harsh performance appraisals, rank staff on a five-point scale, and then fire the bottom 10 per cent of managers – whom he labelled 'C players' – regardless of their absolute performance. In contrast, the top 20 per cent ('A players') were rewarded with bonuses and share options, also irrespective of absolute performance.

But research shows that telling people their weaknesses is a poor management technique that rarely improves performance – largely because of how people are wired.

There are three aspects to this. First, cognitively, as I touched on earlier, our ingrained negativity bias means we remember negative feedback more vividly than positive feedback. We fixate on criticism and downplay praise. This means that negative feedback, especially if insensitively communicated, can have a material damaging impact on employee morale and future performance.

Second, from a neuroscience perspective, criticism activates the amygdala – the brain's threat-detection centre – which triggers elevated cortisol and shuts down the prefrontal cortex, the area of the brain responsible for so-called executive functioning, including reasoning and self-control. Instead of encouraging open reflection, harsh criticism risks making employees defensive and disengaged.

Australian neuroscientist David Rock notes that typically, when our performance is evaluated, the brain tends to shift into 'fight or flight' mode, reducing our capacity to learn.[47] Rock's model outlines how human performance is influenced by factors that trigger either reward or threat responses. He argues that traditional performance appraisals are counter-productive – creating stress, disengagement and ultimately poorer performance.

Third, criticism demotivates. Gallup research shows that when managers focus on employees' strengths rather than their weaknesses, engagement and performance rise significantly – reinforcing the power of a strengths-based approach to productivity.[48]

In a 2008 study, organizational psychologist Hal Whiting and colleagues found that when performance appraisals align with employees' strengths and values, outcomes improve.[49] Their work introduced the Performance Appraisal Congruency Scale and added a psychological dimension to how HR systems are evaluated. It directly challenges the traditional weakness-focused approach.

This doesn't mean we should ignore weaknesses altogether. The key insight is how feedback is framed – and the context in which it is delivered.

Organizational psychology suggests the optimal ratio of positive to negative feedback may be around 5:1. This is known as the Losada Ratio, based on research by behavioural scientists Marcial Losada and Emily Heaphy. In their 2004 study, high-performing teams averaged 5.6:1 positive comments for every negative one, and low-performing teams just 0.36:1.[50] While subsequent criticism of the work by other academics has disputed the exact 5:1 quantification of the optimal ratio, the principle that positive feedback generates better outcomes than negative feedback has not been challenged.

The gist of this evidence is that instead of focusing on what's broken, managers should take an optimistic approach to performance evaluation: they should double down on what's working, emphasizing employee strengths and contributions. This provides a much safer context for dealing with negative aspects of performance in a way that is more likely to lead to subsequent improvement.

I favour this approach partly because I believe there is greatness in everyone – and that it is the role of an organization to help bring this out. At Discovery, Karren Sanderson, chief operating officer of Discovery Health (the South African health insurance business in the Group), started more than twenty years ago as a call centre consultant. And Maia Surmava, chief executive officer of our US business, started with us over twenty-one years ago as a junior software developer. We have underwriters who were in-house baristas, and lots of similarly inspirational stories of people achieving career success beyond their wildest dreams.

This does not happen by accident – it happens in an environment that encourages employees to take risks and that encourages managers to emphasize employees' strengths and achievements, thus liberating greatness at all levels of the organization.

It is an act of optimism to see the potential in others.

Key Takeaway: Attitude Drives Fundamentals

In summary, we are miscoded in relation to how we see positive and negative signals in our environment.

This means that when we make evaluations of external situations, we err twice as much on the side of the negative and struggle to see the positive signals, thus failing to see the full picture and to identify opportunities.

In addition, we miss out on chances to evoke optimism, which is a critical source of energy for success and impact. Society needs our optimism.

This is particularly important in leadership of a system, be it in a small business, a school, a large institution and even a country.

What is exciting is that seeking out positive signals is a teachable tactic, one that if employed is generative in nature, as is spreading positive effects through our networks.

Those who have the fortitude or discipline to resist the negative narrative and to actively seek out positive signals come to understand an inspirational truth: sentiment shapes fundamentals, attitude drives outcomes – not the other way around.

The multiplier effect of the First Principle on impact can be as much as six-fold. Impact depends on (1) identifying the right opportunities and (2) executing on them effectively. On the identification side, Daniel Kahneman and Amos Tversky's work on loss aversion suggests we tend to weight potential losses more heavily than equivalent gains. As a result, we can over-index on negative signals and discount positive ones – leading us to overlook a meaningful share of available opportunities. If that bias causes us to miss, for example, half of the opportunities in front of us, then we act on only half of what is available. Deliberately offsetting the bias does not create new opportunities; it helps us recover the ones we were overlooking – effectively doubling the number of opportunities we identify relative to our biased baseline.

Furthermore, to execute on an identified opportunity effectively, we are required to work with other people, lead companies or manage complex networks. The research shows that these structures can work at least three times better when they are seeded by positive signals and leadership which drives the diffusion of knowledge and pro-social behaviour. The combination of these two powerful forces is multiplicative (the combined effect of enhanced opportunity identification and the increased effectiveness of networks in executing on those opportunities) and can be understood as an indicative six-times effect on impact.

THE SECOND PRINCIPLE: FOCUSED URGENCY

Life is much shorter than we think because of the way time is experienced – we have just 20 per cent of our life to make an impact and leave a legacy, and we need to pursue the important, with focus and urgency.

'Is there greatness in you?'

I have asked this question of new employees at our induction classes over the years. Without exception, the answer is always a resounding 'Yes!' When I then ask: 'Have you used that greatness?' it is generally followed by an equally emphatic 'No!'

The obvious next question is: 'Why haven't you used your greatness yet, and why are you comfortable knowing it's there, unused?'

We induct thousands of people a year, many of whom are actuaries, data scientists and clinicians. By and large, they are brilliant and enthusiastic, and they typically reply that they are 'just starting out' and have their 'entire career ahead'.

If they are sitting there calmly believing this, I point out that it must be because they assume they have plenty of time to live – and therefore plenty of time to make an impact. There are nods all round. The people in the room are typically aged twenty-five to thirty-five, so you can see where they're coming from.

At a deeper level, this mindset echoes something Sigmund

Freud observed: because it is impossible for us to imagine our own death, we carry an unconscious belief in our personal immortality. Subtly, we behave as if we will live for ever. More consciously, people simply believe they have time. And if you believe you have time, nothing feels urgent.

'Okay, let's work it out,' I say. 'How much of your life have you actually lived? And how much do you still have left?'

Let us assume, I say, that you are currently thirty years old and will live to eighty. On a simple linear calculation, you have lived three-eighths of your life – which is around 38 per cent. So that leaves approximately 62 per cent of your life left to realize your potential. And since that is nearly two-thirds of your life, that is plenty of time, I concede.'

'Right,' they answer.

'Wrong,' I say. 'That is not how time works.'

I then introduce the logarithmic theory of time – how we experience time, not how we measure it on a clock – and why our real window to make an impact is far shorter than we think.

I've had this same exchange countless times, both inside the organization and at external events. No matter the audience's age or education, the reaction is always the same.

Shock.

For most people, it is a genuine epiphany.

Let me explain how time actually works.

How We Experience Time – The 20 Per Cent We Have to Make an Impact

When people talk about time, almost everyone says, often wistfully, that it feels as if time is speeding up as they get older. They say things like:

'The last six months just whizzed by.'

'Your children grow up so fast – blink and you miss it.'

'Where did the last year go?'

'I can't believe I've been at this firm this long.'

Or as Dr Seuss whimsically put it: 'How did it get so late so soon? It is night before it is afternoon. December is here before it is June. My goodness how the time has flewn. How did it get so late so soon?'[1]

Have you ever thought about why this is?

Objectively, one year is always 365 days. But subjectively, a year at forty feels nothing like a year at ten. This is the crucial distinction: clock time versus perceived time.

As we age, years feel shorter because each year becomes a smaller fraction of the life we have already lived. Time doesn't just pass – it accelerates. This is known as the log-time hypothesis or the logarithmic theory of time.

Let me elaborate.

When you are one year old, a year amounts to 100 per cent of your life lived so far; when you are ten, it amounts to 1/10th or 10 per cent. By the time you are forty, a year amounts to just 1/40th, or just 2.5 per cent of your lived life.

Clock time is linear – every year is identical in length. Perceived time is non-linear – each year feels shorter than the one before.

A year at forty – 1/40th of your life – goes twice as fast as a year at twenty, which equates to 1/20th of your life, which in turn goes twice as fast as a year at age ten, which is 1/10th of your life.

One of the first thinkers to articulate the idea that our subjective perception of time is relative to the total amount of time we have already lived was the French philosopher Paul Janet.[2] He is credited with formulating the proportional theory of time and, in an 1877 essay, suggested that a year feels shorter as we age because each year constitutes a smaller proportion of our total lived life. Later writers often referred to this as the 'ratio theory' of time perception, since it is based on the ratio between a given time interval and one's lifetime. Although Janet did not use the term 'logarithmic', his theory captured the subjective acceleration and compression of time with age, laying the conceptual groundwork for modern logarithmic models of time perception.

Now let's return to our thirty-year-old.

On a linear calculation, they have lived around 38 per cent of their life. But on a logarithmic basis – how time is experienced – they have lived approximately 78 per cent.

For the mathematically inclined, this is calculated using a relatively simple equation: the sum of perceived years lived is the numerator; the sum of perceived years to age eighty is the denominator. It is depicted as follows:

$$\frac{(1+1/2+1/3+\ldots+1/30)}{(1+1/2+1/3+\ldots+1/80)}$$

$$\approx 0.78$$

$$\approx 78 \text{ per cent}$$

The implication is startling. By age thirty, nearly 80 per cent of your perceived lifetime has already passed. You have just over 20 per cent left. This is why people feel shocked when they see it. It overturns the comforting belief that 'most of life is still ahead.' The following table compares the linear view of time to a logarithmic view.

What percentage of your life have you lived?

Age	Real time	Perceived time
5	6%	37%
10	13%	53%
20	25%	68%
30	38%	78%
40	50%	84%
50	63%	89%
60	75%	93%
70	88%	97%
80	100%	100%

When this is plotted on a graph (see below), how our perception of time behaves becomes clear. We burn through time rapidly until our thirties and then time flattens out thereafter.

Linear Clock Time versus Perceived Time

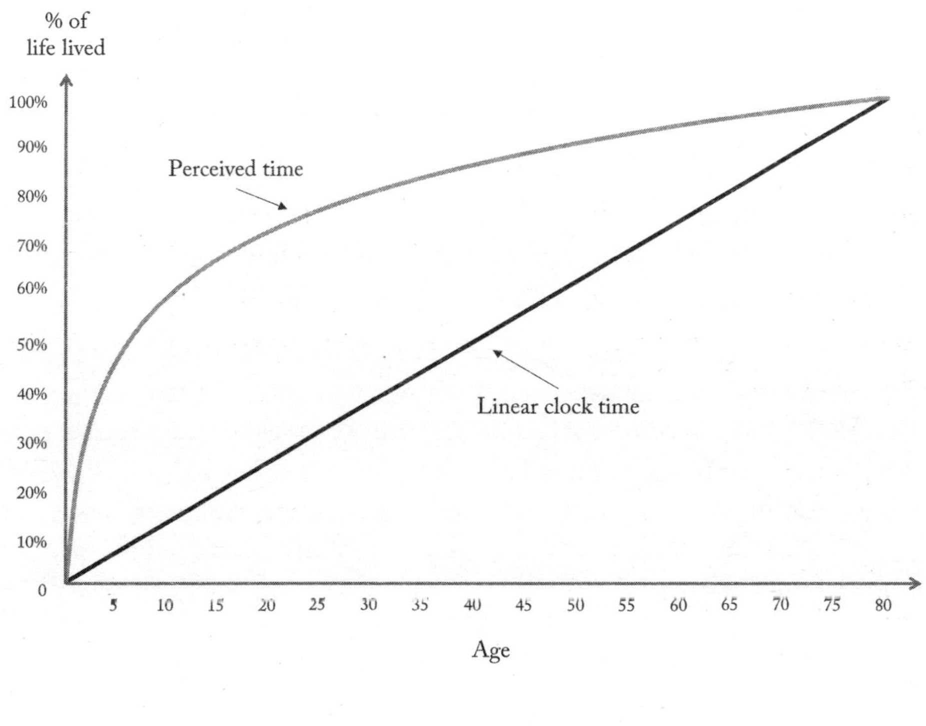

The shocking reality is that by our mid-thirties, we are 80 per cent through our lives in terms of perceived time, and understanding this is crucial if we want to make an impact in life, whatever that is – building a business, seeking to make a charitable impact, spending time with family.

The hard truth for the induction class is – and I reveal this with emphasis – they are 80 per cent through their lives, not the 38 per cent that they came in thinking.

Later in this chapter, I will reveal how we can expand our window for impact and keep ahead of the game. Given the dynamic I have just outlined, however, it is important to break our lives into phases and ensure we are using time optimally. The 20 per cent comes from the simple realization – as depicted below – that there are three broad phases: early life and education, from birth

The 20 Per Cent of Time We Have to Make an Impact

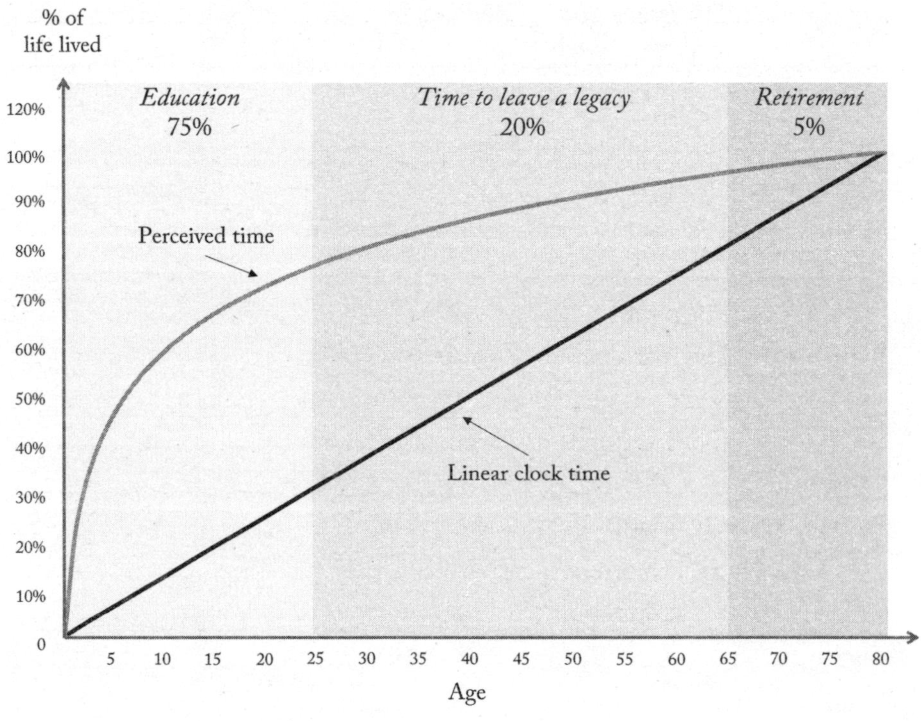

to around age twenty-five (75 per cent); our careers and professional life, from twenty-five to retirement (20 per cent); and retirement (5 per cent).

This leads to a life-changing insight. Your career phase – where impact, contribution and legacy are largely determined – occupies just 20 per cent of your perceived lifetime. People emerge from childhood with vastly different starting points. But for any given set of abilities and opportunities, it is what you do during that narrow career window that determines the difference between unrealized potential and lasting impact.

Understanding how time actually works is not depressing – it is galvanizing, and it leads to the Second Principle: **Focused Urgency**. Your perceived time to make an impact is shorter than you think, given how time is experienced, and recognizing this can act as your greatest motivator.

The implications of the Second Principle are vast and should frame virtually every major decision we make if we want to lead lives of impact. Time lost, opportunities foregone, too little time with loved ones, businesses not started – all leave little time to recover. But all is not lost, there are important tactics that counter this, which, if you employ them effectively, will stretch time considerably to enable you to have more impact and to achieve your goals.

But let me be clear: this is a theory about how years pass, not how moments pass. It is not addressing our perception of short periods of time, for example, where you feel bored and time drags, or when you are engaged and time flies. For me, getting into an ice bath after a long run, each second feels like an eternity. If my plane is delayed at the airport, two hours pass like four. Conversely, if you are engrossed in a good book or film, time passes very quickly. As the Roman statesman Pliny the Younger observed nearly 2,000 years ago, 'the happiest time always appears the shortest'.

The reasons why short periods of time can feel relatively long or short are well-documented in psychology and neuroscience and often comes down to how our brain stores memories. I will be touching on some of these theories later, but for now I want to reiterate that while everyday fleeting examples of moment-to-moment time perception are interesting, they are not what this principle is about.

Instead, logarithmic time perception explains why longer periods of time, such as years or decades, feel shorter as we age. It shows that perceived time doesn't pass uniformly – it accelerates. Whereas our early years feel vast and long, the decades that follow seem to blur, flatten and compress.

Why Should Perceived Time Matter?

Some of our inductees intuitively push back and ask: why should time perception matter if time itself passes at an objectively constant rate? After all, there are twenty-four hours in a day, seven days in a week, and fifty-two weeks in a year, regardless of our age or perception.

The answer lies in how our brains work. Decades of psychology and neuroscience research show that subjective, non-linear time perception shapes how we experience objective time – and importantly, plays a major role in human motivation and decision-making.

Studies in psychology and behavioural economics consistently find that the perceived scarcity of time – our sense that time moves faster as we age – creates a sense of urgency that drives immediate action. It is this perceived scarcity of time – rather than objective clock time – that often motivates urgent choices. For example, time perception research shows that we value immediate rewards more when time *feels* short, regardless of the *actual* time available. According to Zimbardo's time perspective theory, our orientation towards time strongly influences how we make decisions – including how we respond to pressure.[3]

I am not sure why, but I somehow understood this at a young age and it created a deep sense of urgency in me. It is this response to time feeling short – this urgency – that I want to pass on to our inductees and to readers. Because it is one thing to look back when you are older and say, 'How the years have flown', but it is quite another to have the presence of mind to realize, while still young, that this will happen – and to act accordingly.

The timing of when this realization dawns on you is critical – and could be the difference between living an impactful life or not.

I spent my university years listening to the band Pink Floyd, especially when working through mathematical problems. What is ironic, is their take on time. Roger Waters and David Gilmour saw this all too clearly when they were young – and tried to warn us about the perils of wasting our lives. Their famous song, 'Time', which featured on their iconic 1973 album *The Dark Side of the Moon*, was written when they were just twenty-nine and twenty-six years old, respectively. Today, Waters is a controversial figure, but back then they were simply incredibly talented and prescient. They described the fleeting nature of time brilliantly, lamenting that in your youth, life appears long, until one day you suddenly discover that it's all too late – and that because 'no one told you when to run, you missed the starting gun'.[4] The song references the key takeaway of the logarithmic theory of time of succeeding years feeling shorter and addresses our failure to leave a legacy and make an impact, purely because we have misunderstood time.

This, essentially, is my message to our inductees: you think you've got your whole life ahead of you and that you have plenty of time to act, but you don't. So, if you do have something more to say, do it now. Do not delay!

Personal disasters can often act as catalysts for transformation as people respond to the urgency of an external shock with a renewed sense of purpose. For instance, someone facing a life-threatening health scare may develop a heightened energy and clarity, having internalized the realization that they simply don't have time to waste.

Take Stephen Hawking: he was just twenty-one when diagnosed with motor neurone disease and given only two to three years to live. By his own account, Hawking had been an unexceptional student at school and not particularly hard-working during his time at Oxford, where he famously did minimal studying by conventional standards, preferring to work things out in his head and failing to come top of his class. In his final physics exams, Hawking was on the borderline between a first- and second-class degree and only achieved a first because of his convincing viva (oral exam). But that devastating diagnosis changed everything. It gave him both clarity of purpose and a profound sense of urgency. He went on to complete his PhD at Cambridge and became a prolific writer, making ground-breaking contributions to black hole physics, general relativity, quantum cosmology and our understanding of the origins of the universe.

Hawking's transformation into one of the world's most celebrated theoretical physicists was driven by the belief that he didn't have long to live. Fortunately for the world, it was a belief that he spectacularly defied, living another fifty-five years before dying in 2018, aged seventy-six.

'When you are faced with the possibility of an early death,' he wrote, 'it makes you realize that there are lots of things you want to do before your life is over.'[5]

There are countless inspirational stories like this – where bad news or a major shock becomes the turning point that awakens a person to the finite nature of time, sparking them to act with urgency and purpose.

But the message of this Principle – at least as far as the individual is concerned – is different.

Don't wait for unfortunate news – which, hopefully, will never come. Instead, come to this realization for yourself as early as possible in your life. Act now – with proactive urgency – because that is the best way to live your life and make an impact.

There are, of course, other models of time that provide different dynamics, contexts and expectations. But the clarity of time seeming to get shorter as we get older feels directionally correct. For this reason, I use it as a practical lens for urgency and intentionality: it reminds us to act now, before that acceleration catches us off guard.

Let me tell you about my experience of time. I first came upon this theory in my early thirties, and I am now in my sixties, so I have ridden this logarithmic curve personally – and it has felt exactly as the mathematics reveal. My formative years loom large in my mind; the early development of my career and the initial years of building Discovery seem like multiples of the last two decades. I now have a deeper conviction of the importance of the principle of urgency and its 20 per cent consequence.

The question, then, is how to optimize and stretch this 20 per cent to have a greater impact. There is no way to make perceived time feel different, but there are fundamental tools to make that 20 per cent count more effectively. These include making sure you are as productive and as impactful as possible during that effective time – and comes down to health and knowledge.

The Effect of Health on the Time We Have to Make an Impact

The analysis above simply looked at the mathematics of the perception of time, but it ignores how our health and energy – which determine our work rate and productivity – decline as we age.

Even if we maintain good health, our energy declines with age, so tasks take longer to complete and require more recovery time. A 10 km run that takes forty minutes at twenty-five might take fifty minutes at sixty, and your body is likely to need longer to recover. But it is not just physical. Even a desk job can feel harder as our energy wanes.

Combining data from the Global Burden of Disease database with Discovery's data on the effects of lifestyle behaviours on health allows us to estimate the impact of healthy lifestyles on both the length and quality of life – which we capture in the measure termed 'disability-adjusted life years'.

How we manage our health then compounds this effect. A workforce study we conducted in 2023 found that very unhealthy employees lost forty-nine days more in productive time per year than very healthy employees.[6] Over a lifetime, this loss of productivity adds up – not just in what gets done, but in the impact a person is able to make.

The result is reduced output per unit of time. This can make time feel like it is slipping away even faster. Declining health steepens the curve and acts like a drag on our ability to achieve impact, because we do less with each hour, even if the hours themselves remain the same.

But the reverse is also true. If you maintain your health – through regular exercise, good sleep and smart nutrition – you flatten the curve.

The 75:20:5 heuristic ignores the effect of health; it is derived only from the mathematics of the perception of time. Bringing the effect of health as people age into the calculation reduces the 20 per cent.

When we do this, and I have included the detail in the appendix, we see that a person with unhealthy lifestyle behaviours will have only 15 per cent of their perceived life in their working years phase. The antidote – being active, sleeping and eating well, and having appropriate health screenings – will restore this to 19 per cent. The difference between 15 per cent and 19 per cent – between being sick and healthy – is hugely significant, stretching the effective time by close to 25 per cent, a multiple of 1.25.

The idea that health impacts our perception of time is supported by neurocognitive ageing theories, including the processing-speed theory developed by the cognitive psychologist Timothy Salthouse.[7] His research shows that as we age, cognitive processing slows – contributing to declines in memory, attention and overall mental performance. His theory has been foundational in explaining how fewer processed mental events may make time feel as though it is passing more quickly. Later studies have connected this to health, showing that factors such as cardiovascular fitness and sleep quality affect processing speed. This could reverse this effect. So not only does exercise and good health affect productivity but they may also influence processing speed positively.

So, the familiar wholesome advice – 'exercise regularly and look after your health' – proves deeper than it sounds. It is not just good advice: it is a key to preserving or even extending your window of productivity and impact.

This may sound daunting or even out of reach, but the good news is that positive health habits are easy to form.

A 2024 study we conducted with the London School of Economics (LSE) analysed the physical activity and nutrition behaviours of one million Vitality members in the UK and South Africa over a ten-year period. The resulting report, 'The Vitality Habit Index', found that most participants formed a strong habit within seven to fifteen weeks.[8] Crucially, frequency mattered more than intensity. In addition, to get optimal health gains while still being able to maintain a consistent habit, 7,500 steps five or more times a week is advisable. This habit is associated with a 27 per cent overall reduction in the risk of death – rising to as much as a 52 per cent reduction in the risk of death for those over the age of sixty-five.

The key to habit change? Start small and build incrementally – a process known as habit laddering. The effects compound: research shows good habits are correlated. More exercise leads to better nutrition and improved sleep.

None of this will come as a surprise – it is almost a cliché to say that we most appreciate good health as we grow older. Yet from a time perception perspective, it is also profound: good health softens the impact of logarithmic time, giving us the energy and capacity to stay on the curve longer.

The Effect of Knowledge Acquisition on the Time We Have to Make an Impact

Healthy lifestyles and good health have a considerable impact on stretching effective time. The continual acquisition of knowledge is incredibly powerful as well.

It is axiomatic that the more we learn – through education, skills development and experience – the more efficient we become, particularly at more challenging and difficult tasks that require experience and skill to resolve. A task that might take a week when you are just starting out could take just a day when you have more experience.

Crucially, knowledge compounds. At first, learning is slow. But over time, what we have already learned helps us learn more – and faster. What seems difficult in the first year of university becomes foundational by the third. By the final year, students often absorb more in a single term than they did in an entire year as freshers.

This phenomenon is well-documented. As education researcher John Hattie shows in his 2009 book *Visible Learning*, students with more prior knowledge are better able to acquire new material because learning builds cumulatively on what they already know.[9] Cognitive psychologist John Sweller helps explain why: according to his cognitive load theory, as learners develop greater expertise, they reduce their working memory load, enabling them to process more difficult tasks with less mental effort.[10]

People report similar experiences when learning foreign languages: the first is hard, but subsequent new languages are quicker to master.

Learning is not linear – it is exponential. The time it takes to acquire the next unit of knowledge is inversely proportional to how much you already know. In other words, the more you know, the easier learning becomes, creating a positive feedback loop that speeds up mastery.

This is a critical insight – knowledge and time are inversely proportional.

In social science, this dynamic is captured by the Matthew effect – a theory that explains how advantages accumulate over time across domains such as knowledge, wealth and opportunity. It embodies the idea that 'the rich get richer' or 'the smart get smarter' and explains how small initial differences can compound into major long-term impacts – while those starting from behind risk falling even further back.

The term was coined by American sociologist Robert Merton who channelled the biblical verse Matthew 25:29: 'For to everyone who has, more will be given . . . but from the one who has not, even what he has will be taken away.'[11]

Digging deeper, there are also further cognitive and neurological explanations for how knowledge accumulates. For example, cognitive network theories suggest that people with prior knowledge have more 'nodes' (concepts, facts) and 'links' (associations) onto which new knowledge can attach. Prior knowledge acts like a scaffold into which new knowledge can attach.

Because these cognitive networks are underpinned by neural pathways, repeated use of those pathways through learning or practice strengthens them through a process called neuroplasticity.

One such cognitive theory, spreading activation theory, describes how knowledge is stored as a network of concepts and associations.[12] As the network becomes denser and more interconnected, activation – and therefore I argue learning – happens more rapidly.

In neuroscience, neural network growth theories echo this. One of the best known is Hebbian learning, attributed to Donald Hebb, whose principle is memorably paraphrased as 'cells that fire together, wire together'. Repeated activation physically strengthens neural connections, making future activations faster and more efficient.[13]

Put differently, knowledge creates what could be termed pattern recognition at scale. When sufficient situations have been encountered, the mind constructs a vast library of templates against which new problems can be instantly mapped, thereby eliminating the trial-and-error phase that typically consumes considerable time. Consider the surgeon who has performed thousands of procedures: they do not merely work faster, but perceive patterns invisible to more junior surgeons, anticipate complications before they manifest and navigate directly to solutions, while those with less experience remain in the diagnostic phase.

Furthermore, each unit of acquired knowledge does not simply add to existing capabilities – it generates connections with prior knowledge, creating exponential possibilities. An executive versed in psychology, economics and technology will identify opportunities that remain invisible to specialists within any single domain. Knowledge thus multiplies rather than merely accumulating.

Together, these cognitive and neurological forces create a positive feedback loop. Knowledge doesn't just accumulate – it builds on itself and accelerates.

This is the fundamental power of continually acquiring knowledge. Each unit of perceived time gets shorter as we get older, but the time taken to acquire the next unit of knowledge gets shorter as well. Making an impact in life for a given set of skills and work effort is based on how much time you have *and* how much knowledge you have.

If we had infinite time, we'd always make a massive impact because we'd have the time to do whatever we needed to, eventually. And if we had infinite knowledge but limited time, well, we'd write down answers to the world's most pressing problems in seconds. But we have neither infinite time nor infinite knowledge – we have constraints on both.

The breakthrough insight is this: knowledge acquisition slows the perceived passing of time and increases your effectiveness in that time. If you make a habit of learning – say you improve your knowledge base by a few per cent each year – this compounds over time. A simple model in the appendix assumes a 3 per cent annual growth in knowledge after formal education, which is quite attainable (through reading, training and new experiences). Over a career, this compounding can bend the curve of your effective time. Instead of your output peaking early and then stagnating, it keeps growing. Quantitatively, integrating a modest compounding knowledge factor increases the effective impact time of a career by roughly 35 per cent, a multiple of 1.35.

The magic here is visible on the graph below: when you combine the curve of the passing of time and the curve of the accumulation of knowledge, you will see that, conceptually, the composite curve of time to achieve impact becomes much more linear – but only if you keep learning. We can think about this in the form of an equation – impact is notionally knowledge multiplied by time.

Knowledge as an Antidote

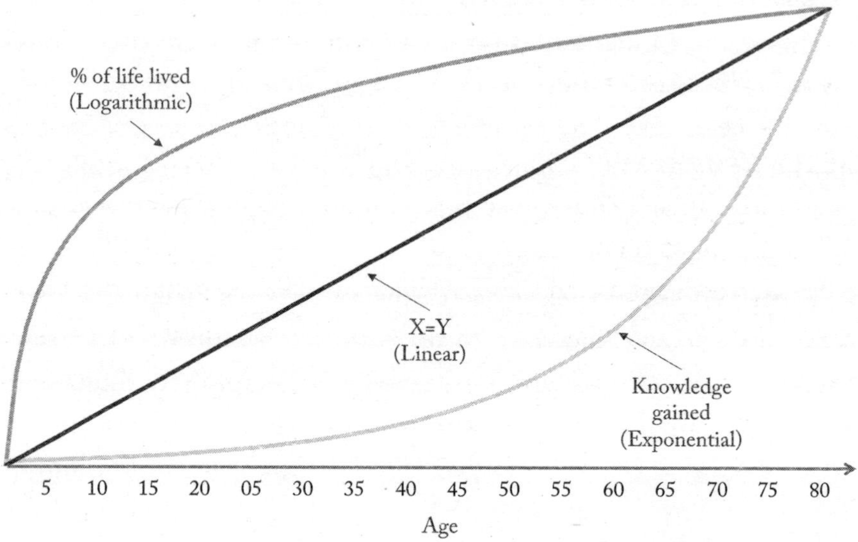

What this means practically is that while each year feels shorter as we age, our ability to learn and apply that learning gets exponentially faster. A difficult business problem that might have taken me weeks or even months to solve at age twenty-five now takes me days – because I have more scaffolding onto which new insights can attach. The learning compounds, and the time to achieve insight compresses.

This isn't just theory – it is something every professional experiences. The doctor who can now diagnose in minutes what once took hours. The teacher who can explain complex concepts with analogies that come from years of seeing where students struggle. Knowledge truly becomes the antidote to time's acceleration.

The exhortations we so often hear to 'keep learning' and to be 'lifelong learners' are not just true – they are mathematically and cognitively profound.

It is clear then that managing your health and continuously

acquiring knowledge has a dramatic effect on stretching your effective time to make an impact.

Why It Is Never Too Late, Even If You Are Older

The legendary coach of the Green Bay Packers, Vince Lombardi, once quipped: 'We didn't lose the game; we just ran out of time.'

The comment reflects Lombardi's relentless drive and refusal to accept defeat, suggesting that he believed his team had the skill to win, but had been unable to deliver within the time constraints of a game. The issue, he seemed to be saying, was not his team's lack of ability, but rather their lack of urgency.

That call for proactive and focused urgency is exactly what this chapter is trying to convey.

Mathematically, as life progresses, you approach the flatter part of the logarithmic time curve, where each year feels more uniform relative to the previous one – and thus more linear.

That is a gift. It is never too late to fulfil your potential and make a meaningful impact. This may sound paradoxical, given that I have said our inductees' time to make an impact is limited by age thirty and introduced the 20 per cent paradigm. So let me be clear: the ideal, of course – and the message I am trying to get across – is that the earlier in our lives we realize the truth about the passing of time, the sooner we can begin to pursue the important, with focused urgency, and make an impact.

The appendix provides a thought experiment: a twenty-five-year-old imagining themselves at age fifty. At fifty, because perceived time has 'sped up', one feels each year fly by twice as fast as at twenty-five (mathematically, using the logarithmic theory of time, the rate of passage of perceived time with respect to real time for a twenty-five-year-old is double that of a fifty-year-old).

If the twenty-five-year-old can internalize that perspective – essentially realizing 'I have no time to waste' – they could double their urgency and drive in the present. In effect, they begin to use their time with the seriousness and focus of someone much older.

This mental trick can significantly accelerate progress on goals, because tasks that might have been put off are tackled immediately. The effect varies with age but quantitatively, instilling an urgency mindset early on could plausibly add an additional indicative 25 per cent boost to effective time, on top of health and knowledge gains, a multiple of 1.25. It is like squeezing more value out of each year by treating time as scarcer than it appears.

Yet there are many powerful examples of people who have made major impacts later in life. Ray Kroc was in his fifties when he turned a small burger stand into the global powerhouse that is McDonald's. Around the same age, Bernie Marcus co-founded Home Depot after being fired from his job. Others, like Sam Walton and Leo Goodwin, launched Walmart and GEICO in midlife, fundamentally reshaping retail and insurance. Even in more technical fields, age was no barrier – Robert Noyce and Gordon Moore founded Intel in their forties, laying the groundwork for the digital age. Chip Wilson, in his forties, created Lululemon and pioneered the athleisure movement, while Ely Callaway, in his early sixties, transformed a small golf-club company into a global brand. These entrepreneurs came from different backgrounds and industries, but they all share one thing: they didn't let age define their trajectory.

I once had a conversation with billionaire entrepreneur Natie Kirsh when he was about eighty and I was struck by his incredible energy and sharpness. While many octogenarians slow down – playing golf, taking naps – he was fully engaged, still actively running his global business empire.

His story demonstrates that it is never too late to reinvent oneself and make a significant impact – as he did in his fifties after losing his South African business empire and fortune in 1986.

Initially building a formidable conglomerate through ventures like the Swaziland Milling Company and Metro Cash & Carry (wholesale and food retail), Kirsh faced a major setback when a partnership with the South African financial services group, Sanlam, led to the sale of his key assets due to a contractual dispute during South Africa's economic turmoil.

Undeterred, he relocated to New York in his fifties, when the time curve flattened, and transformed Jetro Cash & Carry – founded in 1976 – into a multi-billion-dollar company dominating US cash-and-carry food distribution. This business was modelled on his experience running Metro in South Africa, and its success fuelled his global empire. Kirsh businesses now span real estate holdings and private investments across multiple industries and countries.

Despite Natie's considerable achievements, there were still things he wanted to accomplish. His main concern? 'Time is my biggest issue,' he told me.

His words have stayed with me: a reminder that no matter how much success or wealth you build, time remains the ultimate reason to act with intention while you can. His story also exemplifies my earlier point: people can have an impact later in life if they maintain their health and energy and keep learning.

And there are many who do.

Indeed, there is evidence that entrepreneurs in their fifties and sixties are just as likely to start companies as those in their twenties. In the US, people in their forties to sixties are far more likely to become new entrepreneurs than those under thirty-five, according to data from the 2021 Kauffman Indicators of Entrepreneurship.[14]

Furthermore, a meta-analysis of 102 studies, published in the

Journal of Business Venturing in 2021, found that older founders are just as likely to build successful companies as younger founders.[15] This matches other landmark findings, including a 2018 paper in the *Harvard Business Review* that found the average age of the most successful tech start-up founders is forty-five.[16]

Together, these studies confirm that experience, networks and expertise often outweigh raw youthful energy – proving that for those who are motivated and feel the urgency, it is never too late to start and build something extraordinary.

Alternate Theories of Time

You may think my view on time being non-linear is niche, but it isn't. Time is not linear; there are simply varying views on its real properties and the effect on us.

No discussion of time would be complete without recalling the famous intellectual confrontation between the world's most celebrated physicist and one of the most influential philosophers of the era, which took place just over a century ago in Paris.

The 1922 debate between Albert Einstein and Henri Bergson was a clash between physics and philosophy. Put simply, Einstein argued that time does not flow at a single universal rate, but stretches, shrinks and bends, depending on motion and gravity – these are measurable, and governed by physical laws. He dismissed subjective time entirely, saying, in a famously scathing remark, that 'the time of the philosophers' had no place in physics.

Bergson countered that time is not just an objective measurable quantity, but also a continuous, qualitative, lived experience – what he called *duration* – which couldn't be adequately captured by clocks or equations.

Ironically, although Einstein's view came to dominate the scientific world and Bergson's reputation initially suffered after their debate, it was Bergson's ideas that later influenced major research in neuroscience, neurobiology and psychology on how we perceive the passage of time.

This includes a theory proposed by American physicist and engineer, Adrian Bejan, who, in his 2019 paper 'Why the Days Seem Shorter as We Get Older', argued that time seems to speed up with age because the brain's ability to process sensory information slows down. With fewer distinct mental images formed, we perceive time as moving more quickly.[17]

British scientist Rory Maizels extended this idea in 2023, comparing the brain to a camera: 'When we are young, each second of actual time is packed with many more mental images,' he said, 'like a slow-motion camera that captures thousands of images per second.'[18] As we age, this slows down – leading to the perception that time is speeding up.

Today, we can see value in both Einstein's and Bergson's approaches – though they apply to different domains. Einstein's time is objective, measurable and external; Bergson's time is subjective, felt and internal. One explains the universe, the other explains how we experience it. Rather than being contradictory, they can be seen as complementary – and modern neuroscience draws insight from both.

At its core, the key is this: although time is lived forwards, our experience of time is backward-looking – and that makes it subjective and relative.

The question thus becomes: how do we respond? How do we make that 20 per cent really count and maximize our impact? We can consider this from the point of view of the individual and of businesses. Let's take each scenario in turn.

Applications

Optimizing Work-Life Balance

If you were to sit down with your child as they approached twenty-five, what would you tell them about how to make their working life count?

Given what we now know about the scarcity of time, the answer must lie in acting with urgency. But it is not that simple. Working all the waking hours of the day often leads to burnout and an unfulfilled, single-track life. The key question becomes how we can act with urgency and optimize work-life balance to achieve the impact we seek.

There are many theories on work-life balance. One, the four burners theory, popularized by American author David Sedaris and expanded by James Clear, suggests that we imagine life as a stove with four burners: family, friends, health and work. To be successful, the theory says, you must turn one off. To be very successful, you need to turn off two.[19] It is a reminder that we have limited time and energy and that trying to run all four burners can lead to burnout or mediocrity – or both.

Clear advocates for a softer approach that he calls 'burner blending', combining life areas – such as health and friends by running with friends – as an alternative to hard trade-offs.

There are many other theories of work-life balance that hone in on this same issue of how to use your time wisely.

Ray Dalio, founder of Bridgewater Associates, has written about what we might call radical prioritization – accepting that there is no such thing as perfect work-life balance, and instead aligning your time with your personal values, even if it means making hard trade-offs. In his 2017 book, *Principles: Life and Work*, he emphasizes that life is about choosing what you value most and accepting the consequences. 'You can have virtually anything you want, but you can't have everything you want,' he writes.[20]

Dalio encourages people to identify what matters – whether career success, family time, creative freedom or health – and to intentionally allocate time and energy to those priorities. He also advocates treating your life like a business: build systems that support balance, delegate low-value tasks and block time for what matters most. While this advice is sound in principle, it is far easier to apply when you have financial resources, supportive networks or flexible work. Nevertheless, the core idea remains: even small, deliberate shifts in how you spend time can help align daily life more closely with what you value most, so that life becomes more integrated and fulfilling.

Other theories go even more granular, arguing that time isn't the only constraint and that energy is what matters most. You may have eight hours available for work, but they're not all equally productive.

In *The Power of Full Engagement*, Jim Loehr and Tony Schwartz argue that managing energy, not time, is the key to sustainable high performance.[21] They stress that while time is finite, energy is renewable – and should be managed across four dimensions: physical, mental, emotional and spiritual. Time spent in high-energy, high-focus states is far more valuable than simply 'putting in the hours'.

Then there's Stephen Covey's well-known time-management matrix. His key insight is the need to distinguish between what's urgent and what's important – and to prioritize the important. Covey's message is clear: stop living in constant firefighting mode. To be effective, you must invest time in planning and clarifying your values and purpose. That's how you shift from reactive to proactive and focus on the things that make a lasting impact.

Of course, balance – like beauty – is in the eye of the beholder and will differ from person to person.

In my case, my priorities are clear: family, business, fitness and cultivating and maintaining important friendships. I am ruthless about this. There is no compromise. I compromise on other things.

To fit in my four priorities, I am highly structured about my time. I have found several important practices that allow me to be significantly more effective with the limited time I have – this centres on regularity of sleep, early morning productivity and high intensity, short bouts of exercise.

This is what a regular day looks like. I wake up at 3 a.m. and do an hour of work, mostly emails, from bed, and then sleep again until 5 a.m., a light meditative sleep, and get about six hours' sleep in all. From 5.15 a.m. until 8 a.m., I am on the clock: I hit it hard on the treadmill, followed by push-ups and sit-ups and a quick swim – all in all ten minutes of high-intensity training. I have found that this regimen contributes substantially to staying very fit and healthy. I wake up my young son at 6 a.m. and drive him to school. My wife would happily do it, but we agree that me spending this time with him is special and important and I protect it at all costs. I drop him off around 7.10 a.m., make business calls from the car, and typically arrive at the office at around 8 a.m. That 45 minutes in the car lets me prepare for the day on calls and catch up with friends – a time that has proven to be hugely important.

During my workday, I do an unusual thing – between meetings, I run the stairs in our building. My office is on the eighth floor of our building and I run up and down the stairwell as fast as I can several times a day. I typically finish work at around 6 p.m. and head home to have dinner and spend time with my wife and the other children if they are around and put my son to bed. After that, I do a few more emails and work calls, and I am asleep by 10 p.m. On Saturdays, I abstain from work, rest and spend time with my family and friends – I am not available by phone or email, and spend the day reading, learning and at leisure.

I have been following this routine for years, using the first few hours of the day highly intentionally – to exercise, reflect and consciously think through my day. Robin Sharma described the benefits I gain from this very well in his 2018 book *The 5 AM Club*, where he talked about the benefits of waking at 5 a.m. to 'own' the early morning and using those quiet hours with no distractions to 'move, reflect and grow', so as to build health and clarity before the world wakes up and your 'real' work begins. According to Sharma, the early-rising habit is a common one among top performers that has helped them accomplish great results.[22]

It is important to also stress that staying fit need not consume too much time – consistency and intensity trump time. Also, our research shows that consistency with sleep is crucial. Keeping fit and healthy can be achieved with discipline and without imposing too much of a time burden.

You may think that I am living a boring and algorithmic life, dominated by 'work', but it is exactly the opposite. My work is so multidimensional that I find it captivating and liberating. That is the thing about work: if you find something that truly interests you, it becomes a wonderful adventure and a privilege. My work has taken me all over the world and exposed me to many different fields of complexity and geopolitical issues and has enabled me to meet and work with incredibly smart people from across the globe. It is like the famous Thomas Edison quote, 'I never did a day's work in my life – it was all fun.' Edison's point suggests that when you are passionate about your work, it can feel more like a joy than a chore.

Of course, I appreciate that it isn't always simple to find work that engages you: according to the latest Gallup State of the Global Workplace report, the global percentage of 'engaged employees' fell from 23 per cent to 21 per cent in 2024, and in Britain, the figures are even worse – just 10 per cent say they are engaged in their work.[23] My point, though, is that when you do find that kind of work, discipline comes more easily, and the hours invested don't feel like work at all, but like a meaningful life well lived.

At times, I go to extreme lengths to keep that balance. For example, I was in Sun City, a resort about a two-and-a-half-hour drive from Johannesburg, at the Discovery leadership conference which was finishing late at night after the final dinner, and we were due to leave early the next morning. But the next day was also my eldest son's last day of high school. I was determined to be there to take him – I have always taken all my children to school. So, I left Sun City at midnight and drove very carefully and eventually got home at around 3 a.m.

My wife was incredulous. 'What are you doing here?' she asked. 'What kind of person comes home early from his own conference?' But it was worth it. I have never let work get in the way of important milestones. Taking your children to school, having time with them where you prioritize your relationship with them – I'm a strong believer in setting priorities and keeping to them.

In the context of work-life balance, you must understand that your time is a precious commodity and that you have a very limited supply of it. You can't subscribe to other people's perspectives on balance. You need to set your own priorities and pursue these with urgency. Ironically, you have lived a balanced life if you achieve the priorities that are important to you.

How to Create Focused Urgency and Pace Within an Organization

Companies are not like individual people who perceive time in a logarithmic way. Instead, companies move through time in a linear way. Yet time, pace and urgency are crucial for success, competitiveness and sustainability. At Discovery, we have had a surplus of powerful ideas that we know can allow us to compete and win. However, they often take too much time to execute. The paradox is that, with the increasing pace of change, the technology and the time needed to build it slows things down. The central question is how to inject a disciplined pace into a company.

External Shocks and Regulatory Change Lead to Urgency and Pace

One area in which organizations can be forced to address urgency is in response to external shocks. These can be triggered by new technologies, wars, economic upheavals (such as President Trump's tariffs announced in early 2025, which caused companies large and small to completely rework their supply chains, routes to market, and more), or regulatory shocks, often imposed by governments or regulators.

Not all companies interpret these threats correctly – or respond fast enough. But those that pivot in time may not only survive but also emerge stronger, especially if competitors fail to read the writing on the wall.

At Discovery, we faced an external shock that was existential – in the form of a regulatory change that threatened our survival exactly at the point of our IPO. If we hadn't acted quickly, we could have been history.

From a time perspective, what fascinates me is this: innovations that would normally have taken years were achieved in just weeks. That is the power of urgency – the effect of the sword of Damocles.

The episode I am about to recount has become part of our company's lore. Extreme stakes. Exhausting twenty-hour days. Intense collaboration among the leadership team. This is what happened.

Fourteen Days to Save Our Company, and the Genesis of a Global Business Model

The power of deadlines in creating urgency cannot be overstated. In our case, an imposed deadline and the impending threats behind it enabled our entire global business model.

The power of a decree from government or a regulatory body to create urgency within a company is incredibly instructive in seeing how time can be bent and urgency applied.

Seven years after launching Discovery, the government publicly warned us that they viewed our business model as non-compliant with the law and threatened to shut us down – this was front page news in the week of our IPO, not the most ideal message for potential shareholders. This process ebbed and flowed over the next two months, but then we received a letter from the health insurance regulatory body that sent a shiver down my spine.

It arrived at the worst possible time – the day before Christmas in December 1999. Our executive team was away for the millennium holiday period, except for my founding partner, Barry Swartzberg, who was holding the fort in Johannesburg. He picked up the letter and immediately called me.

'Adrian, we have a problem,' he said.

The letter stated that our health insurance products did not comply with new government legislation – and carried a chilling ultimatum:

'You have fourteen days to comply – or we will shut you down.'

We had just signed a fifteen-year lease on a new high-rise building that was still under construction. Barry, standing in our old offices overlooking the rising shell of our future headquarters, looked out and thought, 'Fifteen-year lease, fourteen-day deadline to survive . . .' It didn't compute.

We let the executive team enjoy their festive break but gave them notice that we were calling them back early. On Sunday 2 January, we all went back to the office in Johannesburg. There were about a dozen of us and for the next month we camped out, working day and night to save the company.

Our first step was to buy time. Our lawyers secured a temporary reprieve, extending the fourteen-day deadline to the end of January.

But now we had to do something much harder: design new products that would satisfy the regulator. This was a tough ask because our entire approach to health insurance was in effect being repudiated.

Under the new regulations, insurers had to do three things: accept all applicants (known as open enrolment), not exclude pre-existing conditions, and charge everyone the same premium regardless of age or health (known as a community rate).

This was the complete antithesis of our business model, which was based on actuarial principles: pricing members at entry according to their risk factors, age and gender. The regulatory change would disallow this, forcing us to accept all applicants regardless of risk and to charge everyone the same rate. Such an 'open enrolment, community rating' system is incredibly difficult to impose on an existing business built on opposite foundations. It would mean that healthier members would suddenly pay more, prompting many to cancel their cover and creating what we call a 'death spiral' in the risk pool, where only the less healthy remain insured – costs spiral, premiums rise, more healthy people leave, and ultimately the insurance fund is bankrupted.

The regulations were a manifestation of emerging government policy, but they were also lobbied for by our competitors, many of whom had suffered substantially from our significant growth and success.

So, the dramatic ultimatum, 'fourteen days to comply or be shut down', set an almost impossible task. We had to devise a product that complied with open enrolment and community rating but was also financially viable.

We rolled up our sleeves and devised new products. But every time we thought we had cracked the framework, we were rebuffed by the regulator. For weeks we argued, back and forth – they were desperate times.

Everything we had built over eight years was on the line. One key member of the leadership team came to my house one night just days before the deadline, utterly distraught, and said, 'We've gone through it, Adrian. We've tried everything. We're going down.'

Then, with the deadline imminent, we had a collective breakthrough.

We devised a simple but elegant idea: instead of charging different premiums for the same product, which was now banned, we would offer two different products at two different price points. We created a Standard Plan that offered lower benefits at a lower price, and a Max Plan, with higher benefits at a higher price. The former appealed to younger, healthier members and the latter to older or sicker members. And here was the masterstroke – we allowed customers to pay an additional insurance premium to 'jump up' from the Standard to the Max Plan at any time.

Internally we called this product development process 'Apollo 1, 2 and 3', because it involved three phases of trial and error that to us seemed as difficult as landing on the moon. Apollo 1 and 2 had been rejected by the regulator. Finally, with Apollo 3, we thought we had hit upon a structure that offered open enrolment and community rating, and which segmented the market by benefit instead of by price.

It worked. The regulator gave us approval. We had survived.

What happened next was instructive – because not only did we recover, we accelerated. Our new product structure was more attractive than the one-size-fits-all approach offered by our competitors. Not only that, but international competitors that had entered the South African market after 1994, wanting to be part of the 'new' South Africa, found the new operating environment unfavourable and withdrew. This included the giant US company, United Healthcare. That left the path clear for us to grow our local market share dramatically.

The key issue, though, was a revelation that sustainable health insurance could not be built on solely pricing risk and managing care, but in fact required a much more profound purpose – make people healthier and thereby reduce the demand for healthcare.

You see, that fourteen-day deadline created an intensity and urgency that elevated our business from solving transactional actuarial and regulatory problems to a globally relevant business model.

Typically, this pressure comes from the outside, but I argue that great companies can create this pressure proactively and internally.

Time-Based versus Event-Based Organizations

This is the issue: companies can and often do move quickly with external threats that are imposed on them and can rework their business models in weeks or months because they must.

The more challenging question, however, is how to do this proactively from within, without the pressure of external threats. There is a process and a discipline that can be a powerful solution to this. It involves being 'time based' rather than 'event based'.

As companies mature, they often lose the sharp edge that got them there in the first place. They become reactive – responding to competitors' innovations or market shifts – rather than proactive. These businesses tend to coast until a crisis jolts them into action. While they may still respond well under pressure, they often end up firefighting – tackling symptoms rather than root causes. These are event-based organizations.

Time-based organizations, by contrast, generate urgency from within. They don't wait for competitors or crises to force change – they drive it themselves. By planning and driving for consistent innovation based on internally defined timelines, they don't just stay ahead – they often set the pace for their industries.

Of course, no business can afford to ignore significant external forces, but I believe in the wisdom and discipline of running a business on tight, time-based goals rather than reactive, event-driven responses. Being time based gives you control over your organization's metabolic rate – the pace at which you operate – by instilling urgency from within.

Companies like Amazon and OpenAI embody this proactive mindset. They establish internal innovation schedules and rhythmically deliver change on their own cadence – creating urgency, discipline and anticipation not only within their organizations but also for their customers and often across their entire sectors.

Amazon is relentless in its proactive innovation. Amazon Prime Day – its self-created annual retail 'holiday' on which it offers big discounts on thousands of products to Prime members – drives billions in sales and forces internal breakthroughs in logistics, pricing and delivery. In 2025 alone, Prime Day generated over $24 billion in US online sales, more than double Amazon's Black Friday performance the prior year. In addition, Amazon Web Services releases thousands of new features each year, guided by tight internal schedules and built by small, autonomous 'two-pizza teams' – a term coined by founder Jeff Bezos to describe an ideal team size of 5–8 people, that can be fed with two pizzas and innovate quickly.

OpenAI, with ChatGPT at the forefront, is another exemplar. Since its public debut in late 2022, OpenAI has released a steady stream of upgrades – from more powerful models like GPT-4 and GPT-5 to entirely new capabilities such as multimodal inputs (analysing images, for example), memory (recalling facts shared in prior conversations) and custom GPTs (personalized versions tailored to specific users). The models are not only becoming smarter but also more adaptable and bespoke. These releases follow an internally defined cadence rather than external demand, yet they have generated a cycle of urgency and anticipation among users, customers and even competitors – with rivals scaling quickly.

Both companies demonstrate how self-imposed deadlines foster agility, sharpen internal focus, drive operational innovation and set the wider industry agenda.

Netflix is another interesting example. Launched in 1997, it became a thriving DVD-by-mail service, that by 2005 was shipping over one million DVDs per day. But recognizing that the future of entertainment lay in digital streaming rather than physical DVDs, the company disrupted its own business model, pivoting to streaming in 2007, and building a global content delivery network to handle millions of simultaneous viewers. By the end of 2024, Netflix was available in over 190 countries, and had over 300 million subscribers, massively more than it could ever have achieved by scaling its DVD shipping business. Critically, this 2007 pivot happened during a time of stability – not one of crisis or threats from external competitors.

At Discovery, this proactive, time-based approach is embedded in our DNA. In each of our businesses, we launch material product innovations every year. We set hard launch dates early, and everyone knows – come what may – we go live with new products on that day.

A powerful example is how we expanded our Vitality Shared-Value health insurance model into life insurance. That decision – and the tight timeline we imposed on ourselves – didn't just accelerate execution, it sparked a breakthrough that has made a significant impact on the global life insurance industry.

How a Time-Based Mindset Created a New Model for Life Insurance

In 2000, my former boss at Liberty Life, Herschel Mayers, joined Discovery to help launch our life insurance business. He brought with him the deep, traditional expertise of a large, established life insurer – which was invaluable – and we quickly gained strong traction against large and sophisticated competitors. But the business did not initially integrate our behavioural Vitality model into its life insurance products, and this was a strategic concern. We needed a breakthrough.

Life assurance has operated on a complex set of actuarial principles for centuries – it has had to, because the premiums people pay are generally guaranteed over their entire lifetime. Regardless of how sick they get, how long they live or how investment markets behave, what they pay remains the same. This is a massive and risky undertaking by the life assurance company because this guarantee can endure for fifty years or more, and the amounts of money involved can be immense. The same model is used whether you buy life insurance in New York, London, Tokyo, Hong Kong or Johannesburg.

The challenge was daunting: Vitality is dynamic, but life assurance is fixed. We were determined to find a way to integrate Vitality; however, with just two months left before our annual launch in March, we were running out of time. That's when Herschel, his deputy, Kenny Rabson, and a small group met for a brainstorming session in Johannesburg. The problem had to be cracked, and fast.

At that session, Kenny proposed an approach that was so elegant and impactful that its influence has continued to grow year by year. His idea was this: we would give customers a meaningful discount on their premium at entry, assuming they were healthy. Provided they engaged with the Vitality programme, they would continue to enjoy the same or an even deeper discount. However, customers who failed to engage – and therefore did not make healthy lifestyle choices – would see their premiums increase each year in small but fair increments. The elegance of the breakthrough was that the approach was intuitive and would make sense to customers. Making it work actuarially was difficult, yet doable, enabled by the Vitality structure.

Suddenly, just like that, the Vitality Shared-Value model for life insurance was born.

This seemingly simple dynamic payment structure created a completely different actuarial model that was significantly more efficient and led to better results for both the insurance company and its customers. While we didn't have the data at that stage, with time what has become clear is just how powerful lifestyle choices are when it comes to health and life expectancy, and these choices lie with the customer.

By not taking these into account while people are insured, the insurance company was in effect pooling 'controllable risks', which is inefficient because insurance is fundamentally a mechanism that efficiently pools uncontrollable risks. By removing this inefficiency, we could both enhance the proposition to the customer – pay less, earn incentives, and live a longer and healthier life, while for the insurance company it would be more competitive because it could charge lower prices while generating greater profitability.

What struck me – and this has become increasingly evident over time with our increasing success – is that this is the hallmark of globally disruptive business models; efficiency leads to lower prices for customers and higher profitability for suppliers. In the context of life insurance, the power of this cannot be overstated: the industry is of a considerable scale globally (over $8 trillion) and incredibly capital intensive, with frequent suboptimal returns on that capital. The opportunity for global impact was clearly vast.

What is also critical and hugely gratifying is that the effect on customers would be even more powerful for the sick, chronically ill or the elderly – the data now shows clearly how powerful behaviour change is in these phases of life. It is never too late to make these changes, and the model uses the considerable economic value available from the more profitable insurance pool to incentivize and guide them.

I know it may sound overly grand to say it, but that meeting was the moment that created the potential to dramatically change the global life insurance industry – and the meeting was in response to the time-based discipline of a yearly launch.

Just a few weeks later, in October 2000, we launched Discovery Life linked to Vitality – creating the world's first dynamically priced life insurance product based on behavioural factors and launching what we came to call the Shared-Value Insurance model.

It was only over time that we came to realize the true significance of this new value proposition. Before Discovery Life, the relationship between life insurers and their customers was entirely transactional. The new model, by contrast, was dynamic and engaging. Instead of a handful of touchpoints over a policy's lifetime – it created consistent, ongoing interaction with our customers – associating traditionally boring life insurance products with the positive message of investing in and benefitting from a healthy lifestyle.

The financial impact on customers was profound. People spend a large portion of their savings on life insurance over decades, so a value proposition that rewarded them for managing controllable risks in a transparent, contractual way was immensely compelling.

It allowed those who invested in their health to benefit from richer life cover at materially lower premiums. And so, it turned out that a person who bought an average-sized policy at age forty and engaged in healthy behaviours would save 54 per cent in premiums by age sixty-five – and in addition enjoyed more years of healthy life along the way.

For us as a life insurer, it was equally transformational. It meant we could treat customers fairly while creating a business model that could win new business more competitively – and ensure its sustained profitability over time.

The effect of this is that Discovery became South Africa's leading life insurer in the mid-to-higher income segment, overtaking far larger incumbents that had dominated the industry for more than a century.

In 2007, seven years after that moment which transformed life insurance in South Africa, we took our Vitality Shared-Value model to the UK.

We did it through a joint venture with Prudential, then the largest insurance provider in the country. We first launched PruHealth, a health insurer, and then PruProtect, the first integrated consumer-engaged life insurance company in the UK. Starting with health insurance and expanding into life insurance, the British market represented our first true test of whether dynamic pricing could work beyond South Africa.

The results were extraordinary. Within a few years, PruProtect had captured 12 per cent of the UK's independent financial adviser market for life insurance and had become the fourth largest seller of adviser-based insurance products.[24] In an industry where gaining even 1 per cent market share can take decades, this was a significant result.

What amazed me most was watching British customers embrace the concept. They weren't just buying insurance – they were buying into a completely different relationship with their health.

The structure of the joint venture with Prudential was that we had the right to purchase their 50 per cent of the joint venture at specific points in time. Given the potential of the Vitality Shared-Value model – we jumped at this chance and exercised the so-called 'call option'. In 2014, Discovery took full ownership of the joint venture and rebranded the company as Vitality – consolidating our offering under a single brand that encompassed both VitalityLife and VitalityHealth. This would form the basis of our global expansion. The company was serving more than 800,000 people, a figure that has grown to over 2 million customers today, making VitalityHealth the UK's third-largest health insurer, behind only Bupa and Axa, and VitalityLife the third-largest writer of new business in the British life insurance market, the fourth-largest life insurance market in the world.

Our success in the UK proved that the model wasn't just a South African anomaly – it was a fundamental reimagining of how health and life insurance could work in any developed market.

In 2014, we expanded into the Asia-Pacific region via a strategic joint venture with AIA Group Limited. Our model became a powerful way to differentiate AIA, making life insurance less about death and more about healthy living.[25] This partnership has enabled AIA to offer dynamic pricing and Shared-Value Insurance through Vitality across eleven markets in Asia-Pacific, from Singapore and Hong Kong to Australia and the Philippines; a mutually beneficial partnership that continues to benefit both businesses and AIA's millions of customers.

Next came a partnership with Sumitomo Life in Japan. By the time we entered Japan in 2018, we had insights and learnings from sixteen other markets, and so what followed was a meticulous rollout. Sumitomo Life saw Vitality as a way to address rising medical costs and revitalize life insurance in Japan – and the model has proved highly lucrative for both Sumitomo Life and Discovery.

Around the same time, we took our Vitality Shared-Value model to the US. John Hancock – one of America's oldest life insurers – began offering Vitality as part of its package in 2015, but as an optional add-on to traditional coverage. The results were so compelling that, in 2018, John Hancock made a powerful announcement.[26]

'For centuries, the insurance model has primarily provided financial protection for families after death, without enhancing the very quality it hinges on – life,' declared Marianne Harrison, then president and CEO. 'We fundamentally believe life insurers should care about how long and well their customers live. With this decision, we are proud to become the only US life insurance company to fully embrace behaviour-based wellness and leave the old way of doing business behind.'

Henceforth, John Hancock would offer Vitality on all new life insurance policies at no additional cost – effectively abandoning the traditional life insurance model that had served the industry for over 150 years.

Brooks Tingle, now CEO of John Hancock, put the transformation in context at the time: 'We have smartphones, smart cars and smart homes. It is time for smart life insurance.'[27]

Leading business publications began to write us up in glowing terms. *Forbes* featured our Shared-Value Insurance model, describing it as 'the world's first true shared-value insurance model', and in 2021 named Discovery as one of the companies that was 'transforming people's lives and the industry'.[28] McKinsey & Company highlighted the model in their 2020 report on the future of life insurance, describing 'shared-value life insurance products, such as Vitality' as 'in the vanguard'.

It seems somewhat bizarre now, to look back at that moment in the small conference room with Kenny and Herschel, responding to a local and self-imposed time deadline, and to see how that breakthrough has ultimately had profound global implications. Forcing deadlines, pursuing the important with focused urgency, can change the world. By using the launch date as a catalyst for innovation, we developed an approach to life insurance that created an entirely new category – one that has positively impacted the lives of millions of customers, while generating billions in economic value. Today, the model is becoming increasingly relevant as we move into a world of AI, ageing, rapid advances in health technology, GLP-1 agonists, and more.

A simple but powerful tactic – shifting an organization onto a time-based cycle – can force pace and urgency, which has the potential to create a completely different set of dynamics within a complex and interconnected organization, and a future that is completely different to a company that responds to external events as they occur.

This tactic evokes the power of 'Pareto tail' events, which I cover in more detail in the Fourth Principle.

There are other important reasons why companies operate at a pace that is too slow.

Why Networks Get Quicker as They Get Larger, but Companies Get Slower

I was on a road trip with my family from Johannesburg to Cape Town, and we made a pit stop in Colesberg, a small town in the Karoo Desert, just off the motorway. It is a quiet, sleepy town of around 17,000 inhabitants, and we went into a medium-sized restaurant for a quick bite to eat.

The place was deserted – we were almost the only customers – and they were overstaffed, with about ten staff members in attendance. The weird thing is, no matter what we ordered, it took forever to get our food.

You might expect an empty restaurant in a small town with a high ratio of staff to customers to be faster at delivering your food than a jam-packed restaurant in a big city, but you'd be wrong. When I go to a busy restaurant full of diners in a big city like Cape Town, London or New York, the food comes incredibly quickly. It is a disparity that is particularly evident to me whenever I pass through a small town and feel dismayed by how long things take to get done.

Why is this? Why do cities speed up as they grow larger? And what about companies, I wondered – where do they fit in?

Before addressing this, it is interesting to take a step back and look at the type of complex systems we are talking about.

We know from science that living organisms slow down as they get bigger. Biologists have shown that as animals increase in size, their metabolic rate as a proportion of their mass decreases – a relationship known as Kleiber's Law.[29] That is why larger organisms, such as elephants and giraffes, move more slowly, react less quickly, and have far lower heart rates than small mammals like mice or monkeys. (A mouse's heart races at about 600 beats per minute, an elephant's at just 30.)

Kleiber's insight inspired later models, including the West–Brown–Enquist model, which connects biology to physics.[30] It shows how the way energy flows through blood vessel networks places hard limits on an organism's metabolism and growth. In other words, the very physics of resource distribution explains why big mammals live life in slow motion compared to their smaller, speedier counterparts.

Networks, in contrast, get faster as they get bigger. This is because, according to Metcalfe's Law, as networks (which may be digital, neural or social) grow, the number of nodes or connections increases exponentially, enabling parallel, rather than sequential processing.[31] For example: a modern computer processor can run several instructions simultaneously; the brain processes sight, sound, memory and emotion in parallel through distributed neural circuits; in social networks like the internet, data can be sent over many paths simultaneously.

So, networks achieve dozens of tasks simultaneously and this increases their speed dramatically. Crucially, networks also learn and improve – so the more traffic they handle, the more efficient they become. This creates a positive feedback loop that makes them faster still in a continuously improving cycle.

Let's go back to our bustling restaurant example that experiences high and consistent demand. It can use this demand to generate data about what customers are likely to order, how many covers they should prepare for, when rushes happen and where bottlenecks in the kitchen might be. This allows for task specialization, proactive preparation of food and continuous refinement of the system. In short, the restaurant is operating like a network: it has several systems running in parallel and it is continuously learning and improving from its experience. Chefs and restaurant managers also circulate within the broad network of restaurants in a big city, bringing with them their experience and expertise, thus further diffusing efficiency-linked innovations.

So, busy restaurants both operate like networks and within networks, and hence it makes sense that they should operate more efficiently.

A similar case can be made for cities. The transport links of a large city could incorporate a subway system, overground trains, buses, taxis, cars, scooters and bicycles. But small cities will not be able to justify the expense of subways and trains, and in small towns, it may not even be economic to run a regular bus service, so people are likely to take longer to get around. Again, the bigger the city, the more systems run in parallel, and the more competition there is likely to be – meaning that there is an impetus to learn and become more efficient. Hence, cities too are like networks, and scale leads to efficiency.

Now comes a fascinating question: what about companies? Surely companies are more like networks than organisms – and should therefore become more efficient? When a business gets bigger, it has more employees and greater resources to get things done, so you might think it would speed up.

But that is not the case. Much has been written instead on how companies initially get faster as they get larger and then slow down as they pass an inflection point. Their initial speed comes precisely from behaving more like a complex network – with systems operating in parallel and the learning from scale resulting in positive feedback loops. But at a point, it seems, these advantages of complexity become overwhelmed by disadvantages that come with the territory – namely increased bureaucracy, infighting and competition between internal power bases, all at the expense of the performance of the business and, ultimately, the customer.

This phenomenon of companies slowing down as they become larger was articulated by Chris Zook and James Allen, senior consultants at management consulting firm Bain & Company, who describe in their book, *The Founder's Mentality*, two fundamental types of organizations: insurgents and incumbents.[32]

Insurgents are led by bold founders who are relentlessly customer focused and disrupt the status quo. As start-ups gain traction, their aim is to keep growing quickly and sustainably – otherwise known as rapid scaling.

But over time, insurgents can often become like the incumbents they disrupted – more bureaucratic, less dynamic, and more inwardly focused on their own internal politics than on the needs of their customers. They lose their laser-like focus and risk losing what the authors call their 'founder's mentality': the core strengths and values that helped them become so successful in the first place.

When this happens, the pace of growth slows considerably. Zook and Allen's key insight is that the main reasons for this loss of cadence are internal, rather than due to external market forces such as competition. As companies grow, they become entangled in organizational complexity – which they call the 'southward winds' – that can leave them foundering on the rocks of bureaucracy.

As the authors say: 'Expanding . . . leads to new layers of management and processes . . . which inevitably generates more complexity. Before long, too many management voices are communicating their own versions of strategy and operating plans throughout the corporation. Attempts to manage the resulting dissonance lead to more layers of complexity and soon a good day at the office means creating alignment rather than figuring out how to beat the competition or better serve customers.'

In other words, as companies scale, they add more layers and with that comes more rules, more oversight, more committees – and more rigidity. As complexity increases, decision-making slows, and the focus can shift away from customers and towards managing internal conflict, with loss of speed and reduced agility as the outcome. In short, it dulls the entrepreneurial spirit and blurs the focus of large organizations.

This tendency for organizations to become less efficient as they grow larger raises an even more fundamental question: are companies efficient mechanisms to conduct business, and if not, why do we need them at all?

British economist Ronald Coase won a Nobel Prize in 1991 in essence for addressing the question: why do firms exist at all, instead of all economic activity being coordinated through markets? He asked, under what conditions does it make sense for an entrepreneur to hire staff rather than contract out to achieve their aims?[33] The answer, he showed, was that there are initial advantages to internalizing costs within the firm, because this is more efficient than bearing the costs of numerous external transactions required for outsourcing. However, at a certain point, the size of the firm and the internal complexity this creates means that internal transaction costs come to exceed the costs of outsourcing externally, implying that outsourcing can be more efficient once firms reach a certain size.

He wrote: 'In general, making the firm larger will initially be advantageous, but decreasing returns will eventually kick in, preventing the firm from growing indefinitely.'

Both Coase and Zook and Allen are in broad agreement: at a certain point in their development, companies tend to get slower as they get larger. The good news, though, is that because the slowdown is internally driven, the solution to avoiding it is within the grasp of the organizational leadership.

Key Takeaway: Act with Self-Imposed, Focused Urgency

We think we have plenty of time to make an impact, driven by our linear view of time.

But we don't.

The results are regret later in life for dreams and aspirations unfulfilled, and the sense that time ran away from us.

But if you can grasp that time – as you truly experience it – is logarithmic, then the refrain that 'no one told you when to run, you missed the starting gun' will not apply to you.

The key to making an impact is to realize the 20 per cent window *now* – to act urgently and intentionally, whatever age or stage you are at – so that you don't have any remorse. For individuals, acquiring knowledge and staying healthy are critical, and all three tactics combined can significantly stretch your impact in the time you have.

For me, I have always felt the urgency of time knocking insistently at my door. The sense of time becoming more compressed as we age has been a powerful driving force – and it continues to inspire urgency in me to this day.

The multiplier effect of the Second Principle on impact is approximately two times. The tactics for extending your effective time fall into three areas: maintaining good health so your energy and activity levels don't decline unnecessarily; pursuing knowledge so that each unit of time yields greater wisdom and more effective action; and cultivating a conscious awareness of how limited time is, so you operate with urgency. Actuarially adjusting life years for disability due to ill-health, we can demonstrate that maintaining good health generates a multiplier of approximately 1.25 between healthy and unhealthy lives. In the acquisition of knowledge, cognitive theory demonstrates the exponential nature of learning – the more you know, the faster you can learn the next unit of knowledge – amounting to a 1.35 multiplier. And by developing a sense of urgency, you can create an additional 1.25 multiplier. Assuming the increased healthy time can be used to broaden and deepen knowledge, and then applied with increased urgency, these produce an overall indicative multiplier of two times effective time (1.25 × 1.35 × 1.25 = 2.1). In other words, pursuing these three tactics together indicatively doubles the time you have available to make an impact.

THE THIRD PRINCIPLE: DECLARED GOALS

When we set goals and declare them to make them visible, either personally or publicly, we create something to lose. This has a multiplicative impact on our motivation because potential loss motivates more than potential gain. That's why setting goals isn't childlike or mundane – but crucial for impact.

In September 2022, I set myself a very public personal goal: to run a 5-minute mile.

It was a completely mad idea. I was fifty-eight years old, and, although in reasonably good shape, the fastest I could then complete a mile was in just over six minutes. I had given myself only eight weeks to cut around 70 seconds off my time – a massive improvement that most people familiar with running thought was unattainable.

The distance was chosen deliberately. The mile has a notorious reputation in running. When twenty-five-year-old Roger Bannister broke the elusive 4-minute mile on an Oxford track in 1954, he made history by achieving what many believed was impossible. At the time of writing, the fastest mile ever run is 17 seconds faster at 3:43, set by twenty-four-year-old Hicham El Guerrouj of Morocco in 1999 in Rome.

The appeal of the mile is that it is neither a sprint nor a marathon, requiring a combination of sustained speed and endurance – strong legs, strong lungs and mental fortitude.

In my quest, age would be a factor. The world record for a sixty-year-old is 4:49, set in 2020 by Dan King, a former University of Colorado athlete. While I am disciplined about my exercise and run seven days a week, my training is casual in its duration and intensity – and critically, I am no athlete. Yet I would be trying to run just 11 seconds slower than the world record for my age.

I hired a coach and – to make everything transparent and public – announced my goal on LinkedIn. I also approached running experts for their opinion and advice – including Sebastian Coe, the British 1500-metre Olympic gold medallist and one of our Vitality ambassadors, and Wayde van Niekerk, the South African 400-metre gold medallist and world record holder. I encouraged followers of my LinkedIn page to engage with my journey and set stretch goals of their own.

How did this work out? I will return to that later. First, let's get under the skin of what was really going on. Why would I do this? Why would I set myself up for potential failure in such a public way? And why then?

On a basic level, the challenge was an opportunity to bring Vitality and its compelling data to a wider audience – to demonstrate the importance of physical activity and encourage others to lace up their running shoes. For example, our data shows that moving from no exercise to just one physically active day per week reduces the risk of death by 36 per cent, with positive knock-on effects for other healthy behaviours and mental well-being. The 'Strive for Five' challenge, as we called it, came out of a conversation with my executive team about how best to use our LinkedIn platform to share this data in a compelling, real-world way.

Second, it was an intensely difficult time – both locally and globally. We were emerging from the Covid pandemic, facing intensifying power outages amid South Africa's electricity crisis, and dealing with global uncertainty triggered by the war in Ukraine and its inflationary effects. There was a general sense of doom and despair. An outlandish physical challenge might be distracting, but in a good way – a sort of left-field tonic to provide hope.

But most importantly, I did it out of a deep, long-standing conviction: to illustrate the power of setting and declaring goals – and how setting them takes you infinitely further than not setting them. Not only would I be motivating myself, but by declaring it publicly and encouraging others to set their own goals, I hoped to spark a chain reaction.

It might sound superficial – even banal – to set goals, but behavioural science explains why goal-setting is profoundly effective. What do I mean by this? It starts with some powerful insights into how we respond to losses and gains.

A Deeper Dive into Prospect Theory and Loss Aversion

As rational decision makers facing options under conditions of risk and uncertainty, we think we are motivated to choose the most rational option – the one with the best combination of value and likelihood of occurring. This thinking – codified in the 1940s as 'expected utility theory' by game theory founders John von Neumann and Oskar Morgenstern – dominated decision theory for decades.

According to expected utility theory, when presented with a guaranteed gain and a riskier option with a higher upside but ultimately the same expected value, a rational decision maker would be indifferent – both are considered equally valuable. For example, choosing between a sure gain of $1,000 and a 50 per cent chance of winning $2,000, the decision maker is indifferent because the expected value in both cases is $1,000. However, if the probability of winning $2,000 drops to 40 per cent, the expected value falls to $800 – making the guaranteed $1,000 the rational choice. Similarly – and critically – losses are treated proportionately: losing $1,000 is considered exactly twice as bad as losing $500.

Expected utility theory assumes a linear relationship between rival potential gains – and between potential gains and losses. But this linear model was challenged in 1979 by Daniel Kahneman and Amos Tversky. As I alluded to in the First Principle, their theory – prospect theory – proposed that losses loom larger than gains, a phenomenon known as loss aversion.

In one experiment, participants reported feeling much worse about losing $100 than they felt good about gaining $100 – despite the amounts at stake being the same. A foundational reason is that people evaluate outcomes relative to a reference point, typically the status quo, rather than in absolute terms. This reference point determines whether an outcome is perceived as a gain or a loss. Once a loss is perceived, loss aversion kicks in – an emotional response in which the pain of loss far outweighs the pleasure of gain. As discussed in the First Principle, losses are typically felt to be twice as impactful as gains of the same size.

This was depicted there in graph form – and for ease is repeated below – as a non-linear, S-shaped curve showing two key insights. First, our perceived value of gains diminishes as we acquire more – an idea known in economics as the law of diminishing returns. For example, the utility of the first week of annual leave is higher than that of subsequent weeks. Second, and most importantly, the curve is steeper for losses than for gains, illustrating how losses are felt more acutely. And it is not just a bit steeper – the curve has been shown to be twice as steep. This, in essence, is loss aversion.

Prospect Theory

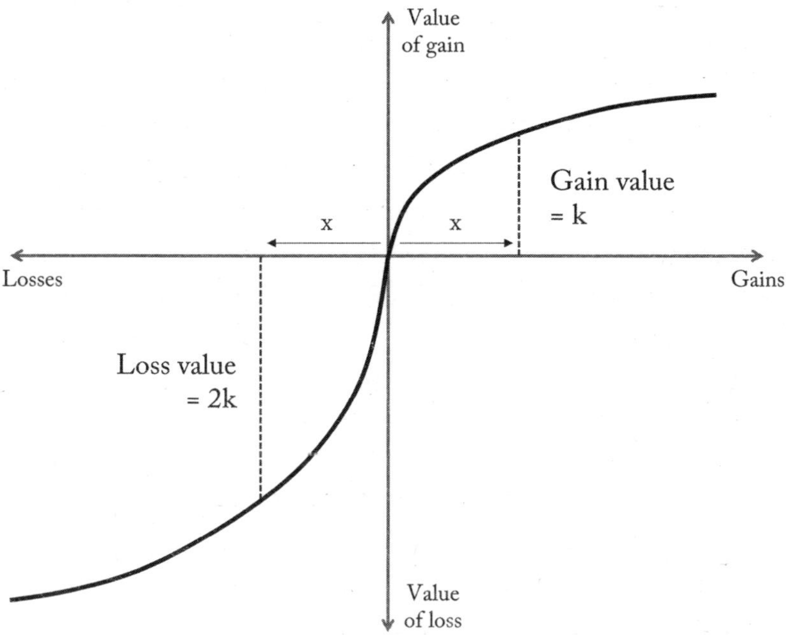

So, in a nutshell, loss aversion is the idea that the fear of losing something is a much stronger motivator than the prospect of gaining something of equivalent value. We might believe we are driven by the pursuit of gain, but avoiding loss or defeat compels us to act more decisively.

In the four decades since this theory was put forward, the concept of loss aversion has become well-established, but it is the largely unexplored link between loss aversion and goal-setting that is, in my view, fundamental to impact.

The logic is this: by setting and declaring a goal, we put ourselves on the line. By putting something at stake, we create something to lose. And by having something to lose – according to the concept of loss aversion – we galvanize motivation and action.

I will explain the power of this insight in more detail later, but the critical thing to note here is that the act of setting and declaring goals creates a reference point from which emerge two possibilities: the possibility of failure and the possibility of success. By setting and declaring a goal, we tap into our deep psychological predisposition to avoid the personal or public disappointment that goes with loss – that is so powerful a motivator.

So, declared goal-setting activates loss aversion. And it is this 'hidden power' of goals that makes it such a powerful tool for creating impact – in our personal lives, our businesses and even in how we run a country.

This is the revelation of the Third Principle: **Declared Goals**. Because avoiding a loss feels psychologically twice as valuable as achieving a gain, setting and declaring bold goals triggers this force, unlocking radical motivation and decisive action.

The power of loss aversion is remarkable. Not only is the asymmetry between loss and gain significant, but loss aversion is pervasive across nearly every domain of life – from global financial markets to deeply personal choices. This is why the Third Principle is so important. It is everywhere.

In financial markets, loss aversion causes investors to hold onto losing assets longer than they should, hoping to avoid realizing a loss, and to sell winning assets too early to 'lock in' gains. This is known as 'riding their losers and cutting their winners' – a pattern that contradicts optimal investment strategy.

A classic 1985 paper by American behavioural finance scholars Hersh Shefrin and Meir Statman was among the first to link real-world investor behaviour to prospect theory and loss aversion.[1] They introduced the disposition effect – the tendency of investors to sell winning stocks too early and hold on to losers too long – and argued that loss aversion drives this bias. Later empirical studies, such as those by Terrance Odean in 1998, quantified the effect by analysing 10,000 accounts at a large brokerage house and found that individual investors are 50 per cent more likely to sell winning stocks than losing ones (after controlling for the number of potential selling opportunities for each) – providing robust evidence that loss aversion leads to systematically suboptimal investment choices.[2]

In healthcare, patients' treatment choices are strongly influenced by how information is framed. Highlighting what someone stands to lose by declining a treatment tends to be more persuasive than explaining what they'll gain by accepting it – an insight consistent with prospect theory.

For instance, in cancer-related studies, participants have been shown to respond more strongly to messages that emphasize avoiding a 10 per cent chance of death than to messages that the same action will result in a 90 per cent chance of survival – even though the two outcomes are statistically identical. A foundational 1987 paper on breast self-examination by Beth Meyerowitz and Shelly Chaiken found that loss-framed messages – emphasizing what women might lose by not conducting self-exams – were more effective in promoting preventative behaviour than gain-framed messages.[3] The authors cited this as a textbook demonstration of prospect theory and loss aversion in action.

In consumer behaviour, marketers frequently leverage loss aversion to prompt action. Tactics such as 'limited-time offers' and 'only a few left' are examples of scarcity messages, which heighten perceived value and create urgency by tapping into consumers' fear of missing out. A 2011 study published in the *Journal of Advertising* found that scarcity-framed advertising significantly increases consumer response, with consumers driven by a desire to avoid losing a fleeting opportunity – a behavioural pattern consistent with loss aversion.[4]

Across all these contexts, ranging from health and wealth to everyday purchases, loss aversion is shown to be pervasive and powerful.

Loss Aversion Is Pervasive, Powerful and Unavoidable – Consider Sport

Sport is an excellent laboratory for testing loss aversion and goal-setting. It involves set rules and clear goals that make for explicit reference points, and importantly, athletes at the highest level of discipline illustrating human behaviour at its extreme.

A fascinating 2011 paper by behavioural scientists Devin Pope and Maurice Schweitzer – titled 'Is Tiger Woods Loss Averse?' – explored the role of loss aversion in professional golf. They analysed over 2.5 million putts from the 2007 PGA Tour, covering around forty-five tournaments, using precise laser measurements to compare how professional golfers performed when putting for par as opposed to putting for birdie (one shot better than par).[5]

Would the best golfers in the world – including Tiger Woods – exhibit signs of loss aversion?

The authors noted that such a result would be surprising. In golf, scoring works by counting the number of strokes it takes to complete a hole, and then aggregating those strokes for all eighteen holes to get a total for the entire round. So, putting for birdie versus for par is no more impactful to your overall score than putting for par versus for bogey (one shot worse than par). Logically then, you would expect not to find any difference. As Pope and Schweitzer put it, golfers 'should only care about their overall tournament score', so why would they 'be influenced by the salient, but normatively irrelevant, reference of par when they attempt putts?'

To test this, they corrected for obvious variables – such as length and difficulty of putts – and were able 'to match par and birdie putts within one inch of each other on the exact same hole in the same tournament'.

The researchers found that professional golfers putt significantly better for par than they do for birdie. At every distance, whether the putt was easy or hard, players were more successful when putting to avoid a bogey than when putting to gain a birdie. The performance gap was 2–4 percentage points – a meaningful difference. For example, if Tiger Woods, who ranked number one in 2007, had putted as well for birdies as he did for pars, he would have improved his average score by one stroke per tournament – boosting his 2007 PGA earnings by around $1 million. Other golfers, like Jim Furyk, who played more regularly on the tour, would have gained even more – over $1.5 million across twenty-three tournaments, equivalent to around $2.5 million in additional prize money today.

The conclusion: professional golfers try harder and take more care when putting to avoid a bogey than to secure a birdie.

The authors concluded that the data suggested a tendency towards loss aversion. According to prospect theory, golfers will be more driven to avoid a bogey than to achieve a birdie – even though the effect on their overall score is identical.

This is because missing a par putt (and scoring a bogey) is perceived as a loss, while missing a birdie putt is merely the absence of a gain. And since losses loom larger than gains, golfers are more motivated to avoid them – even at the highest level.

This finding is profound: it reveals how deeply embedded, stubborn and persistent loss aversion is coded into our ways of thinking and feeling. Even elite athletes like professional golfers – among the most disciplined individuals on the planet, rigorously trained to perform under intense physical and psychological pressure – are not immune.

In football, behavioural economist Michael Bar-Eli and colleagues found that while 29 per cent of penalty kicks go down the middle, only 6 per cent of goalkeepers stay in the centre. Yet when they do, they save 60 per cent of those shots – a much higher success rate than diving to either side.[6]

Why don't goalkeepers stand still more often? Because of action bias and loss aversion. Conceding a goal while standing still feels like a passive failure – a loss. On the other hand, diving and missing feels like a foregone gain – you tried but were unable to stop the shot which you were not expected to stop anyway.

Several studies show how professional coaches and athletes often adopt conservative strategies – not necessarily to win, but to avoid failure or criticism.

In basketball, professional teams that are slightly ahead often shift to overly defensive strategies or foul to protect their lead, rather than continuing the aggressive play that built the lead in the first place. In these situations, the fear of losing the lead outweighs the potential benefit of increasing it. One study found that professional basketball teams trailing by ten points display significantly increased effort.[7] As the authors put it: 'We find a "losing motivates" effect so large that an average team scores like a league leader when trailing by ten points.'

The study linked this behaviour to loss aversion: when players are behind, they are powerfully motivated to close the gap. Avoiding a loss becomes a stronger driver than securing a win – highlighting the impact of loss aversion on performance at the highest level.

Across professional sports, loss aversion quietly creeps in – overriding training and tactics and having a profound impact.

How We Tapped into Loss Aversion to Motivate Our Customers to Exercise

We discovered the power of loss aversion in our emerging data on how people respond to incentives aimed at changing their levels of physical activity. Physical activity is one of the most effective ways to improve and maintain health, and therefore, methods and tactics that get people physically active can have a massive impact.

In late 2015, we offered our health insurance customers an Apple Watch for free, if they exercised. It was a huge moment in the development of our company and our brand, both in South Africa and internationally – I tell this story in full later in the Fourth Principle – but the point I want to make here is this: once we understood the power of loss aversion, it became an integral and intentional part of our programme design.

Let me elaborate. By 2015, because of all the data we had accumulated on our Vitality members, we already understood the role of loss aversion in driving behavioural change. We structured the benefit carefully; customers received the Apple Watch for a small upfront activation fee (in a sense, almost free) and then paid monthly instalments for twenty-four months. The key mechanism was that the instalments would vary based on achieving weekly physical activity goals. If met, the instalment was zero; in effect, the watch was free if members achieved their goals consistently. If they didn't stay active, monthly charges would apply. This flipped the psychology: rather than working to earn the Apple Watch, customers had to work to avoid losing its free status.

The results were compelling.

A report published in 2020 by independent research firm RAND Europe, covering around 422,000 Vitality members across the UK, US and South Africa over three years, compared two distinct groups:[8]

- *Group 1* – members receiving Vitality Active Rewards only: a gain-framed incentive where physical activity was rewarded with a range of modest rewards on a weekly basis (such as a free Starbucks coffee, free movie tickets).

- *Group 2* – members receiving Vitality Active Rewards with the Apple Watch benefit: a loss-framed incentive where monthly repayments for the Apple Watch were waived if activity goals were met.

In Group 1, gains started at zero and accumulated over time as people exercised more. This aligned 'effort now' with 'reward now' and deployed the cognitive bias of hyperbolic discounting, which I discuss in the Fourth Principle.

In Group 2, the gains started at 100 per cent, with an Apple Watch that people owned. But the gain could be lost if people failed to exercise enough to meet the activity thresholds, resulting in them having to pay towards the cost of their watch at the end of each month. This deployed both hyperbolic discounting and loss aversion.

The difference between the two groups was, for the most part, due to loss aversion.

The results were striking and definitive. Members in Group 2 – those with the Apple Watch – put in an additional 4.8 days of physical activity a month, the equivalent of being 34 per cent more active than Group 1. Although there was some variation across country samples – with South Africa showing the largest increase of 44 per cent, followed by the US on 30 per cent, and the UK on 28 per cent – the relationship held. What is more, it persisted over time – at least for the twenty-four-month duration of the repayment cycle.

From both a customer health and business performance perspective, the results emerging subsequently have been striking:

- Vitality members who increased their physical activity became healthier.

- Health insurance claims dropped substantially among the most engaged.

- Mortality risk was significantly lower in the Apple Watch group.

This allowed us to reprice our insurance products based on reduced sickness and death. It led to us lowering our premiums, undercutting competitors and expanding our market share – creating a positive flywheel effect.

In summary, goals and their power to invoke loss aversion are remarkable, pervasive and unavoidable. This is well demonstrated in sport and physical activity, where reference points are well defined and externally set. But life isn't sport – in our everyday lives, there often aren't clear reference points and goals for transformative action. That is the power and necessity of the Third Principle – we must consciously set and declare appropriate goals. But how?

How We Set Goals for Impact in Life

Before we delve further into how to tactically harness the power of loss aversion through goal-setting, let's first examine what we mean by goals. What are goals, really? And how do they differ from plans and dreams?

Goals versus Plans

Many people use the terms 'goals' and 'plans' interchangeably – but they're not the same thing.

Goals are desired outcomes or end states – what an individual or organization ultimately wants to achieve. They are future-focused, and typically motivational or aspirational in nature. For example: to run a marathon, lose 10 kg, publish a novel, graduate with honours, save $10,000.

Plans, on the other hand, are the specific sequences of actions, strategies or tactics used to reach a goal. They answer the question: how will I get there? For example: follow a training schedule, cut out sugar, write 1,000 words a day, set up a structured study schedule, or automate savings and reduce expenses.

In their landmark 1990 book, *A Theory of Goal-Setting and Task Performance*, psychologists Edwin Locke and Gary Latham made a critical distinction between goal-setting and goal striving:[9]

- *Goal-setting defines the 'what'* – identifying a clear, specific and challenging target.

- *Goal striving refers to the 'how'* – the sustained effort, planning and adjustment required to reach that target.

Their book synthesized hundreds of studies across fields including business, sport and education. Their findings were replicated in real-world settings to improve performance, making their theory one of the most influential models in organizational psychology. It helped shape everything from corporate incentive schemes to elite athletic training.

Some of their core insights included:

- *Clarity and ambition matter:* The clearer and more challenging a goal is, the more it directs attention, effort and persistence.

- *Difficulty drives performance – up to a point:* As goals get harder, performance improves – until the goal becomes so unrealistic it turns demotivating.

- *Feedback is crucial:* Regular feedback enables adjustment and sustained progress.

- *A goal without a plan is not enough:* Intent alone won't drive action – you also need a roadmap to get there.

Put simply, a goal without a plan is just a wish. A plan without a goal is directionless. Goals are destinations. Plans are the mapped-out steps that get you to your destination.

Goals versus Dreams

Like goals and plans, goals and dreams are often used interchangeably in everyday language – but they, too, are fundamentally different.

A dream is a vision or desire for something you hope will happen one day. Dreams are aspirational, open-ended and often abstract. They are powered by imagination, emotion, values and ideals.

Goals, by contrast, are tangible, concrete, actionable and often time-bound. A goal is a dream made specific – something that has been concretized with a deadline and direction.

Something like 'writing a novel' could live in either category. It might start as a dream, but it only becomes likely to materialize when it moves from the dream column to the goal column. Conversely, not all goals need to be inspired by dreams; some are practical, task-driven and smaller in scale.

Interestingly, while children are encouraged to dream, adults often come to view dreams as childish or impractical. As children, we're told: 'You can be anything you want to be.' Dreams are seen as healthy expressions of curiosity and self-worth.

But as we grow up and take on financial and social responsibilities, society subtly – and sometimes overtly – signals that dreaming is naive. The education system and workplace reinforce this by measuring us primarily by tangible results and productivity, rarely valuing idealism or imagination. Big, risky dreams can come to seem indulgent, even counterproductive. Many adults learn to suppress imaginative thinking as a result.

Evolutionary biology offers insight into this shift. In childhood, risk-taking, creativity and 'what-if' thinking are seen as crucial for learning and adaptation. At this stage, the prefrontal cortex – responsible for judgement and risk assessment – is still developing and does not inhibit dreams to the extent it does in the mature adult brain. Dreaming is a mental tool that helps children simulate possibilities, navigate uncertainty and prepare for the future.

As we age, evolutionary pressures prioritize survival and social conformity. Adults become more risk-averse, striving to maintain social status and avoid ostracism. Evolution tends to reward behaviours that maximize practical outcomes and resource security. Consequently, we dream less – not simply because we grow up, but because we are conditioned, biologically and socially, to avoid uncertainty and minimize risk.

The damaging effect is that we stop dreaming. I use the word damaging because dreams are essential. Human progress depends on adults who continue to dream and can imagine better futures.

Interestingly, while many assume that dreams give rise to goals, American psychologist Eric Klinger proposed the opposite. In a 2013 essay, he argued that our goals influence our inner mental life and shape the content of our thoughts and dreams.[10]

Rather than dreams fuelling purpose, he suggested that dreams are often reflections of our ongoing concerns and what matters to us – mirroring the goals we've consciously or unconsciously committed to. In other words, he positions goals as organizational anchors of mental life. His work has influenced how psychologists understand the relationship between goals, mental focus and emotional life.

This insight flips a common assumption: if you want to understand what drives someone, don't just ask what they dream about – also ask what goal or goals their dream is linked to.

So perhaps we can think of it like this: goals transform dreams into destinations – and plans make concrete the actions needed to achieve those goals.

Where We Set the Goal Is Crucial

Goals create a 'line in the sand' that puts something at stake and unlocks a powerful non-linear source of motivation.

This was the core argument in a classic 1999 study by Chip Heath, Richard Larrick and George Wu, experts in behavioural decision-making. They proposed that goals act as psychological reference points that trigger loss aversion.[11] People don't evaluate outcomes in absolute terms, but relative to their goals. This aligns with prospect theory: falling short of a goal is felt as a loss, while exceeding it is experienced as a gain.

In this way, the goal – not the result – becomes the ultimate arbiter of our perceived success or failure.

Take the example of a top-100-ranked tennis player who sets a goal of reaching the fourth round at Wimbledon. If they make it to the quarterfinals, that's a success. But if they fall in the third round, it feels like failure – even though in neither case have they won the tournament. The goal itself shapes the emotional outcome.

Where we set the goal, then, is crucial. Set it too low, and you won't trigger the motivating power of loss aversion. Set it just right, and the discomfort of falling short may propel you across the line. The negative feeling of missing a goal is stronger than the positive feeling of exceeding it – which is why well-judged, challenging goals can be such powerful motivators.

Consider the 4-minute mile.

Elite runners had been trying to break it for nearly seventy years – since the first officially recorded mile time in the 1850s – before Roger Bannister finally did it on 6 May 1954. His time of

3:59.4 followed a nearly decade-long plateau, during which Gunder Hägg's 1945 record of 4:01.4 stood unbroken.

But then the barrier fell. Just forty-six days later, John Landy of Australia ran it in 3:58.0. Three years after that, it fell again. And over the next two decades, it tumbled still further, culminating in the current world record of 3:43:13 by Hicham El Guerrouj. Since Bannister's historic run, more than two thousand athletes have run a sub-4-minute mile – including high-schoolers.

So, what changed? In the seventy years before Bannister, only one man achieved it. In the seventy years since, thousands have. Why?

Because once someone proved it was possible, it changed the belief landscape. What had seemed physiologically impossible became a reachable goal. And when it became a goal – not just a fantasy – people pursued it. Bannister's feat shattered the mental barrier that had been holding runners back, resetting what they believed they could do and creating a new line in the sand, a new goal. This is well-established, known as the 'Bannister effect'.

Yes, training methods have improved, and so have running shoes, track surfaces and nutrition. But none of that really mattered until belief shifted where the goal was set.

Of course, where the stretch goal is set is only important if it is accompanied by a credible plan to get there. In James Clear's popular 2018 book, *Atomic Habits*, he says that while goals are a useful first step for setting direction, it is the system you put in place to achieve them that ultimately produces results.[12] He is referring, of course, to the habits, routines and small actions you repeat daily in pursuit of your goal – in other words, breaking up bigger goals into daily, weekly and monthly goals. In the Second Principle, I talked about habit laddering, which is precisely this – breaking up your stretch goals into smaller, bite-sized, manageable chunks that allow you to continue making visible progress.

Motivation Intensifies as We Near the Goal

There is also data showing that people exert more effort as they approach a goal – what's known as the goal-gradient effect. This phenomenon was first observed by psychologist Clark Hull in the 1930s, who found that rats ran faster as they approached a food reward in a maze.[13] This goal-gradient hypothesis suggested that motivation increases non-linearly as the goal gets closer.

Later studies have confirmed this pattern in humans as well:

- A 2006 study showed that customers in a loyalty programme accelerated their purchases as they neared a reward threshold.[14]
- In charitable fundraising, donations spike as campaigns near their targets.
- In education, students study more intensively as exams approach.
- In health and fitness, our own data shows that people increase effort as they near weekly fitness goals, like step counts.

To harness the goal-gradient effect, it helps to establish clear staging posts along the journey – milestones that spark renewed bursts of effort, not just a final sprint at the end. This builds on the goal laddering I mentioned above. A simple but powerful example can be seen in *The New York Times* Spelling Bee game, which motivates players by awarding incremental titles such as 'Good', 'Solid', 'Great' and 'Amazing' en route to the top-tier status of 'Genius'.

We Can Always Work Harder in Pursuit of Our Goals

The central question is how hard a person is genuinely prepared to work to achieve a given goal.

Loss aversion creates intrinsic motivation. But when this motivation sets in, it must be converted into action: how intensely a person is willing to work, what they are prepared to sacrifice, and how far they are willing to go in pursuit of success.

Intrinsic motivation is critical, but conscious desire and commitment are required too. Meaningful goals require sustained effort, discipline, and a sequence of deliberate choices made under pressure, fatigue, and competing demands. Progress is not determined by intention, but by how consistently effort is applied when it becomes uncomfortable.

I hold the view that, within broad limits, no matter how hard you believe you are already working toward a goal, you can work harder. This jars with contemporary narratives around work-life balance – but that tension is precisely the point. Work and balance is not a moral question; it is an optimization problem. How important is the goal? And what are you genuinely prepared to sacrifice to achieve it?

As explained earlier in the chapter, sport provides a particularly clean lens through which to examine this question, because both the goals and the rules are externally defined. Talent is largely fixed in the short term. What remains is effort, discipline, and a willingness to suffer. In elite sport, the rewards of success are unambiguous – and so are the costs of falling short. This makes it possible to isolate how far individuals are truly prepared to push themselves.

Repeatedly, we see that even when athletes appear to be operating at their limit, they are often not.

I was struck by an article in *The New York Times* published shortly before the 2026 Winter Olympics, describing the extremes to which Jessie Diggins, the US cross-country skier, was willing to go in pursuit of victory.[15]

In the Beijing Olympics in 2022, she raced after being ill the day before. When Diggins crossed the finish line, she collapsed, face in the snow, 'a marionette whose strings had been cut. Her eyes were open, contacts frozen to her eyeballs, but she couldn't see. Her breathing was a shallow panting. At first, she didn't know where the sound was coming from. "Then I realised, oh my God, that's me," she says.'

Her mentor and former Olympic skier Liz Stephen says: 'My best races, there's no noise. A lot of people lose sound. They lose their sensory experience. Taste, smell, sound – those things go away. Even vision. It's just what you're focused on: kick and glide.'

While anecdotal, the example reinforces a powerful idea: the boundaries we believe define how hard we can push are far more malleable than we assume. We are almost always capable of more.

This intuition is given theoretical weight by Tim Noakes, the renowned sports scientist's central governor theory. Noakes argues that fatigue is not simply the result of muscles reaching their physiological limit, but a protective mechanism regulated by the brain. The brain acts as a 'governor', deliberately down-regulating effort to prevent perceived harm. In this framework, the sensation of exhaustion is not evidence of failure, but a conservative warning signal.

The implication is profound. Our true physical and mental limits lie far beyond where we usually stop. The constraint is not the body, but the brain's risk-management system – and that system can be trained, reframed, and, in certain contexts, overridden.

Noakes captures this idea with a deliberately provocative thought experiment: the athlete who finished second did not push hard enough – the proof being that they did not die in the attempt to win. The statement is extreme, even offensive. But intellectually, it forces an uncomfortable conclusion. Short of catastrophic failure, there was still margin left. The absolute limit had not been reached.

A similar idea appears in mathematics through the concept of an open set – a set that does not include its boundary. Consider the set defined by $x < 100$. The boundary, 100, is excluded, as opposed to a closed set $x \leq 100$, in which the boundary, 100, is included. For any number in the set – 90, for example – there is a number larger that is still in the set: 91. If it's 99, then there is 99.9; and for 99.9, there is 99.99, and so on. There is always another number closer to the boundary that still lies within the set. No matter how close you get, there is always room to move further. The boundary in this mathematical construct is analogous to a physical or work-related limit.

It is instructive. While limits exist, we almost never operate at them. For any given level of effort, there is almost always more that could be applied without crossing the boundary. The stopping point is rarely absolute; it is self-imposed. Work is an open set.

The implications for goal-setting and impact in life are stark. The real constraint is not capability, but importance. When a goal truly matters, people can tolerate far more discomfort, exert far more effort, and make far greater sacrifices than they initially believe possible.

In life and in organizations, we rarely frame goals with the seriousness that Olympians bring to winning a medal. And this is the key issue: people don't think about their careers or other pursuits with the conscious intensity they need, as a competition with discrete and defined goals. Yet doing so can be clarifying. It forces an honest reckoning: what am I prepared to give up, and how hard am I genuinely willing to push? This consciousness activates the motivational force of loss aversion created by the goal.

Instead, we retreat behind comforting platitudes: 'I need to be realistic now'; 'I've done all I can'; and 'Enough is enough'. These statements sound reasonable but are often self-protective rather than truthful.

The uncomfortable truth remains: in most cases, no matter how hard you are working, you can work harder. The counterfactual is mediocrity.

The Transformative Nature of Goal-Setting – How My 5-Minute Mile Panned Out

I started this chapter with the story about setting myself the challenge – to run a 5-minute mile. How did it work out?

I went public with my challenge on 28 September 2022 with a post on LinkedIn headlined: 'Can a 58-year-old CEO run a 5-minute mile?'

From thereon out, there was no pulling back and no place to hide. I had to deliver.

I began, as all strenuous physical challenges should, with a health check and a baseline fitness assessment. The former showed no major areas of concern, and the latter gave me a cardiovascular fitness VO_2 max result of 47.7, well above the 41 classified as 'excellent' for men my age. I felt reassured and was up and running.

My coach, JP van der Merwe, who had trained World Championship and Olympic winners, set me a brutal training plan, which he thought could – if all went well – slash my time by up to 30–40 seconds. It involved running twice a day, morning and evening, and getting my speed up through hill running and fartlek training (alternating between sprints and slow paces). If I did that, I could get down to around 5.30, he thought – around 30 seconds short of my goal. Sebastian Coe weighed in; he asked to see my data and opined that getting to 5 minutes would be 'very difficult', probably beyond me. Other running experts said I would need two years of consistent training to make that sort of improvement.

The public weighed in, too. One man, Denzil, wrote on my LinkedIn page: 'A mile at around 5 min is just over 3 min per km. I don't think people realize how fast that is. Your goal to achieve this in such a short space of time is REALLY MAD.'

Yes, I would need to run at a 3:06 per kilometre pace. Or 18.6 seconds per 100 metres. The fastest I could run 100 metres was around 15 seconds. So, for someone like me, it was almost a sprint for the entire mile. Yet the naysayers spurred me on. I began my training with excitement and relish.

Over the next month, I stuck rigidly to my training routine and posted weekly 'performance dashboard' updates on LinkedIn. My time was improving – I managed to whittle it down to 5:40; a stellar improvement, but still a long way off 5 minutes. I was training at altitude in Johannesburg but would make the final attempt at sea level in Cape Town, which would shave a further 10 seconds or so off my time. Running with the wind behind me would give me another 5 seconds. So, I needed to gain another 25 seconds over the course of November to have a stab at it.

The main purpose, of course, was to inspire people to set profound goals, and I was amazed and humbled by what people wrote on my LinkedIn page. Momin wrote: 'I was diagnosed with a rare progressive autoimmune disorder that induces neuromuscular weakness in my right hand and both feet. I stopped running almost a decade ago. I was inspired by your post to set a goal of my own to run a mile.' Siphiwe posted that he had 'suffered depression and gained excessive weight, weighing 127 kg', and that he was inspired by my crazy challenge 'to return to the gym and lose 27 kg in 12 months'.

One of the most moving posts was from Lida, who wrote: 'I was diagnosed with cancer in 2020 and have been going for chemo every second week. I'm setting a goal that's a lot less impressive but almost as ambitious considering my current fitness level – to run 5 km in under 30 min before the end of Nov.' In November, Lida wrote another post: 'I did it!!! A 5 km run at a pace of 6 min/km.' She added: 'At first I regretted setting a personal challenge on a public platform but it had worked.'

At the same time, I was conducting podcasts with eminent athletes, coaches, scientists and business leaders to glean their perspectives on how to optimize performance through the framework of goal-setting – and I was posting those interviews on LinkedIn. They included Alex Honnold, the American rock climber known for being the first to 'free solo' – ascend ropeless – the formidable 3000-foot El Capitan in Yosemite National Park, the most important piece of rock on earth for rock climbers and described in *The New York Times* as 'one of the great athletic feats of any kind, ever'.[16] Honnold told me that goal-setting was fundamental to how he picked his challenges, and added: 'What's the point of living a long time if it is not full of things you care about?' It's hard not to think of his 2026 ascent of Taipei 101 in this context – a 101-story skyscraper in Taiwan and another vertiginous test of nerve and ambition.

In my conversation with Dan Ariely, professor of psychology and behavioural economics at Duke University, he also told me that goals are not just about the end, they are about the path they create. Some of my other high-achieving interviewees also emphasized the importance of 'the journey' and how it enriches lives.

In the meantime, I was intensely focused on the endpoint and, after my initial time improvements, was struggling to make further headway. About six weeks into my training, I got impatient. I thought: how can I run at close to 3 minutes per kilometre when I don't train at that speed? As a result, I pushed a little faster than my coach had suggested. Then, after my run, I went into a full-day board meeting where I sat, barely moving, for ten hours.

I went home to do an easy run up a steep hill, and to my horror, I suddenly felt a sharp pain in my calf – I had torn the calf muscle. I tried everything to fix it, including platelet-rich plasma therapy and hyperbaric oxygen therapy. I was gutted but had to face it – my challenge was over.

Of course, I was devastated that I didn't achieve my goal. I had made the rookie error of going too fast too soon and I was bitterly disappointed. But I also saw the bigger picture: I had got my time down to 5:35, the equivalent of 3:28 per kilometre, and my VO_2 max had risen to 58, a level considered excellent for a man under thirty. I was faster and fitter than I had ever been and my running would never be the same again.

Moreover, people all over the world got involved. My thirty postings over eight weeks had reached close to 12 million members. In some ways, the fact that I had tried but not succeeded widened the appeal, with quite a few people posting: 'thanks for being vulnerable Adrian'.

So, was it a success or a failure? In the final calculation, it was a success for several reasons. First, it engaged people in the importance of physical activity. Second, it proved my hypothesis: setting and declaring a goal takes you further than you would ever have gone without one. Because it creates a reference point and loss aversion as a result, you arrive in a fundamentally different place relative to not setting a goal at all. And third, even if you fall short of the destination, the goal – and the journey – will change you.

After my injury, one of my key takeaways was that I had nevertheless made remarkable progress as a runner. So, I set myself another goal: could I run a marathon again – something I hadn't done in two decades – and do so at a reasonable pace, given my age?

This time, I stuck to my training plan and avoided injury. And this time, the answer was an emphatic yes.

In 2025, I ran the London Marathon in 3 hours, 37 minutes and 40 seconds, a time that put me in the top 20 per cent of all finishers, and a time I could never have achieved twenty years ago, let alone before my 'Strive for Five' 2022 challenge.

So, in my case, one declared goal led to another, my limits expanded, and in the process, I experienced – directly and personally – the transformative power of setting goals.

In conclusion, declared goals are transformative in themselves. Even if you miss them, even if you 'fail', you are never the same. The simple acts of setting goals, declaring them and striving for them make you better than if you had never set them at all.

The Impact of Setting Goals on Our Psyche

It turns out that in addition to enabling achievement and meaningful impact, goal-setting profoundly benefits our psychological wellbeing.

Goals, Loss Aversion and Happiness

In the Olympics, you might assume that after a race, the gold medallist is the happiest, followed by silver, then bronze. Yes, that is true for gold, but research tells us that bronze medallists are often happier than silver medallists.

This counter-intuitive finding was explored by psychologists Victoria Medvec, Scott Madey and Thomas Gilovich in their influential 1995 paper, 'When Less Is More: Counterfactual Thinking and Satisfaction Among Olympic Medallists'.[17] They analysed video footage from the 1992 Barcelona Olympics and found that bronze medallists consistently displayed more positive facial expressions than their silver counterparts – both immediately after their events and during medal ceremonies.

The explanation for this pattern once again lies in loss aversion.

Silver medallists tend to use gold as their reference point – focusing on how narrowly they missed the top prize, which can lead to disappointment. Bronze medallists, in contrast, are more likely to compare themselves to fourth place – just missing the podium – which evokes gratitude and relief. The emotional frame of reference, not the objective result, determines how satisfied they feel.

This pattern has been repeatedly confirmed. A 2021 study by researchers at the University of Iowa, covering five Olympic Games (from 2000 in Sydney to 2016 in Rio), analysed 413 medallists across 142 track and field events.[18] The results strongly supported the original findings: silver medallists often felt the pain of missing gold more than the pride of beating bronze, while bronze medallists were relieved not to leave empty-handed.

The reason is that goals create reference points that act as psychological anchors. When we fall short of a goal, it feels like a loss – even if the outcome is objectively positive. We saw this, too, with the earlier example of professional tennis players who tend to feel a success or failure based more on what their goal was than their actual achievement in a tournament.

This means that goal-setting – while motivational – can also be a delicate matter. A stretch goal should be ambitious enough to inspire effort, but it also becomes the benchmark against which outcomes are evaluated, shaping how we feel in the aftermath.

This links to a deeper relationship between goals and happiness. Dan Ariely told me: 'We have the simplified notion that happiness means sitting on a beach drinking mojitos. But that's not true. If you talk about what really drives happiness, it is things like starting companies, writing books, having kids, running marathons, climbing mountains – things that are difficult and challenging and painful. When people run marathons, they don't smile in the middle. It doesn't feel like fun. But of course, they're having a very different sense of fun.' He added: 'Goals are not just about the end – they're about the path they create.'

Numerous studies support the link between goal-setting and wellbeing. A 2022 study found that participants who completed a 'happiness through goal-setting training' reported significantly improved psychological functioning, including greater life satisfaction, higher levels of positive emotions and reduced negative emotions.[19]

There is also an interesting link between happiness and success. In his 2025 article, 'The Success-Then-Happiness Fallacy',[20] and his recent book *The Happiness Files: Insights on Work and Life*, Harvard professor Arthur C. Brooks argues that while most people believe that pursuing success brings happiness, the sequence is flawed.[21]

'Success alone rarely delivers lasting satisfaction', he wrote. 'Instead, happiness is a strong predictor of success.' That is not to say, he added, that you must choose between success and happiness, just that you 'have to reverse the order of operations and expectations. Instead of trying first to get success and hoping it leads to happiness, start by working on your happiness, which will enhance your success.' Importantly, this finding links back to the First Principle – attitude is causal and drives fundamentals.

Workforce studies back this up. They show that although people believe large pay increases will have a large impact on their job satisfaction, the effect is both small and transitory. Brooks points to a study which shows job satisfaction rising from 6 out of 10 to 6.5 if your boss doubles your pay, but then falling back to 6.2, showing a much smaller happiness bounce than one might have anticipated. Much stronger effects emerge, however, when researchers swapped the order and evaluated happiness's impact on success in many realms of life – 'including marriage, friendship, health, income, and work performance'.

So, if goal-setting improves happiness, and seeking happiness leads to success, then goal-setting is the precursor to both happiness and success.

Bringing this all together, I have come to see that setting goals may create challenge in our lives, but goals also create purpose. And feeling purposeful is one of the strongest drivers of lasting happiness.

That was exactly my experience with the 'Strive for Five' challenge. Setting a meaningful target over which I had control was immensely empowering – and gave me a sense of agency, direction and fulfilment.

Goals and Hope

Goals are also integral to creating hope. Hope theory, developed by American psychologist Charles Snyder in the 1990s, suggests that goals act as the anchor for hopeful thinking.[22] His theory proposes that hope is not just an isolated emotion, but a dynamic cognitive process involving three key interrelated components – 'goals, pathways, and agency' – that drive individuals to pursue desired outcomes.

Goals, he said, provide the critical first step because they identify the desired outcomes and set the direction of travel. The next stage – 'pathways thinking' – is about generating strategies, plans and routes to achieve those goals. The third step – 'agency thinking' – involves the belief in one's capacity, the motivational component that produces the 'I can do this' mindset, fostering effort and persistence.

Snyder's research spanned decades and showed that goals are central to hope, and that hope correlates with better mental health (lower levels of depression and anxiety), higher academic performance, and even physical wellbeing.

Goals, Legacy and Living Obituaries

In trying to define what matters in life, some people have turned to writing their obituaries while they are still alive. The idea is simple: by imagining how they want to be remembered, they clarify what's truly important – then set goals and allocate their time accordingly.

In a *New York Times* article titled 'Why I Write My Own Obituary Every Year', Columbia University professor and author Kelly McMasters describes how she begins each new year by writing her obituary.[23] She uses it to reflect back and sometimes to project forward to 'an aspirational obituary', detailing or imagining her accomplishments in work, home life and community – and how people might remember her.

'Writing your obituary while you're still alive can offer clarity about your life and, mercifully, if you find something lacking, you still have time to revise', she wrote.

The article was striking on its own, but what fascinated me even more was the response it provoked: a spate of letters from readers who also use obituary-writing as a tool for focus and direction.[24]

One reader wrote: 'Writing my own obituary has helped me stay true to myself . . . and to the person I want to be.' Another described how he once read an obituary about 'an ad guy' whose life mirrored his own – and realized he didn't like what he saw. In response, he wrote two obituaries: one for the life he had lived so far, and one for the life he aspired to live. Then he made changes. He quit his job at the ad agency, got a job at a radio station, played jazz, started a novel, published short stories in magazines, and became an adjunct professor at a local college.

Writing your own obituary may feel uncomfortable, but as a tool for aligning your goals with your values, it can be highly effective.

Goals Can Create Purpose in Bad Times

I have discussed the importance of goal-setting to drive motivation as part of an overarching aim to have maximum impact, but what about when things are bad and we are just trying to get through the day?

The role of goals in helping us to handle personal trauma is just as powerful. Setting goals is part of a cognitive process that gives us agency – or, in Snyder's theory of hope, a feeling that 'I've got this', which is essential for maintaining hope.

One of the most powerful accounts I have heard is from Dan Ariely, who used goals to recover after suffering third-degree burns over 70 per cent of his body. At age eighteen, Dan was caught in an accidental flare explosion. He was bandaged from head to toe, and his recovery required prolonged hospitalization and three years of painful treatments – including excruciating daily dressing changes, multiple surgeries, and intensive physical and psychological therapy.

The enormity of the pain and the duration of the healing process could have been overwhelming. But in his 2010 book *The Upside of Irrationality*, and in various interviews, Dan describes how he used goal-setting to break down the ordeal into manageable chunks. He set small, achievable goals and focused on immediate milestones to get through each day.[25]

Some of these involved managing his pain relief – carefully planning morphine injections to last the day. Others, as he wrote in his 2008 essay 'Painful Lessons', involved fiercely controlling the speed at which bandages were removed during an especially painful treatment called 'the bath'.[26] Having lost control over so much of his life, setting goals and taking control of what little he could became essential.

These goals gave him structure, a sense of agency and a way to measure progress – all of which helped him stay motivated during some very dark days.

As Ariely later reflected, what allowed him to manage the pain was structure. When faced with something too big, too painful or too distant, you need to shrink your world to just the next step.

Later, after becoming a behavioural economist, he recognized that the strategies he had used aligned with behavioural science concepts such as effective goal-setting.

A Personal Note on Loss Aversion – Motocross and Me

Research shows that loss aversion isn't consistent throughout our life, albeit present in each life stage. In particular, the transition to parenthood is accompanied by increasing risk aversion for both mothers and fathers alike. Changes begin a year before childbirth and are most pronounced in the year the first child is born. Several years after the birth of the first child, risk attitudes of both parents return to their initial level.

I have a personal story that captures how dramatically behaviour can shift when loss aversion kicks in – in my case, seeing my behaviour and what I had to lose through the eyes of my son.

As a teenager, I did a lot of risky things – foremost among them, motocross: aggressive off-road motorcycle racing at speed. My parents had originally bought a bike for my older brother, but when he lost interest, I took over and quickly became obsessed.

I was fiercely competitive and eventually started entering national contests. Motocross is incredibly high-risk, demanding perfect balance and lightning-fast decision-making at speed, over rough terrain, with big airborne jumps – and I loved it.

Races were thrilling and adrenaline-fuelled highs. But I wasn't as good as I wanted to be – and in chasing faster lap times and better results, I had a lot of crashes. Some were bad. Once I hit a brick wall at high speed, lost consciousness, and woke up in hospital with a broken collarbone and a concussion. This kind of thing happened more often than I liked to admit.

One day, after yet another crash and blow to my head, my mother had had enough. She marched me off to see a psychiatrist. Not a doctor, mind you, but a psychiatrist. I was seventeen or eighteen at the time. She was furious and kept repeating: 'You've got to stop, Adrian. You're going to kill yourself.'

Although my mother had likely not read Kahneman, she was, in effect, trying to use his newly minted concept of loss aversion to try to get me to see reason and change my behaviour.

Her concern wasn't misplaced. The statistics are alarming. A comprehensive twelve-year study analysing 15,870 athletes in off-road competitions during the 1980s – the era when I was riding – found an injury rate of 23 per 1,000 riding hours. That meant I was statistically likely to injure myself 23 times every 1,000 hours I rode. Almost a quarter of those injuries were fractures, 6 per cent head trauma or spinal fractures, and 3 per cent of head trauma injuries resulted in a coma. The overall injury rate was three times higher than rugby or American football, and ten times that of skiing or snowboarding. Another study showed that in the US alone, motocross crashes cause nearly 700 adult and 175 child deaths per year.

At the time, I was oblivious to all this. But my mother wasn't. So, while my peers were being taken to see career counsellors, I was unceremoniously hauled off to a psychiatrist. There, I was told bluntly that if I kept smashing headfirst into walls, I risked doing permanent damage to my brain – so much so that I would be unlikely to manage university. Not getting a degree – well, for my parents, that was the ultimate failure, and I was read the riot act.

Reading those statistics today, I can see it clearly: with my degree of fearlessness and level of expertise, I was heading for a serious brain injury that really could have changed the trajectory of my life.

So, did I stop?

Yes and no.

Yes – I retired my beloved racing machine to a dark corner of the garage and stepped away from motocross.

No – fifteen years later, I started again.

By then, I was married with three young children and several years into my Discovery journey, responsible for a company and several thousand employees. This time, I bought a much faster, far more powerful off-road machine and began riding on weekends with a few mates. The old excitement and passion flooded back. It was exhilarating.

To the dismay of my mother – and now of my wife – my old hobby was back.

One weekend, I took my young son with me to the track to show him what it was all about. He sat on the sidelines while I went round and round, pushing harder and faster, testing myself. Then, out of nowhere, I must have hit something – I somersaulted through the air and landed badly.

At first, I thought I had broken my leg because I couldn't get up. Even more worrying, blood was coming out of my helmet. The shocked look on my son's face said it all.

I was taken to hospital for an urgent brain scan. That's when it landed. You have kids. This is insane. Enough.

It wasn't the injury itself that triggered the change – it was seeing myself through my son's eyes. I saw the potential loss, not just to me, but to him. The fear of what he could lose – his father – finally overpowered and trumped the excitement and thrills I would gain. Loss aversion had finally kicked in.

That moment of clarity brought everything into sharp focus. And that shift changed my behaviour. I quit motocross. This time for good.

Applications

These insights also have important implications for companies, large and small. Businesses that are purpose-driven, articulate a clear ambition, and use declared goal-setting as part of their strategy tend to outperform the competition.

Netflix is a great example. In *Harvard Business Review*'s 'Top 20 Business Transformations of the Last Decade', Netflix ranked number one, a key example of what the authors called a powerful 'infusion of higher purpose into the culture' to guide strategy and give clarity to everyday actions.[27]

In 2013, CEO Reed Hastings published an eleven-page memo to employees and investors detailing a shift in purpose: from simply distributing content to becoming a premier producer of original programming – including shows that could win Emmys and Oscars. Since unveiling that new purpose, Netflix's revenue, as of 2025, has roughly tripled, its profits have multiplied 32-fold, and its stock compound annual growth rate has increased 57 per cent annually, compared to 11 per cent for the S&P 500.

The HBR report noted that companies using purpose to drive strategy were the most successful at refocusing their organizations and achieving profound transformation. As it concluded: 'In an era of relentless change, a company survives and thrives based not on its size or performance at any given time but on its ability to reposition itself to create a new future, and to leverage a purpose-driven mission to that end.'

So articulating purpose is critical, but without declared goals to hold your feet to the fire, it is just rhetoric. Purpose sets the frame for transformation, but declared goals are needed to get you there – to set targets and achieve rapid growth.

Rapid Scaling

The theory of rapid scaling holds that once a product or system reaches a critical threshold of readiness, it can expand exponentially – far faster than linear growth. But getting to that threshold requires more than just market fit. It takes purpose to align teams and ambitious stretch goals to activate energy and urgency.

Google is famous for its '10X targets' – goals that aim not for a 10 per cent improvement, but for a 1,000 per cent leap. These so-called moonshot goals are designed to provoke breakthrough thinking rather than incremental change. As co-founder Larry Page is renowned to have said, 'you need to do some crazy things'.

Not every Google bet has paid off – their cloud gaming initiative, for instance, failed – but many have succeeded with spectacular impact. They have achieved: global domination of the search engine market with around 90 per cent market share; 100 times more free storage on Gmail at launch than competitors offered; a revolutionary mapping platform in Google Maps; and Android, a free open-source mobile operating system that now powers over 70 per cent of the world's smartphones.

Similarly, SpaceX set audacious 10X goals: cut space travel costs tenfold, land reusable rockets and eventually colonize Mars. Starlink, its global internet venture, merges that same clarity of purpose with stretch goals, aiming to bring high-speed connectivity to even the remotest parts of the world.

Google and SpaceX are not just innovating – they are deliberately engineering impact. By combining clear purpose, bold goals and market readiness, they unlock exponential potential.

Of course, there is now the reality of AI to contend with – and understanding how AI will affect your business and how you might use it to forge a competitive advantage is going to be utterly crucial to even the best-laid plans.

There is less evidence on how small and medium-sized companies benefit from purpose-driven goal-setting, but it is clear to me that this advice is even more important to them. Declared goal-setting tends to be part of the culture of large corporates, but smaller operations, caught up in the business of survival, may neglect to set or declare them – at their peril.

For small to medium-sized enterprises (SMEs), goal-setting can be a tool for navigating complexity, attracting capital, and determining organizational identity and direction. Investors, employees and collaborators are more likely to back SMEs with bold, measurable and time-bound goals. Indeed, empirical research shows that firms with formal, measurable objectives are more successful in securing external resources. And accelerator cultures reinforce this by focusing founder teams on aggressive, time-bound growth targets to display intent and momentum to stakeholders.

When I started Discovery, my clear purpose was to make people healthier, and my first clear declared goal was to create some new health insurance products that could do so.

Today, our stated ambition is to be the best insurance and financial services group in the world and to achieve this by using our disruptive Vitality Shared-Value model – as explained in full in the Fourth Principle – to correct for the inefficiency of traditional insurance. We have set and shared this ambition, together with operating growth and return on equity targets five years into the future. And we have created clear paths to get there.

I am a firm believer in the Simon Sinek 'Why, How, What' model, also known as the Golden Circle. It posits that successful organizations inspire by starting with their 'Why', then articulating their 'How' and finally detailing their 'What'.[28]

Purpose defines the 'why'. Your strategies to achieve the purpose – in our case the Vitality Shared-Value model – determine the 'how'. Stretch goals define the 'what'.

Where these align, rapid scaling becomes not just possible but likely – and perhaps even inevitable.

Social Programmes: Use Loss Aversion and Targets to Boost a Country's Health and Education

Engaging the public in social programmes that benefit them can be a challenge for governments – but could loss aversion be used by politicians and civil servants to drive healthy behaviour?

The experience of Brazil suggests that it can.

In 2003, Brazil launched its flagship Bolsa Família (Family Allowance) programme under President Lula da Silva, aiming to do two things: alleviate immediate poverty and build human capital to break the intergenerational cycle of poverty. To address the former, it provided cash transfers to low-income families to improve short-term living conditions. For the latter, it set health and education targets.

Cleverly, the system was designed so that receiving the former was conditional upon meeting certain thresholds related to the latter. In doing so, Bolsa Família leveraged both goal-setting and loss aversion to achieve its twin aims.

Recipients are required to meet clear behavioural goals regarding school attendance, vaccinations and prenatal care. These goals are then loss-framed, such that families lose benefits if:

- Their children do not achieve at least 85 per cent school attendance for ages 6–15, or 75 per cent for ages 16–17.
- Children under seven are not up to date with vaccinations and growth monitoring (weight and height checks).
- Families fail to comply with scheduled health check-ups.

- Expectant mothers fail to attend prenatal appointments, follow health guidelines, or participate in nutrition and educational programmes.

Non-compliance triggers a series of consequences: warnings, followed by temporary suspension, and ultimately cancellation of benefits. The system frames non-compliance as a loss. In other words, it encourages compliance through loss aversion – because losing financial support represents a painful setback that families are strongly motivated to avoid.

The programme is massive. Latest figures show it supports 20 million families, reaching around 26 per cent of Brazil's population.

The data show that Bolsa Família has had a significant positive impact. It is credited with being a key contributor in cutting poverty by more than half – from 9.7 per cent to 4.3 per cent – in its first decade, according to a study by the Institute for Applied Economic Research.[29] It also led to a 9 per cent reduction in infant mortality in its first five years, according to Health Affairs.[30]

It further significantly boosted school enrolment. Before the programme, school attendance among low-income children was low due to economic pressures and unstable home lives. But after Bolsa Família, attendance changed dramatically: by 2017, over 93 per cent of children aged 6–15 met the required attendance threshold, as did 84 per cent of older teens – an increase of roughly 7 percentage points. These improvements were attributed to loss aversion, which incentivized families to ensure regular attendance to avoid losing their cash transfers.

Several other countries – including Argentina, Colombia, Mexico, Peru, Indonesia, Philippines and Zambia – have also used loss aversion in their conditional cash transfer (CCT) programmes. While not all are as well documented as Brazil's, many have shown long-term benefits, including reduction in inequality and improved health and education outcomes.

Interestingly, Singapore has taken a different path.

Singapore uses incentive-based schemes to encourage healthy behaviours – but through a more universal, tech-enabled and gain-framed approach. Their system resembles our own Vitality rewards model. For example, citizens who enrol with a family doctor and attend regular health check-ups earn health points redeemable for rewards such as supermarket vouchers or health products. Their National Steps Challenge tracks physical activity and healthy lifestyle choices, awarding Healthpoints that can be redeemed for vouchers or healthier food options. There are rewards for attending health screenings as well.

Singapore's system is light-touch, broadly inclusive, and designed for a sophisticated population that is already relatively health-conscious and motivated. It aligns with their national vision of a 'first world oasis in a third world region' where all goals and strategies support their aim to build the world's most competitive economy. Even ministers' salaries are linked to economic growth – another way to set stakes and tap into the asymmetric power of loss aversion.

Which approach works better – Brazil's loss-framed or Singapore's gain-framed method?

Comparative studies are limited, but the partial evidence suggests that while both loss-framed and gain-framed incentives are effective, the former may have the edge. This is due to the psychological power of loss aversion. For example, a study published in the *International Review of Social Psychology* found that loss-framed messages were more persuasive and motivating than gain-framed ones in promoting healthy behaviours.[31]

Overall, the success of programmes like Bolsa Família offers strong, real-world evidence that loss-framed goal-setting works

– especially when behavioural insights are baked into programme design. For maximum impact, the goals must be clear, actionable and monitored – and, critically, there must be a clearly articulated cost to non-compliance.

Our Experience of Using Goals and Loss Aversion to Drive Public Projects

In the First Principle, I described how we used disciplined optimism and seeking out positive signals to tackle South Africa's electricity crisis and reduce the number of potholes in Johannesburg.

But I did not reveal the full story. We also used loss aversion and declared goal-setting to motivate people and to galvanize action. This was, I believe, a key part of why we were successful.

In the case of the potholes, the declared stretch goal was to fix every pothole. And in the case of the electricity crisis, it was the pledge signed by over 150 CEOs that laid the foundation for a successful partnership between business and government to help turn the corner on load-shedding. In each case, we used declared goals to activate loss aversion and to create common purpose and hope.

Of course, we have not fixed 'every pothole'. But we have filled more than 300,000 of them so far – a pretty impressive rate of 75,000 a year, or 200 a day – and, of course, far more than the zero we would have filled if we had not set and declared the goal in the first place.

The electricity crisis, one of the greatest challenges faced by South Africa since becoming a democracy in 1994, is no longer a crisis, with load-shedding down dramatically – and with Eskom, the country's electricity provider, declaring the problem 'fixed' and the chances of significant load-shedding again 'small'.

As part of tackling the electricity crisis, we also engaged with the South African government to help it create a framework for GDP growth. Our public-private partnership focused on three priority areas that we believed were pivotal to unlocking growth: energy, transport and logistics, and crime and corruption. In each instance, we established clear targets and deliverables, bringing structure and discipline to the ideals articulated in our pledge.

A year after the launch of the public-private partnership, we added a bold top-down target of 3 per cent GDP growth by the end of 2025, as mentioned in the First Principle. At the time of publishing, the IMF and World Bank both estimated 1.3 per cent growth in 2025.

So, was setting the goal of GDP growth of 3 per cent a folly – a failure?

Earlier, I explained how where we set the goal matters – stretch goals drive behaviour and propel action. I believe that with urgent reforms in our chosen areas of focus, this target was the right one because it shows what can be achieved if these reforms were to be implemented. In other words, it is within reach if we act urgently and appropriately. Analysis from South Africa's Bureau of Economic Research (BER) supports this view, suggesting that if the country implements key economic reforms in energy, logistics and crime, the resulting boost to exports and investment would raise growth to 3.3 per cent.[32] Sustained growth at that level could generate 1 million additional jobs by 2030 – a transformative outcome.

In short, setting and declaring an ambitious yet realistic, clear goal, along with a plan for deliverables, lays down a marker. It aligns effort, sharpens focus and triggers the motivating force of loss aversion to power progress.

Key Takeaway: Set and Declare Goals to Galvanize Action

As children, we are encouraged to have dreams and set stretch goals to develop and grow as people, but as adults, many of us fall out of the habit of setting goals. The business and the busyness of life, the pressures of making a living – all these and other things distract us. Even the advice – to 'set goals' – can seem mundane, commonplace and obvious.

Loss aversion tells us why setting and declaring goals is such a big deal. It shows that when we set and declare a goal, we create a charged reference point – a line in the sand – which makes us doubly motivated to avoid falling short of that line, and which drives us to action.

The message is clear: declared goals unlock motivation and amplify our impact toward an effective and meaningful life.

The multiplier effect of the Third Principle on impact is approximately two times. Impact is a consequence of prospect theory – the research that illustrates how individuals are more motivated by potential loss than potential gain, known as loss aversion. The research reveals that our fear of loss is approximately twice as great as our perception of the positive effect of an equivalent gain. When we set and declare a goal, we immediately create something to lose – not achieving that goal. Without goals, there is little at stake – only vague potential gains, which are half as motivating.

Now here's the kicker. If you do grasp the importance of seeking out positive signals, living your life with focused urgency, and of setting and declaring goals, you will be perfectly positioned to activate the Fourth Principle of this book – to act in the Pareto tail. This concept is the subject of the final section of this book and it is arguably the most powerful. It shows how impact can happen very quickly and very dramatically. It certainly did for me.

THE FOURTH PRINCIPLE: THE PARETO TAIL

Only a few decisions and actions determine the impact of our lives. This is because our lives are governed by the Pareto principle, also known as the 80:20 rule, which explains how a small number of causes generate a disproportionately large share of the effects, and in which actions in the 'Pareto tail' determine our impact.

It was after my daily run, lying in the bath one day in 1997, that an idea came to me – one that would change the trajectory of my life and our business, and disrupt the global health and life insurance industry.

It seems remarkable to consider that, having worked twelve-hour days for more than three decades – over 6 million minutes in total – a thought that took just a few seconds could have such a disproportionately powerful impact.

At its core, the idea was to reimagine health insurance – from simply paying for sickness to actively incentivizing people to be healthy. It centred on guiding people to do healthy things, for which they earn points and rewards, like an air miles programme – that yield significant and valuable rewards and incentives. It may sound obvious in hindsight, but at the time it was a radical shift: from transactional and passive insurer to active partner in our customers' health and wellbeing. Nothing like it existed in our industry then.

That single moment marked the beginning of an extraordinary journey for Discovery, and for me personally:

- It encapsulated our core purpose: to make people healthier.
- It became the foundation of our business model, *Vitality*, which incentivizes healthy behaviour.
- The model proved profound and repeatable, enabling our expansion into health insurance globally.
- We applied it to disrupt other financial sectors – including life insurance, banking and motor insurance.
- It led to new industry-defining partnerships – such as our collaboration with Apple, allowing customers to finance Apple Watches through exercise; and more recently with Google, bringing AI-powered health guidance to millions more people.
- And it became an exemplar of what is now known as the Vitality Shared-Value model – taught at Harvard Business School and studied as a case in creating simultaneous value for companies, customers and society.[1]

To grasp the scale of its impact, it is useful to compare where we were before that moment to where we are now.

Before 1997, Discovery operated only in South Africa and served around 200,000 customers. We had launched just five years earlier and were still in the early stages of our development.

Today, Discovery's revenue exceeds £3 billion, with over 50 million customers globally, and operations in 37 countries.

I tell this story – a moment in the bath juxtaposed with a global business – to illustrate that a few critical decisions can have disproportionate impact and transform lives, businesses, industries and even nations.

This, as I will explain, is the power of acting in the Pareto tail.

The Profound Cognitive Error that Distorts Our Worldview

To understand the Fourth Principle and its power, we need to confront a profound error in how we've been taught to see the world.

The error is this: we are taught in school that many phenomena follow a bell-shaped curve – a normal distribution. This symmetrical curve has an average (or mean) in the centre, with small, mirror-image tails spreading out on either side. It is a comforting idea. It matches our preference for fairness, balance and predictability – with most outcomes clustering around the average and outliers fanning out on either side.

But this mental model is misleading. In reality, very few things in life follow a normal distribution. Typically, only naturally occurring and statistically independent factors shaped by biology and physics – like height, weight, IQ and blood pressure readings – tend to approximate a normal distribution, as depicted in the graphs below.

Outside of nature, such neat patterns are rare. In fact, I challenge you to find a single major real-world system that reliably conforms to a normal distribution. Almost none do – because real-world systems are rarely random and independent. Instead, they're connected, dynamic, and influence one another.

IQ as an Example of a Normal Distribution

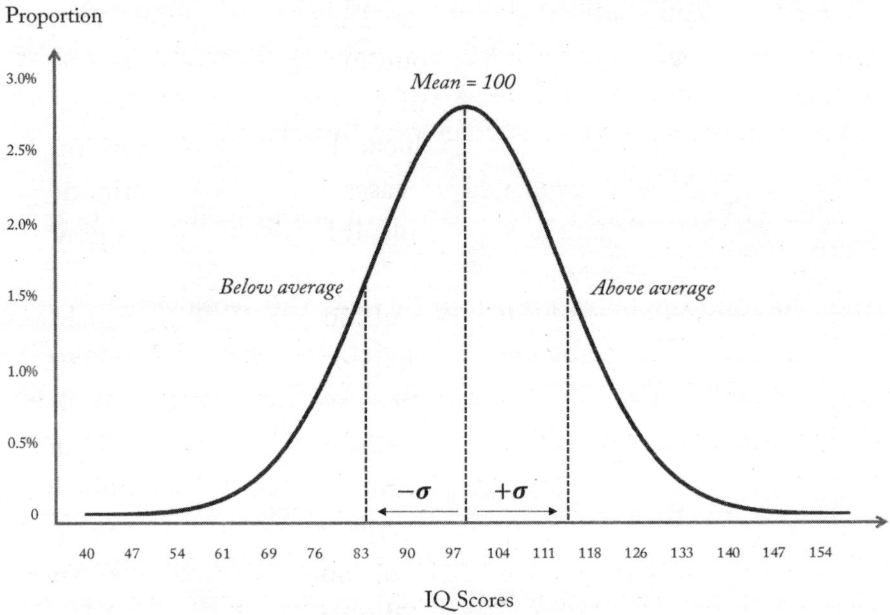

Height as an Example of a Normal Distribution

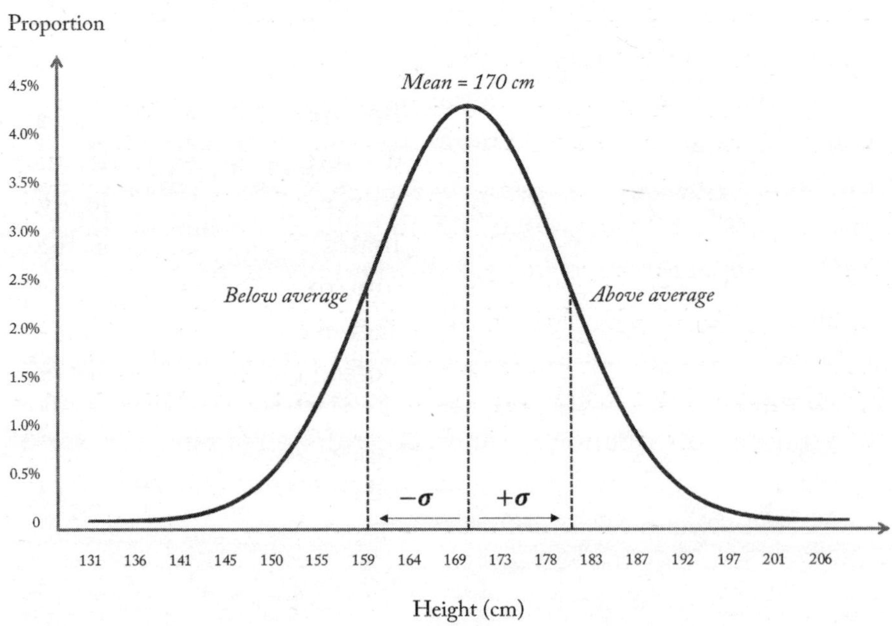

In a Pareto distribution, by contrast, a small number of causes generate a large share of the effects. This is the essence of the 80/20 rule: roughly 80 per cent of outputs stem from 20 per cent of inputs. For example, 80 per cent of a company's sales may come from around 20 per cent of its products. This empirical pattern is known as the Pareto principle. In cases where the distribution follows a precise mathematical formula, it is referred to as a power law, or a Pareto distribution.

These skewed outcomes are both ubiquitous and inescapable. That is because in today's world – shaped by technology, globalization and accelerating complexity – we live inside systems: the global economy, supply chains, social networks and digital platforms. In these systems, outcomes are driven largely by network effects. In such networks, the value of participation increases with the number of users or 'nodes', creating positive feedback loops that lead to compounding advantage and winner-takes-all dynamics. Put simply, nodes interact with and amplify each other, accumulating influence and producing reinforcing, cascading effects that are non-linear, multiplicative and far less predictable.[2]

On a graph, see below, the Pareto distribution appears as a steep drop, followed by a long tail that stretches along the X-axis – getting closer and closer to zero, but never reaching it. Visually, it has an L-shape. The 'head' dominates the left side of the graph, while the long 'tail' stretches out to the right. The head contains high-frequency but low-impact events. In contrast, the tail holds rare but high-impact events, often referred to as 'Pareto tail' events.

The Pareto Distribution: Power Lies in the Tail

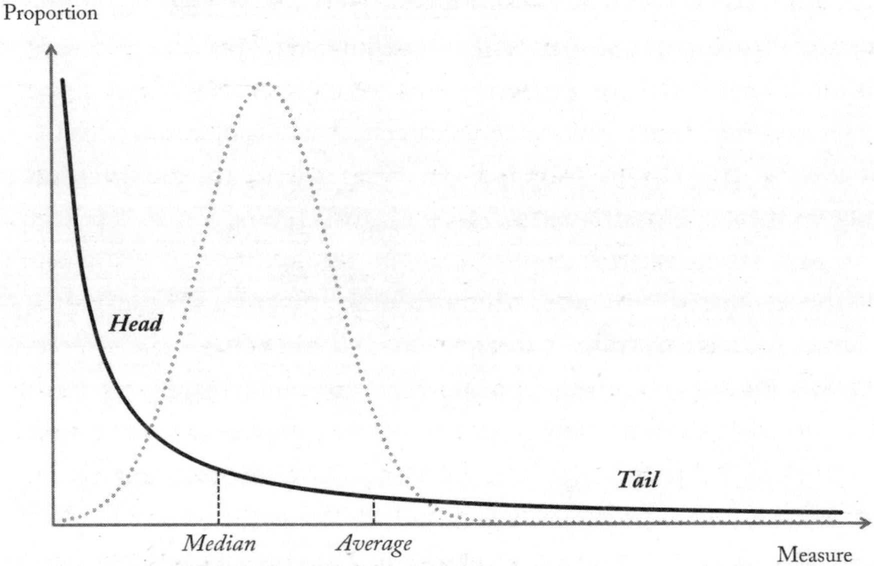

Comparing graphs, the skewed Pareto distribution looks nothing like the elegant symmetry of the bell curve. In the bell curve, the average (mean) is central, and most data falls within two standard deviations of the mean. In a Pareto distribution, the long tail of the distribution drives the average – it is pulled far to the right by a small number of extreme outliers. In fact, some versions of this distribution are so extremely heavy-tailed that an average does not even exist.

What is fascinating is that Pareto is pervasive. Once you start looking, you will notice the skewed Pareto pattern across nearly every field.

Take sport: at the Paris 2024 Olympic Games, the top 20 per cent of countries took home just over 83 per cent of the medals. In academia, the top 20 per cent of papers typically receive 80 per cent of all citations. In publishing, it is well known that a handful of bestsellers – roughly 20 per cent of published titles – generate around 80 per cent of total book sales. Medicine, too, is no exception. Preterm births – deliveries before thirty-seven weeks of gestation – represent around 10 per cent of global births, yet they are the leading cause of complications and deaths in newborns. In health insurance, just five chronic conditions – cardiovascular disease, cancer, respiratory illness, obesity-related conditions and diabetes – account for over 60 per cent of global deaths.

From our own health insurance data, we know that 20 per cent of lives account for 94 per cent of claims costs. The same applies to oncology: 20 per cent of cancer patients comprise 73 per cent of cancer costs. In our motor insurance business, the worst 30 per cent of drivers are responsible for 60 per cent of serious accidents.

Pareto is so pervasive that it should no longer surprise us: it is the norm, not the exception.

How Pareto Applies to Our Lives and Our Impact

The key issue is this: our lives are also complex, interconnected systems shaped by network effects. In the case of our lives, the 'nodes' creating feedback loops are the decisions we make – each with varying degrees of impact. There will be an infinite number of low-impact, everyday choices. But a few decisions in the tail – like who we marry, where we live, what career we choose, whether we start a business – will have repeated and consequential effects on the rest of our lives with disproportionate, long-lasting consequences. They can effectively change our lives by orders of magnitude.

Psychologist Sean Hechtlinger and colleagues offered a framework for understanding why big decisions, like emigration, marriage or career changes, have a greater impact on subsequent decisions than smaller, everyday choices, most notably including:[3]

- *Change of self:* Big decisions like emigration or leaving a religion can shift one's identity, beliefs and life trajectory.

- *Irreversibility:* Many big decisions are difficult or impossible to undo, which leads to cascading consequences from the point at which they are decided, for example, the decision to have children.

These dimensions mean that big decisions are not isolated – they reconfigure the context in which future decisions are made. Because they shape so many of the choices that come afterward, new decisions tend to connect back to them – and they naturally end up becoming the most influential anchors in the whole system.

Pareto: Impact on Your Life

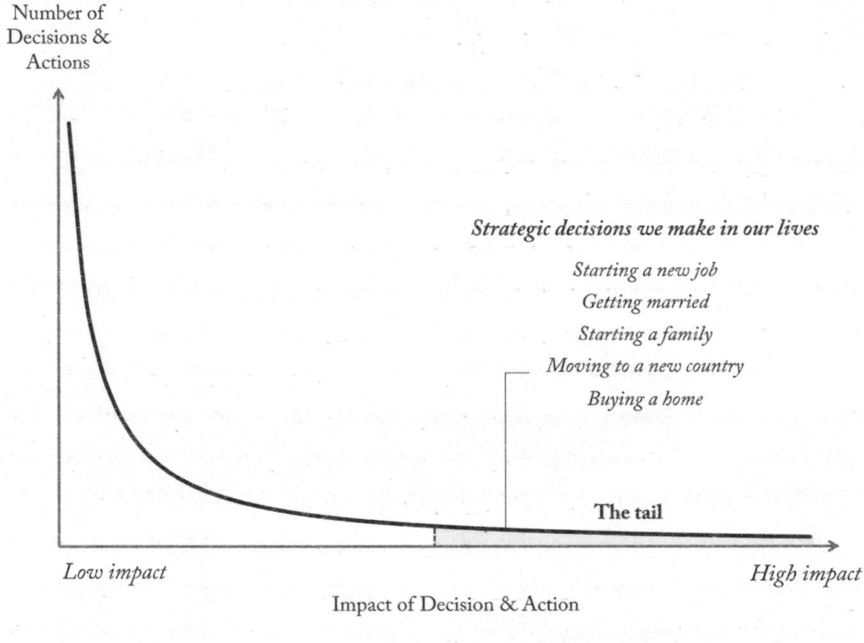

This key insight leads to the Fourth Principle: **The Pareto Tail**. If only a few key decisions and actions determine the impact and trajectory of our lives, then learning to identify and target these decisions – harnessing the Pareto tail – determines our impact.

The implications of the Fourth Principle are profound and multidimensional, and to appreciate them requires deeper understanding of Pareto, how it works, and its dynamics.

Progress in a Pareto World Is Determined by the Tail

A well-known quip often used to illustrate the impact of Pareto goes like this: 'Steve Jobs walked into a bar, and everyone in the bar instantly became a millionaire – on average.' The operative words are 'on average'. Jobs had not given away any money. None of the patrons were any richer. But if Jobs, worth around £8 billion when he died, walks into a bar with 100 people, the average wealth per person jumps to £80 million. That's the Pareto principle. One person, one outlier, one event can dramatically shift the average, not just marginally, but rapidly and into another stratosphere.

The realization that we live in a largely Pareto world – inherently asymmetric, unpredictable and 'unfair' – may feel disconcerting at first. But the upside of this Fourth Principle is that achieving systemic change in such a world is much easier and faster, because in shifting these distributions, you can shift the average and create enormous impact in the Pareto tail.

As the two comparative graphs below show, impact is all about shifting the average. In a normally distributed world, changing a system requires shifting all the elements within it to move the average – a laborious, time-consuming process that is often impractical or incremental, at best. However, in a Pareto world, systems can be transformed by activity in the long tail of the distribution. Sometimes, even a single action or outlier in the tail can drag the average and reconfigure the system.

The fact that this applies to our lives is the essence and power of the Fourth Principle. We can make changes and impact quickly by acting in the Pareto tail.

Progress in a Normal Distribution World

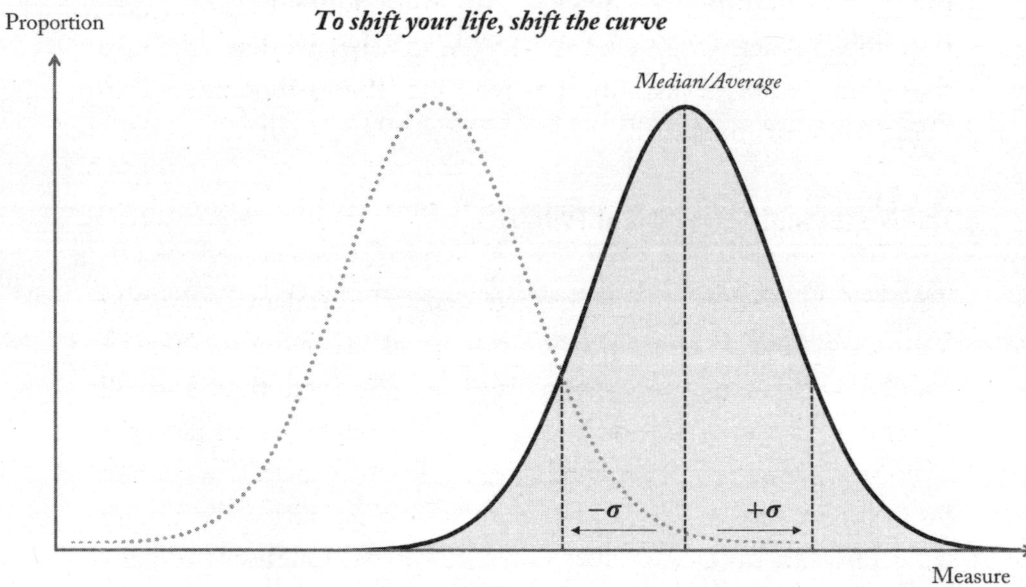

Progress in a Pareto World

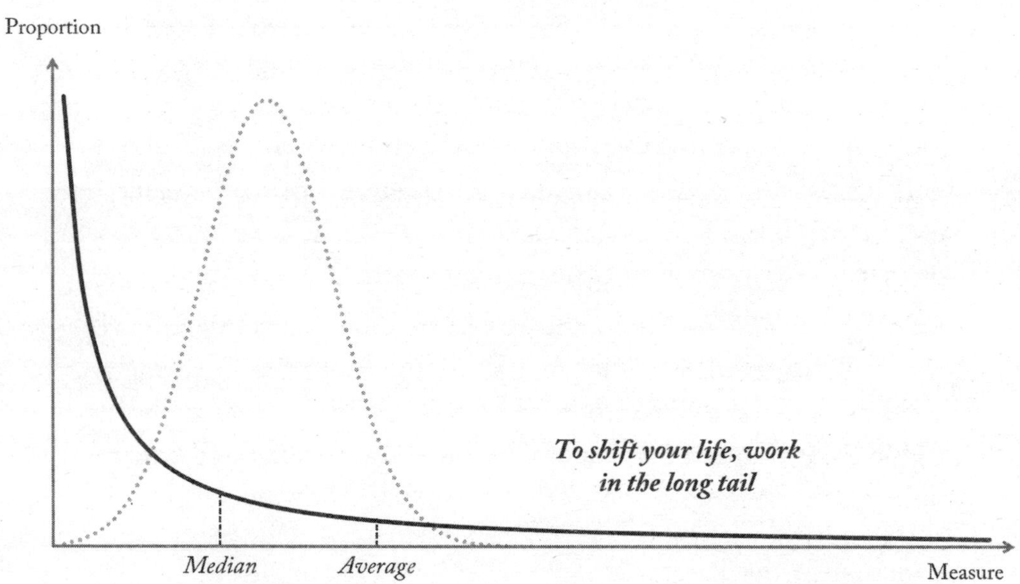

The implication is that a few decisions and actions in the tail can shift our entire lives, quickly and profoundly – both in direction and impact. It is never too late, and what we have done to that point is not necessarily that relevant. This is fundamental to living a life of impact.

The Origin and Evolution of Pareto

The Pareto distribution is named after the Italian economist Vilfredo Pareto (1848–1923) who, in 1906, conducted a mathematical study of economic inequality. He observed that a small fraction of Italy's population (around 20 per cent) controlled the majority (about 80 per cent) of its land and its wealth. Expanding his research across Europe, he found that this pattern of wealth concentration persisted across countries and throughout history.

Ironically, it was not Pareto himself who coined the term 'Pareto principle'. That distinction goes to American engineer and management consultant Joseph Juran, who in the late 1940s and early 1950s, recognized the broader applicability of Pareto's insights – particularly in quality control on the factory floor, and in business management. Juran observed that roughly 80 per cent of defects in manufacturing stemmed from about 20 per cent of causes or components, an insight that proved significant for systems efficiency and process improvement. It was Juran who reframed Pareto's findings into a more general 80/20 principle, which he called the Pareto principle, and it was he who coined the phrase 'the vital few and the trivial many', emphasizing the importance of focusing on the most impactful factors.

The Pareto pattern may appear simple at first glance, but the more closely you examine it, the more nuanced – and powerful – it becomes. That is why it is important to understand its core attributes.

Crucially, Pareto should not be viewed as a strict 80/20 mathematical rule, but rather as a broad heuristic – a rule of thumb that highlights unbalanced, asymmetrical relationships. The 80/20 ratio is simply a benchmark – the actual distribution might be 90/10, 70/30 or even 80/10 (the two numbers don't need to sum to 100), because one number refers to effect and the other frequency. The key insight remains unchanged: a small number of inputs drives a disproportionately large share of outcomes.

The Two Key Attributes of Pareto – Stubborn and Recursive

Pareto is remarkably stubborn. Regardless of what policies or interventions are implemented, a small percentage of factors tend to account for a disproportionately large share of outcomes.

This is evident in income distribution – the very origin of Pareto's insight – where inequality is frequently viewed as a problem to be overcome. Yet while it presents real and tragic consequences, the reality is that even where systems have been explicitly designed to reduce inequality, Pareto-like patterns of inequality are stubbornly resistant to change.

In historically communist and socialist-leaning countries, such as China, Cuba and Vietnam, where emphasis has been placed on economic equality, they still have a Gini coefficient – the standard measure of income inequality – higher than that of advanced capitalist countries such as France, Japan, Germany and the UK. In China, the Gini coefficient is 36, in Cuba it is 40 to 50, and in Vietnam it is 36.1 – whereas France has a measure of 31.8, Japan 32.3, Germany 32.4, and the UK 32.4, according to latest World Bank data. (The higher the Gini coefficient, the higher the inequality, with 0 representing total equality and 100 representing extreme inequality.)

Several factors explain this: the rise of shadow or informal economies; corruption and state capture; limited economic growth opportunities for the general populace; and challenges in enforcing redistributive policies. It is also important to note that Gini coefficients do not capture everything. For example, access to housing, education and healthcare can be much more equitable in socialist-leaning countries, especially if those services are universally provided.

But the general point stands: income inequality is not exclusively a capitalist phenomenon and structural inequality – often modelled by Pareto distributions – can stubbornly persist, even where income redistribution is a stated government goal.

City sizes, too, often demonstrate the stubborn Pareto pattern, resisting planners' attempts to spread the population. According to Zipf's Law for Cities, the population of a city tends to be inversely proportional to its rank – so the largest city in a country is roughly twice as large as the second, and three times as large as the third – and this pattern holds remarkably steady over time.

For example, America's largest city, New York, has a population of about 8.5 million – over twice the size of Los Angeles (3.9 million) and three times the size of Chicago (2.7 million). A similar pattern exists in Brazil, with São Paulo at 11.9 million, Rio de Janeiro at 6.7 million, and Brasilia at 3 million. In the UK, France, Argentina, South Korea and Thailand, the country's premier cities – London, Paris, Buenos Aires, Seoul and Bangkok – dominate even more extremely than Zipf had observed.

Urban migration and planning efforts rarely break this hierarchy.

The second attribute – and perhaps most importantly – Pareto is recursive. This means that within every Pareto tail, there is another Pareto tail inside it. Inside the 20 per cent of the vital actions or causes, another 80/20 split applies – and within that, yet another. It is like a Russian Matryoshka doll: layer upon layer of concentrated, asymmetrical impact.

Vilfredo Pareto observed this recursion in his original study – not only did the top 20 per cent own 80 per cent of the wealth, but the lion's share of that wealth was concentrated within the top 5 per cent, and even more so in the top 1 per cent.

We see the recursive nature of Pareto in our own business. For example, within the 20 per cent of lives that account for 94 per cent of total claim costs in our health insurance business, the top 20 per cent of the top 20 per cent account for 63 per cent of the total costs of that group. Drill down again and the top 20 per cent of the top 20 per cent of the top 20 per cent account for 48 per cent of total costs in that subgroup. Ultimately, the top 1 per cent of all claimants account for over 33 per cent of total pay-outs – a figure that has remained remarkably consistent over time.

Another word to describe the recursive nature of Pareto is 'fractal', a term coined by mathematician Benoit Mandelbrot in the 1970s.[4] It refers to a complex geometric pattern that exhibits 'self-similarity' – meaning the pattern repeats itself at every scale. Fractals exist in nature – snowflakes, fern leaves and coastlines all display fractal patterns – as well as in mathematics, and they offer a powerful analogy for understanding the recursive nature of Pareto.

In summary, extensive research by scientists who study complex systems has confirmed that Pareto distributions arise naturally in virtually all adaptive systems, emerging automatically from the dynamic interactions between agents in these systems, without requiring any central coordination or design.

The ubiquity and recursiveness of these patterns suggest they represent a fundamental organizing principle of complex systems, not merely a statistical curiosity.

As Nobel laureate American physicist Philip Anderson observed in his reflections on complex systems: 'Much of the real world is controlled as much by the "tails" of distributions as by means or averages; by the exceptional, not the mean, by catastrophe, not the steady drip.'[5] To put this in context, Anderson wrote those words in the 1980s – long before the advent of the internet, social media and AI. One can only wonder how much more emphasis he might place on the 'tails' of distributions today.

In short, the Pareto pattern is now so pervasive that it is arguably more 'normal' than the so-called 'normal distribution' of the bell curve. Instead of being surprised by it, we should expect it.

The Question Is: How Do We Act in the Pareto Tail?

Considering the power of Pareto, its pervasiveness, stubbornness and recursiveness, the fact is our lives are governed by it, and this has profound implications. No matter what we do, our lives and their impact are determined by the tail that inevitably forms. The challenge is that to live a life of impact requires us to take deliberate decisions and actions in the tail – not to let the tail define us – and crucially, to shift the tail as far to the right as possible.

The question is: how? The answer lies in the first three Principles. They are enabling with learnable tactics, while the Fourth Principle, Pareto, is defining and explanatory. The Fourth Principle is where the rubber hits the road – decisions and actions, and their impact.

The First Principle, Disciplined Optimism, enables us to resist automatic declinist narratives and seek out positive signals to identify opportunities others don't see. In addition, it enables us to execute on opportunities which inevitably require working through webs of organizations, structures and people in today's networked world. The Second Principle, Focused Urgency, addresses our distorted perception of time and ensures we act quickly or face the reality of running out of time – and of never identifying the opportunity that brings out our real potential. The Third Principle, Declared Goals, creates motivation, action and additional drive to avoid the loss that comes with falling short of that goal.

Applying these three Principles will place us in easier reach and proximity of the Pareto tail – making decisions and taking actions that are in the tail and pushing the tail to the right. The tail is our personal tail, based on our own circumstances, abilities and talents. Action in the tail is so powerful – that is how Pareto works – and it has a multiplicative effect on the impact of our lives.

This power can be illustrated because the Principles are mathematically demonstrable. The cumulative effect of the first three Principles – I argue – is multiplicative, because each Principle operates on a different axis – opportunity (Optimism), availability (Urgency) and drive (Goals). So, their effects compound rather than overlap.

Scaled Up Impact in a Pareto World

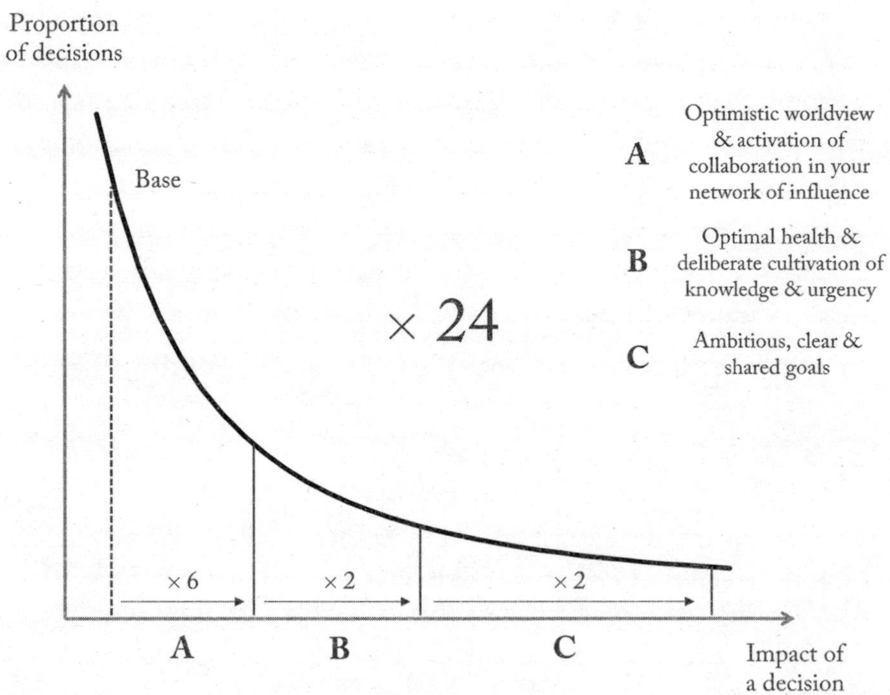

For example, as shown in the graph, doubling your effective time (Urgency) allows you to pursue twice as many opportunities, and if with Optimism you are six times more likely to find and leverage value from them, the total impact is 2 × 6 = 12. Then, if your motivation to act on those opportunities is also doubled (Goals), the final impact becomes 12 × 2 = 24.

This 24-times multiplier may sound fanciful or unlikely, but it is not – and that is precisely the power of the long tail of Pareto. A 24-times higher impact is hugely significant in a Pareto distribution of actions, getting us into the top per cent of actions by impact. So, by embracing these three Principles, we cumulatively move into the far tail of the distribution, putting ourselves in a prime position to reap the benefits of rapid and transformational change and impact.

The cumulative power of the Four Principles also explains the paradox that first sparked my curiosity – curiosity that led to decades of observation and research, and ultimately to this book. Successful, high-impact people come in all shapes, sizes and abilities because the Four Principles are so powerful that, when pursued, their impact can dwarf differences in skills and capacity.

This is a good segue to my bath story, because it was a moment in time that I arrived at because of the power of the first three Principles leading me deep into the tail – and the Fourth Principle.

Back to the Epiphany in the Bath

It was 1997, three years into the fledgling 'new' South Africa, and Nelson Mandela was South Africa's president. Discovery was still the new kid on the block. We were nimble, innovative and profitable, but we were small and had yet to expand beyond South Africa.

One day, Neville Koopowitz – now the CEO of Vitality, our

global business – approached me with a business proposal involving the Health & Racquet Club, a group that operated around eighty-five gyms across the country. Neville has been a principal driver of Discovery's success and his proposal caught my attention.

What intrigued me about the gyms was how they had disrupted their industry and redefined what a gym could be. Keep in mind that in the late 1990s, the world was experiencing a wellness revolution, driven by an appreciation for preventive approaches to health rather than solely focusing on treating established conditions. Against this backdrop, the commercial fitness industry was changing. What had once been a fragmented market dominated by small, locally owned gyms was transforming into a sophisticated retail sector with global chains and mainstream appeal.

In South Africa, the Health & Racquet Club had emerged as a dominant player in this market transformation. Their timing was perfect: post-apartheid, the rapidly expanding middle class was creating strong demand for lifestyle services previously accessible only to a small subset of South Africans. Their gyms were not traditional boxing or weightlifting facilities; they were high-end and modern, designed to appeal across generations and genders. They helped shape a new consumer mindset around health, mainstreaming wellness as a lifestyle goal. Also important was the unique aspirational position that the Health & Racquet Club held: membership was expensive, but it offered a refuge from the fears and stresses of a country in transition.

The idea that had been proposed to Neville was a traditional cross-sell strategy: the Health & Racquet membership base was supposedly young and healthy, and in our target market. So, we would offer our health insurance plans to them. During the quieter midday hours, when their staff had little to do, they could earn commissions by selling our insurance policies to their gym members.

As a road runner, these exclusive gyms were not my usual habitat, but I kept mulling over their offer. I fully appreciated the scale of the gyms and the appeal of their target market. My instinct told me there was something much larger and more interesting buried in their proposal – but I couldn't quite figure out what.

That evening, after my usual run, I was lying in the bath, turning their offer over in my mind, when I suddenly had an epiphany: what if we flipped it? Instead of selling our health insurance to their gym members, what if we offered their gym membership to our health insurance customers? And what if we made it free? In other words, if you had health insurance with Discovery, you could walk into any Health & Racquet Club across the country – at no extra cost.

I instantly knew it would be a game-changer. If we secured this partnership, no other insurer would be able to compete. It would differentiate us – instantly and powerfully.

But there were significant obstacles to overcome – the affordability seemed an impossible barrier. Gym memberships were expensive; per member, the cost was significant as a percentage of the cost of our health insurance products themselves. How could we make the access 'free' if you were our member?

What if we paid Health & Racquet Club a small, fixed fee for each member, regardless of how often our members used the gyms – known as a capitation fee? Crucially, it would be only a fraction of the actual cost of gym membership. In addition, to reduce our costs further, we contemplated an approach in which our members had to 'earn' their gym membership by engaging in healthy behaviours – by working out. If customers were physically active, the gym stayed free; if not sufficiently active, they would pay a portion; and if they were inactive, they had to cover the full membership themselves. This approach would have the dual benefit of encouraging our members to remain active and healthy, while also reducing the cost to our business of this amazing free gym offer.

This idea would ultimately evolve into a dynamic system of

earning points for doing healthy things, and those points gave the member a status. We would call the programme Vitality, and the points Vitality Points – and we would create four statuses: Blue, Bronze, Silver and Gold.

We duly completed the deal with Health & Racquet Club and launched. I still remember the impact with newspaper headlines proclaiming: 'Free gym with Vitality' and 'Discovery members to go to Health & Racquet Club for free'.

The offer was a novel concept, but not everyone was convinced. We faced scepticism from competitors, some media and many health policymakers who either called it 'a waste of money' or insisted that trying to boost people's wellness was a fool's errand. At that time, there was no data that could illustrate the causal effect of physical activity and healthy lifestyles on health outcomes and healthcare costs.

But our critics were wrong.

Vitality was a profound breakthrough. We saw a surge in new customers signing up, many of them switching from older, more established insurers. One might have expected the initial excitement to fade as people struggled to maintain their fitness targets – but our data showed the opposite: five years in, more members were 'active' than in the first year. And that number kept growing.

Over time, we added more benefits – like travel discounts and active rewards for physical activity – in return for meeting a wide range of healthy activity targets. Being a Gold Vitality member became a badge of honour, like the wealth-signalling effect that banks create by issuing credit cards in various colour tiers. But in our case, we were doing only good – trying to make people healthier.

Indeed, it turned out that our business model was doing something extraordinary: it was changing people's behaviour – and yes, making them healthier. This was long before we understood the real causal effect of these activities on health and mortality, and before we really understood the principles of behavioural economics that we were applying.

Reasons Why the Gym Deal Became a Tail Event

To grasp why Vitality became such a powerful event in the Pareto tail, it helps to understand the context in which we operated and the interplay between three key factors: South Africa's dire healthcare landscape, the inflationary pressures facing health insurers globally, and several powerful behavioural science concepts that we had inadvertently stumbled upon.

The South African healthcare system was facing considerable challenges. The country had both a shortage of doctors and a severe health burden comprising four overlapping epidemics: infectious diseases including HIV and AIDS, TB and others; maternal, newborn and child health issues; non-communicable diseases such as high blood pressure and diabetes; and high rates of violence and injuries.

In addition, South Africa's transition from apartheid and its deep levels of discrimination brought about legislation rightly focused on promoting equality, fairness and access. In the health insurance context, this translated, as discussed earlier in the Second Principle, into a radical shift to 'community rating' – all members paying the same premium, regardless of individual risk, with guaranteed acceptance of cover.

This combination of high need and structural reform created fertile ground for 'adverse selection', as actuaries call it, where the sick buy health insurance, while the healthy delay joining until they're older or unwell. The spectre for health insurers was stark: escalating claims, runaway premium inflation, financial instability and, ultimately, the potential collapse of the business model.

When we founded Discovery, the hypothesis was that a business built on sound actuarial principles and backed by strong shareholders could offer funding models and products that were sustainable in a fast-changing environment such as we faced. But as we built the business, the primary challenge remained how to curb medical inflation.

Around that time, a deeper understanding of the impact of lifestyle choices on health and mortality was emerging. But the health insurance industry was wrestling with a persistent imbalance known as the 'healthcare consumption paradox' – a dynamic in which healthcare is over-consumed while wellness and prevention are under-consumed. This mismatch is a major driver of rising premiums. Healthcare is over-consumed because, for insured individuals, it is free at the point of delivery. Its value is immediate, substantial and evident. Wellness, by contrast, has a cost: you must go for a run, skip the dessert or say no to the sugary drink. These are uncomfortable choices and their benefits – better health and longer life – are not immediate as they only manifest in years to come.

This behavioural tendency – in which we prioritize smaller, immediate rewards over larger, delayed ones – is well documented in behavioural economics and is known as hyperbolic discounting. It explains why many people abandon exercise routines, break diets, overspend or give up on New Year's resolutions before the end of January. It also explains why wellness is under-consumed and highlights the scale of the challenge: a growing imbalance between the over-consumption of healthcare and the under-consumption of wellness – and the impact being both inflationary and unsustainable.

We knew intuitively that part of the solution lay in trying to tame the demand for healthcare. A simple analogy haunted us: what would food inflation look like if people paid a fixed monthly fee to supermarkets, then took whatever they wanted off the shelves at no additional cost? Naturally, they would take everything – caviar and bread alike – and within months, the supermarkets would go bust.

Yet that is exactly how unmanaged health insurance works: customers pay a fixed premium and access whatever healthcare they believe they need.

At Discovery, we became obsessed with solving this. Our first breakthrough was to introduce Medical Savings Accounts (MSAs) – a mechanism to pay for routine, day-to-day medical expenses. The idea was that a portion of each customer's monthly premium went into their MSA. When they visited a doctor or bought prescription medication, the cost came out of that account – in effect, a pot of their own money. Of course, for chronic medication or hospitalization, healthcare services which were much less in our customers' discretion, coverage was provided separately without affecting their MSAs. This model completely changed customer behaviour: it made them more mindful of how they consumed care. They went from wasteful to prudent because the payments for more discretionary services came out of their own MSAs and they did not want to run short. The effect was dramatic, and we were able to offer more competitive premiums. As a result, we gained considerable market share.

While this was an important first step, it only dealt with one side of the healthcare consumption paradox – the inflationary effect of over-consumed, out-of-hospital care. The next major leap was to tackle under-consumed wellness. To our knowledge, no one had done this at scale before.

As it turned out, our Vitality structure that emanated from the original gym partnership was the breakthrough. Almost by accident, we had created a behavioural mechanism that helped overcome hyperbolic discounting – bridging the psychological gap between 'effort now' and 'reward later'.

That was because the gym benefit – and the broader Vitality

programme – aligned 'effort now' with 'reward now', removing the psychological barrier of delayed benefits in the future. Without realizing it at the time, we had tapped into a profound motivational truth – one with enormous business potential.

The results were striking. First, many of our less healthy customers began exercising and saw real improvement in their health. Second, the model attracted a wave of new customers – particularly people seeking better health, and low-risk individuals who liked the idea of being rewarded for exercising. Third, it helped us retain our most engaged customers, who appreciated being recognized and incentivized for their effort. Less engaged customers, who were often higher risk, were more likely to lapse. The combination of these dynamics enabled us to lower our premiums and undercut our competitors – while offering a dramatically better and fundamentally different value proposition.

This created a successful flywheel – a positively reinforcing system that kept gaining momentum. It allowed us to dramatically outperform our sector both in growth and profitability, and it rapidly disrupted and reshaped the South African health insurance market.

Despite this extraordinary early progress, little did we know that in fact it was only the beginning. We did not know it then, but that single idea would lead to extraordinary outcomes – ones that extended beyond our business, beyond our industry, and eventually beyond South Africa to the global stage.

To be clear: at the time, nothing like our model existed in any health insurance market – not in South Africa, not in the US, UK, Europe or Asia. We had no concrete data yet on how incentivized wellness would impact sickness or mortality rates, and in its absence, there continued to be heated debates – both inside our business and across the industry – over whether it could truly work.

The granular data would come later. But even then, we could already see that we had created a compelling win-win-win model:

- For individuals, who lived longer, healthier lives and paid lower premiums than they would elsewhere;
- For our business, which grew market share and profitability as reduced claims enabled us to offer lower premiums than our competitors;
- For society, which benefitted from less pressure on healthcare systems and a healthier, more productive population. Even the sick gained – as balanced risk pools kept premiums affordable for everyone.

There is no doubt that my story illustrates the Fourth Principle well – a thought, a decision in a single moment that changed the direction and impact of both my life and that of our organization. It is evidence of the power of the Pareto tail, pure and simple. But what is fascinating and instructive is just how the first Three Principles got me into the tail in that moment. I have reflected a lot on this dynamic.

Consider the First Principle, Disciplined Optimism: in a South Africa under threat and undergoing dramatic political change, the gyms were an aspirational tonic. By seeking out positive signals, we were able to see – amid the prevailing despair – their aspirational nature as a business opportunity. Importantly, by that stage we had written 'Optimism' into our set of core values.

In terms of the Second Principle, Focused Urgency, not much more needs to be said: I was flat out and used every single awake moment focused on our growth and scale – on almost every run and in almost every bath I had, as it turned out.

And in terms of the Third Principle, Declared Goals, our goal at the time was to build the best health insurer in South Africa, which we had publicly stated. It drove us to not accept conventional wisdom or to follow what others were doing. Rationally, the cross-sell proposal put to us should have been clear and we should have accepted it, but our stretch goal required us to go beyond and think through every single detail looking for competitive advantage, which led to the flip from selling health insurance to young and healthy gym members to attaching gyms to health insurance and making all of our members healthier.

The question is whether you can extrapolate this to all breakthroughs or innovations, with the relevant question being whether breakthroughs are a singular moment, a fluke of timing, or the culmination of a process of intense thinking, questioning and internal wrestling, which the first three Principles drive?

It seems clear to me that it was the latter. Innovation is often romanticized as the product of sudden brilliance, but those moments are typically hard-fought, involving a lot of work carried out below the radar by many people.

It reminds me of what the champion golfer Gary Player used to say when he holed out from a bunker: 'The harder I work, the luckier I get.' Or how Albert Einstein put it: 'It is not that I'm so smart, it is just that I stay with problems longer.' While I would not be so bold as to compare myself to Einstein or Player, I do believe that my colleagues and I share that drive and persistence. Acts in the Pareto tail may seem miraculous, but more often than not, they are hard-won.

The power of the Fourth Principle is not just in its first-dimension effect of creating a point of inflection in a life or a business, but its attribute of being recursive creates an exponential ongoing effect. The recursive property means that within the tail, there is another tail, and so on. It is a gift that keeps giving.

In our case, what we didn't yet fully realize in launching Vitality in its initial basic form, based on the gym benefit, was that we had not just stumbled upon a repeatable, scalable business model – but an exemplar within the increasingly widespread debate around acceptable and effective forms of capitalism. It would lead to further innovations that would augment the groundbreaking nature of Vitality and further enhance the Pareto effect – and demonstrate the recursive power of the tail.

The Vitality Shared-Value Model – The Healthier Our Customers Are, the More Profitable We Are

The Shared-Value model is a groundbreaking business concept introduced by Harvard professors Michael Porter and Mark Kramer in 2011. Their *Harvard Business Review* article, 'Creating Shared Value: How to Reinvent Capitalism – and Unleash a Wave of Innovation and Growth', described how businesses could simultaneously enhance profitability while generating meaningful economic and social benefits for customers and society at large.[6] The idea was significant because it aligned profit-making with social impact rather than seeing them as opposing forces, and it showed that profit and purpose could coexist. At its best, it created a virtuous cycle of 'good for us, good for our customers, good for society' and redefined the role of business in shaping a better world.

We had invited Michael Porter to address our annual Discovery Summit in South Africa, a platform that brings together thought leaders, business strategists and influential figures. Over the years, we have hosted an array of world-class speakers, the Clintons, Al Gore, David Cameron, Richard Branson, Sebastian Coe, Malcolm Gladwell, Arianna Huffington, Joseph Stiglitz and David Beckham, to name a few.

Porter headlined our 2012 summit, delivering a fascinating

presentation on the Shared-Value model. As he illustrated the concept – using companies like Nestlé and Unilever which he cited as strong examples – we had a sudden realization that our Vitality business model was, in fact, a perfect embodiment of the Shared-Value model.

We had pioneered this approach over a decade earlier, recognizing that the healthier our customers were, the more profitable we became – and that society benefitted in the process. Our industry is perhaps unusual in this regard in that we are completely aligned with the interests of our customers – we are more profitable when they are healthier and so making them healthier creates economic value that can be shared by way of incentives. So, our model didn't just align with the principles of shared value, it was a textbook example.

The formal naming and framing of the Shared-Value model by Porter and Kramer was significant for us. First, it expanded the relevance of our business model beyond the insurance sector, illustrating its applicability across industries. Second, it connected our work to the broader crisis facing capitalism, positioning our model at the forefront of a movement aimed at making global capitalist economic systems more sustainable. Third, we became active players in a wider conversation of how business models need to change for good, which was in turn, key to our evolution in terms of how we framed ourselves. In marketing terms, our business model had become a great example of a timely economic model.

For context, I should add that the Shared-Value model came at a time when dramatically rising inequality was fuelling growing concerns about an economic system that produced too few winners. Such debates had already been happening within academia, NGOs and think tanks, but the model thrust these ideas into the business mainstream where they then gained traction.

Shared value was distinctive in that it marked a departure from the traditional neoliberal doctrine of shareholder capitalism, most famously articulated by Milton Friedman, which prioritized maximizing shareholder wealth above all other considerations. Instead, it embraced stakeholder capitalism, a model that considers the interests of a broader group of stakeholders – including customers, employees, suppliers, communities and society at large. Porter also highlighted the limitations of traditional Corporate Social Responsibility (CSR), which often treats social impact as separate from the core business operation – a 'nice to have' add-on rather than an integrated business imperative. Shared value, by contrast, integrates social good directly into the business's core operational strategy.

The Shared-Value approach we adopted at Discovery reflected our broader philosophy: business success and societal progress don't have to be at odds – they can, and should, reinforce each other.

This inherent alignment between the interests of our shareholders and our customers created a repeatable model enabling us to expand both globally and by industry. We applied it to motor insurance, incentivizing people to drive better via Vitality Drive within Discovery Insure, and in banking, incentivizing people to manage their money better via Vitality Money within Discovery Bank.

All from that moment in the bath.

It also led to repeatable innovation as technology and data emerged. Consider our experience with Apple.

Apple Watches for Free – The Recursive Power of Pareto at Work

In the spring of 2015, Apple Inc. launched the Apple Watch in nine countries to overwhelming acclaim. They flew off the shelves in the US, UK, Germany, France, China, Canada, Australia, Hong

Kong and Japan – with about four million sold in the first three months. The Apple Watch was so incredibly appealing, and I found myself wondering whether we could leverage its appeal to make health and life insurance exciting as well.

Having thought this over for some time, I put the following question to my colleague Neville Koopowitz: what if we replicated the structure of the gym reward by offering our customers a discounted – or even free – Apple Watch? And what if they had to earn it by being physically active?

By this time, Vitality had globalized and was being used by Ping An in China, AIA across Asia-Pacific, John Hancock in the US, and many smaller insurers around the world. Also, our Vitality business was achieving considerable success with a concept called 'Active Rewards' – in which members were rewarded weekly with a coffee from Starbucks or the equivalent local coffee chain if they met their weekly physical activity goals. This tech-enabled reward achieved incredible engagement – the user experience was simple and appealing, with the coffee voucher available on your phone. Once earned, I typically emailed mine to my daughter who was at the time a student in Cape Town, a wonderful feeling mixing getting healthier with gifting to your children. Nothing better.

The point is that Active Rewards gave us deep insight into physical activity – how to drive engagement, and the causal effect of that engagement on health and mortality. The Apple Watch seemed a potentially compelling addition to Active Rewards, as well as a natural fit within our Shared-Value model.

Our idea was to apply the same behavioural science mechanism that we had first stumbled upon with gym memberships. In other words: could we make the watch work like the gym? Could the Apple Watch become the fulfilment vehicle for incentivizing healthy behaviour?

The question wasn't flippant but backed by data.

For eighteen years, our team of more than 200 actuaries and data scientists had been meticulously collecting and analysing behavioural health data, giving us one of the world's most comprehensive datasets. Today, this includes more than 60 million life years of health claims and clinical data alongside over 35 million life years of exercise and lifestyle data. These datasets painted a clear and compelling picture of the dramatic impact that physical activity has on health status and lifespan.

Specifically, they showed that the impact of behaviour on risk is causal:[7]

- When someone aged 45 to 65 went from being inactive to highly active, their mortality risk dropped by 58 per cent.
- Even a shift from inactive to low activity levels resulted in a significant 36 per cent reduction in mortality.

They also showed that the impact of behaviour on risk is elastic – with mortality risk being highly responsive to changes in behaviour, especially when you're older. For instance, if you are aged 45 to 65 and you go from no physical exercise to a healthy habit of moderate physical activity, your mortality risk reduces by 38 per cent, but if you are older than 65 and similarly step up from no exercise to a moderate habit, your mortality risk reduces by 52 per cent.

Encouragingly too, the data showed that good habits are easy to form.

We could further prove that frequent exercise reduces the cost of hospital admissions. Our data showed that going from no exercise to a moderate habit of physical activity (two or three active days a week), reduced average hospital costs by 10 per cent. Our data also proved that becoming physically active acted as a powerful 'gateway' to other healthy behaviour changes; for example, a person who first began to exercise was 12 per cent more likely to begin buying health foods, and 24 per cent more likely to undertake preventative care.

Backed by all this data, and our deep conviction about what we could achieve with Apple, we reached out to Apple's leadership team.

When we arrived on Apple's sprawling Infinite Loop campus in Cupertino, Silicon Valley, I had this sense of an amazing journey of scale – from that moment in the bath to an audience with senior leaders of the most valuable business in the world. We had secured a 45-minute meeting with Jeff Williams, their former chief operating officer and number two to CEO Tim Cook, but back then, Apple's senior vice president of operations, responsible for the development of the Apple Watch.

I was taken aback by Jeff's approach, humble but intense, and hugely impressive and smart. We took him through our model and came to the core intellectual proposition – by making people more physically active, we would bend the sickness and mortality curves downwards and use the consequent savings to fund the Apple Watch.

The discussion that followed was highly engaging and challenging. I was struck by how quickly he picked up the core actuarial concepts and by his pragmatic, purpose-driven approach. By the end, it felt like we were aligned on our vision of using the Apple Watch as a mechanism to change behaviour to achieve good. We left with an agreement that turned out to be transformational for us and enabled us to significantly turbocharge our Active Rewards product, by changing it to 'Active Rewards with Apple Watch'.

It meant our Vitality members could apply for and receive an Apple Watch – worth around £250 – funded entirely within the Vitality Shared-Value model.

The day we launched in South Africa, in December 2015, there were massive queues outside all the authorized Apple Watch dealers. There had been a swirl of publicity, and our offer was clearly cutting through. South Africa's biggest online news site, *News24*, had run the headline, 'Discovery launches free Apple Watch initiative',[8] while *BusinessTech*, the largest online business news site in South Africa, splashed: 'Discovery to give away a free Apple Watch to Vitality members'.[9] Even *Forbes* would later report on our initiative, headlining their piece, 'How Incentives – And a Free Apple Watch – Make People Healthier'.[10]

In that first week alone, we gave away 10,000 Apple Watches. Demand from our Vitality customers was so intense that dealers across South Africa quickly ran out of stock. That week, Apple's global sales data flagged South Africa as a statistical outlier – an anomaly given the massive global numbers they typically achieved.

That single deal was a huge shot in the arm for our South African business. It achieved exactly what we had envisioned: allying our brand with one of the world's most aspirational consumer products. By the end of that year, a remarkable 10 per cent of all Apple Watches sold in South Africa had been distributed via our business.

A few months later, in 2016, we rolled out the same offer to our Vitality customers in the UK – again with dramatically positive effects. And this was just the beginning. Soon after, we expanded into other international markets. In the US, the launch of the Apple Watch benefit helped position our partner, John Hancock, as the standout innovator in the North American life insurance market. We launched similar schemes to make the Apple Watch available to our customers in Japan, Germany, Austria and Australia.

To date, we have provided close to one million Apple Watches to Vitality customers globally – at a modest upfront cost to them.

Our offer was highly creative. Vitality members could get an

Apple Watch for a nominal upfront payment of as little as £1. They then entered into a twenty-four-month payment agreement with us for the balance of the cost. Each month the customer would be charged the monthly instalment less a credit for how physically active they had been, as measured by the 'Move' ring on the Apple Watch. If they met their physical activity goals, their payment was zero and the watch remained free. So, they were in effect being incentivized to earn their watch through being physically active each month of the twenty-four-month contract.

Part of the brilliance of the design was its framing, as mentioned in the Third Principle, to evoke the behavioural bias of loss aversion: our deal put the Apple Watch on the wrist of our customers who were then motivated to exercise to keep it (or more accurately, to avoid the 'loss' of having to pay for the watch that month) – more so than they would have been had they only earned the Apple Watch later on, as a consequence of adhering to their exercise goals over a twenty-four-month period.

The data we later accumulated showed, as I touched on in the Third Principle, just how powerful this framing was: people who had Vitality Active Rewards with an Apple Watch became 34 per cent more active than before – the equivalent of an extra 4.8 days' physical activity a month.[11]

These changes would make our customers even healthier and lead to a reduction in health insurance claims from our most engaged members, evidence of the closing of the gap between the over-consumption of healthcare and the under-consumption of wellness. Most tellingly, our data showed that customers with an Apple Watch had a significantly reduced risk of mortality compared to their counterparts without the watch. It meant that we could confidently start banking material reductions in the mortality rates of our customers in pricing our model and setting premiums.

In the intervening years and thereafter, we would roll out our

Vitality Rewards programme and license our intellectual property to health and life insurance partners in dozens of countries. Discounted gym, Apple Watches, and all the other incentives in our programme would transform our business and present a new model to disrupt the health and life insurance industry around the world.

I hope I have made the power of the Fourth Principle clear – it is the culmination of the first three and enables us to profoundly change the direction of our lives, the power of our leadership, the impact we can make, and the legacy we will leave.

Having said all this, what Pareto can create, Pareto can take away – and not all Pareto experiences are positive.

The Sting in the Pareto Tail: What if Richard Branson Won't Play Ball?

So far, we have looked at the upside of Pareto, but there is peril too. If you don't clearly identify those elements that are the key drivers for your business's success, then everything can unravel if the fundamentals change, and those key drivers come under threat. Such threats could be industry specific, or they could relate uniquely to your business.

Negative Pareto tail events that have brought down entire sectors include, for example, the devastating impact of digital mobile phone photography on traditional camera and film businesses, such as Kodak, and the obliteration of the video and DVD hire industry and its leaders such as Blockbuster, due to advances in streaming technology that changed the way people watched movies, and led to new giants such as Netflix.

Some negative Pareto events are foreseeable and happen slowly, allowing you time to adapt. Others require you to pivot at warp speed. In our case, we have faced existential Pareto tail events twice – and in both cases the speed and intensity of response was critical. In the first instance, it was a change to the regulations governing the health insurance sector in South Africa at the turn of the millennium that threatened us. (I told this story in the Second Principle under the headline 'Fourteen Days to Save Our Company', but it also fits here as a critical Pareto moment.)

Our second existential moment happened soon after, when the Health & Racquet Club business went bankrupt in 2000 and was about to be taken over by Richard Branson's Virgin Active. The deal we had agreed with Health & Racquet Club three years earlier, giving Vitality members who exercised regularly free gym membership, had become the central pillar of our business model, and so, when we discovered that we were not part of the forward plans of the new owner, Virgin Group, we were deeply concerned.

Just as the epiphany of linking free gym membership to our health insurance had been a Pareto moment in the tail with exponential positive consequences, so the decoupling of it threatened to be a Pareto moment in the tail with equally devastating negative consequences.

Sir Richard Branson, the founder and owner of the Virgin Group, was close to Nelson Mandela at the time and was a big promoter of South Africa. He arrived in the country with his negotiating team to buy these gyms out and rebrand them as Virgin Active. We were told that his team was going to tear up the deal we had with the gyms.

Now, Virgin Group's team were telling us that this model had been good for us but bad for the gyms. This was a flawed understanding of the deal, as in fact the gym group had benefitted greatly from the partnership. Nevertheless, their negotiating team was intent on shutting it down and dumping us as partners. We were staring down the barrel because there was no other aspirational gym group of the same scale that we could partner with. We realized that unless we came up with a compelling argument and a better deal, our Vitality product would lose its marquee offer – and with it, the goose that laid the golden egg.

We knew we had to do something to change the dynamic and our team began a series of meetings with theirs, fully mandated to fight tooth and nail to keep the contract alive. I decided to make a personal appeal to Branson himself. I knew this was a small thing for him, but huge for us. I chatted to Branson and found him humble and tremendously creative, and we got on easily and well, but he was adamant that his team were dealing with it.

His team, however, were still playing hardball; properly prepared to shut the deal down. So, we decided to play a bit of hardball ourselves. We had obtained an option on many of the property leases housing Virgin's flagship gyms. We had hoped not to have to play this card, but with our backs to the wall, this meant we had the power to evict them. Once our fallback position was revealed, the whole power balance shifted and their negotiating stance began to soften considerably.

After that, instead of being locked in conflict, we started to focus on common ground. We offered them a better deal with a higher capitation fee. It wasn't as good for us as it had been, but, after further negotiation, we found the sweet spot that was workable for both of us.

In time, that hard-won initial deal would evolve and mature – and we would become a great partnership and good friends. Today, our deal with Virgin Active remains in place, not just in South Africa, but also in the UK, and our fee structure has become a substantial part of Virgin Active's worldwide revenue. The amount we pay them has grown in rough proportion to our expanding client base and these days we pay them tens of millions of GBP per year. In summary, it quickly became win-win – a great source of revenue for them and a huge benefit providing competitive advantage for us.

Life is made up of millions of decisions, but a precious few determine everything. This was one of them. Events in the tail require you to fight harder to protect and pursue your interests – otherwise they can wipe you out. If we had got this wrong, our competitive advantage would have collapsed. Just like getting the gym membership deal had been a game-changer, so losing it would have been one too. You must act in the tail. Because that tail will wag the dog.

Applications

Corporate Philanthropy - Work in the Pareto Tail to Transform a System

Corporates donate vast amounts to charity – a commendable and necessary expression of social responsibility and a way to reinforce the legitimacy of capitalism. But given the vast scale of these contributions, businesses have a real opportunity to drive meaningful, lasting impact in the causes they support.

Philanthropy, by its very nature, is a network process, working through different nodes and systems to get optimal effect. In addition, many of these causes – such as healthcare and education – are complex networked systems that are powerfully shaped by the Pareto principle. This means that focusing on high-leverage points in the Pareto tail can significantly move the dial.

I want to share our experience because it is instructive given the South African context of record levels of unemployment and inequality, which manifests in unique needs of corporate philanthropy. A key area of need is our public healthcare system – which is underfunded, under-resourced and overburdened. The challenge is immense: the country faces a quadruple disease burden and a critical shortage of medical professionals.

Overall, South Africa has just 8 doctors per 10,000 people – only 25 per cent of the physician density of the UK, 22 per cent of the US, and 18 per cent of countries like Germany and Switzerland. This places the country below the World Health Organization's recommended threshold of 10 doctors per 10,000 population for a functional healthcare system.

In the public healthcare system, it is even worse, with doctor density dropping to just 4.5 per 10,000, and in rural areas it is often fewer than 3 per 10,000. The consequences are stark: South Africa's mortality burden from disease is dramatically higher than in developed countries, with deaths from causes like TB, HIV and AIDS and violence far outpacing rates in the UK and US. While exact comparisons vary, studies consistently show that South Africa's years of life lost – especially among younger populations – are roughly 3 times higher than in the UK and about 2.5 times higher than in the US, reflecting the devastating impact of under-resourced health systems on population health.

The central question was: how – with limited resources – could we make a meaningful impact on the national healthcare system?

A healthcare system is a complex network of funding systems, universities, tertiary and primary systems, hospitals, doctors, nurses, pharma companies, regulations, and much more. Our solution was to apply Fourth Principle thinking by targeting the Pareto tail. Let me explain.

An area in the tail of the healthcare system is its medical specialists (known as consultants in the UK) because, in addition to the criticality of the care they provide, they are also central to the standards of education, and the ability to train at scale. South Africa has just 1.7 medical specialists per 10,000 people, according to 2019 estimates, far below international norms. In the public sector, that figure drops further to just 0.6 specialists per 10,000.[12]

By contrast, the country is relatively well served by nurses and midwives, with a combined density of around 60 doctors, nurses and midwives per 10,000 people[13] – placing it above the WHO's recommended threshold of 44.5 per 10,000 for a functional healthcare system.[14]

The challenge we set for ourselves was this: could we meaningfully increase the number of medical specialists – and, by doing so, influence the healthcare system through the Pareto tail?

Given that the current ratio of 1.7 specialists per 10,000 people is the same as one specialist per 5,882 people, rounding up, it means that each additional specialist would serve almost 6,000 people – and every 100 specialists, an additional 600,000 people. The leverage was clear.

When we launched one of our key philanthropic ventures – the Discovery Foundation – in 2006, we chose therefore to focus exclusively on training and developing medical specialists – particularly those committed to working in underserved rural areas. We prioritized disciplines facing acute shortages. This included oncologists, nephrologists, paediatricians, urologists, cardiologists, trauma surgeons, neurosurgeons, orthopaedic surgeons and family medicine specialists.

Our model required recipients to remain in the public sector for at least two years after qualifying. It also actively promoted black economic empowerment – stipulating that at least 75 per cent of those funded be black doctors to help reverse the effects of apartheid, which had denied many talented black South Africans access to medical education.

So, how have we done?

Since 2006, we have funded the training and professional development of close to 600 medical specialists through scholarships, research grants and fellowships.

We have also supported more than 450 undergraduate medical school students who did not qualify for government grants but could not afford to fund themselves – the so-called 'missing middle' – by guaranteeing their bank loans. This initiative was delivered through a partnership with Standard Bank, the largest bank in Africa, and two leading universities: the University of the Witwatersrand in Johannesburg and the University of Pretoria. For these students, the loans have been transformative. For us, the financial risk has been minimal, with default rates below 1 per cent.

At a systems level, the impact has been significant. Despite limited resources, our focused approach has increased the country's number of medical specialists by approximately 5 per cent, and the number of sub-specialists by approximately 10 per cent. That translates to several million more people gaining access to specialist care, not to mention the downstream benefits to the wider healthcare system. The idea that you can change a society with 1,000 PhDs rings loudly here.

We have also acted in the tail of the tail, applying the recursive power of Pareto. In partnership with Massachusetts General Hospital (MGH) – Harvard Medical School's largest teaching hospital – we launched a pinnacle fellowship programme to train a select group of 'super specialists'. This initiative was challenging and expensive. It required carefully selected South African specialists to spend a year at MGH and involved navigating regulations about foreign medical professionals.

The concept sat deep in the Pareto tail: to develop a cadre of elite specialists who would not only bring cutting-edge healthcare to South Africa but also operate on a 'train-the-trainer' basis to ensure the perpetuation and expansion of their impact.

The recipients of the fellowship have been remarkable. Their contributions have powerfully vindicated our belief in the tail. Consider just a few beneficiaries of the Discovery Foundation MGH Fellowship Award and what they have achieved for the country:

- *Dr Nelisiwe Gogela (2013)* – A liver disease specialist from the University of Cape Town (UCT) who became the inaugural MGH Fellow, her hepatology expertise and groundbreaking work set the tone for future fellows.

- *Dr Brian Allwood (2017)* – A pulmonologist who organized the world's first post-tuberculosis symposium, he brought together global experts to tackle the long-term health challenges of a still-prevalent disease.

- *Dr Salome Maswime (2018)* – Head of global surgery at UCT, her research in maternal and foetal medicine has improved outcomes for women and babies locally and internationally.

- *Dr Sean Chetty (2019)* – Anaesthesiologist and department head at Stellenbosch University, his work in pain management has significantly improved patient quality of life.

Many other Discovery Foundation alumni have become leaders of South Africa's top academic and medical institutions – and some have made landmark medical breakthroughs. The list includes:

- *Professor Mosa Moshabela* – Vice chancellor of UCT.

- *Professor Zukiswa Zingela* – Executive dean of Health Sciences at Nelson Mandela University.

- *Professor Hopewell Ntsinjana* – Head of Paediatric Cardiology at Nelson Mandela Children's Hospital.

- *Professor Ntobeko Ntusi* – President and CEO of the South African Medical Research Council.
- *Professor Elizabeth Mayne* – South Africa's first specialist immunopathologist and a pioneer in cancer immunotherapy.

The point I am trying to make is relative to South Africa's total health budget of just under R300 billion (over £13 billion), our contribution has been small – yet its impact has been wildly disproportionate.

The truth is, you cannot meaningfully change a healthcare system by focusing only on the 'head' of the Pareto distribution – for example, increasing the number of nurses or expanding primary care – unless you are prepared to spend vast sums of money. Instead, systems are changed by achieving leverage in the Pareto tail.

Applying this understanding – and the power of the Fourth Principle – to corporate philanthropy can lead to dramatic, outsized and disproportionate impacts in the causes businesses care about.

Strategic Planning – Think Your Way into the Pareto Tail

Strategic planning involves several key components that, together, form a roadmap for an organization to achieve its goals. These include defining their purpose or vision, developing strategies to realize it, and establishing mechanisms for evaluation and control – such as assessing preparedness for multiple possible futures.

Crucially, each of these elements requires careful analysis of the Pareto tail.

Scenario planning is a key tool within the broader strategic planning process, used to analyse potential future events or conditions to enhance organizational resilience.

When evaluating plans for multiple possible futures, should we rely on the mathematical probability of outcomes, or on our imaginative sense of what is possible? In other words, how should we frame choice? And can the Pareto principle help determine the best approach?

The probability-based approach is the conventional method of scenario planning. As the name suggests, it assigns likelihoods to a defined set of outcomes and then ranks decisions from most to least favourable. It is the standard approach taught in many MBA programmes.

It rests, however, on two problematic assumptions: first, that the range of possible outcomes (often labelled 'worst case', 'budgeted case' and 'best case') can be reliably identified using available data and trend analysis; and second, that we can assign accurate probabilities to each scenario.

The approach has profound weaknesses in that we obviously cannot identify all scenarios, and we cannot then assign probabilities to them – which statistically should add up to one for completeness. At best, we end up with broad and blunt scenarios to consider and plan around.

An interesting counter-theory comes from George Shackle, one of the early pioneers of behavioural economics, who rejected probability-based models and said they were inadequate for decision-making under conditions of uncertainty. He argued that focusing on possibilities – rather than probabilities – offers a more useful framework.

Shackle – who completed his PhD at the London School of Economics under the supervision of Nobel laureate Friedrich Hayek and later served in Winston Churchill's war cabinet during the Second World War – developed what he called potential surprise theory. It challenged the idea that we can assign objective probabilities to future events. Instead, he emphasized the role of imagination and surprise in decision-making.

There are striking parallels between Shackle's surprise theory and Pareto thinking in how they approach scenario planning. Both recognize the outsized influence of outlier events – the tail phenomena that defy conventional modelling yet profoundly shape outcomes.

Surprise theory is not widely known beyond niche academic and economic circles. I highlight it here because I believe it offers an interesting lens for strategic thinking – and one that helps us imagine our way into the tail in a Pareto world.

As the British Australian behavioural economist Peter E. Earl wrote in his 2018 paper: 'Shackle's key insight was that the concept of "potential surprise" could be used instead of statistical probability for understanding how individuals cope with choosing when they envisage a range of possible outcomes for their options. Instead of asking ourselves what the probability of an outcome is, we may ask ourselves how surprised we would be if it eventuated.'[15]

Shackle, he added, believed that we imagine a spectrum of outcomes that we rank based on how powerfully they capture our attention. 'The somewhat plausible loss that most causes fear, and the somewhat plausible gain that most excites hope are the main focal points for choice. With limited human attentive capacity, the other imagined outcomes for a scheme end up getting ignored.'

In other words, when creating a framework for making strategic decisions, Shackle thought it more productive to focus on the best- and worst-case scenarios we can plausibly imagine. He thought that real-world decision makers are often less concerned with small, probable gains or losses, and more focused on high-impact scenarios that could be surprisingly disruptive – positively or negatively. As an alternative to probability-based approaches, surprise theory reconciles creativity with analytical rigour – both of which are essential when planning for Pareto-type outcomes in a networked world.

Shell's strategic planning approach exemplifies surprise theory. As a major international oil and gas business, its scenario planning explores a range of possible futures by testing various assumptions and outcomes. Crucially, this process is not limited to probabilistic models; it also draws on expert insight and considers different versions of the future.[16] For example, imagining a cohesive and strong OPEC cartel enabled Shell to prepare for a scenario in which OPEC successfully coordinated oil production and influenced global prices. This foresight helped Shell respond effectively to the 1970s oil crisis, when an OPEC embargo led to severe petroleum shortages and sharply rising prices across the Western world.

Another real-world case is the 'Mont Fleur' scenario exercise in South Africa, undertaken in 1991–2.[17] This initiative convened twenty-two prominent and diverse leaders to envision the country's transition from apartheid to democracy. Named after the conference centre that hosted it outside Cape Town, the group developed four narrative scenarios to imagine South Africa's future into the next decade. Three warned of potential pitfalls:

- Ostrich, where the minority white government sticks its head in the sand and ignores calls for change.
- Lame Duck, where transition drags on, producing a weak government that pleases no one.
- Icarus, in which an unconstrained government comes to power on a wave of popular support and embarks on an unsustainable public spending programme, which crashes the economy.

Notably, there was one bright vision of a future in the tail to work towards – Flight of the Flamingos – in which the transition is successful because all the key building blocks are put in place, with everyone in the society rising gradually, together.

By embracing an imaginative approach, the process generated systemic insights into what might happen – and, alongside other critical factors, helped bring about the scenario in the tail: a decisive political settlement, followed by fiscal conservatism, and the creation of conditions that would provide the best chance for sustainable economic growth and steady social redistribution.

My takeaway from Shackle is this: whenever we imagine the future, we should begin from a place of unbounded possibility, not bounded probability. Potential surprise theory offers a valuable supplement to traditional scenario planning by encouraging us to search for a tail view of what the future might hold. We shouldn't simply rely on past statistics to define safe, and likely inaccurate, probabilities – but look rather to the future for plausible downsides if we fail, and plausible upsides – the surprises – if we succeed.

This opens the door to more intuitive thinking and keeps us agile and alert to emerging opportunities. Only after we have fully explored the realm of possible surprises do we begin to work backwards to identify constraints. That way, the constraints don't defeat us before we have even left the starting blocks.

In Risk Assessment – Anticipate Events in the Pareto Tail

Risk assessment is another essential component of strategic and scenario planning.

Businesses typically use a bell-shaped approach in their risk assessments. Traditionally, their approaches have focused on quantifiable, predictable risks – often downplaying extreme, highly unpredictable events because they were considered too rare or difficult to model.

But in a Pareto-shaped world, we should do the opposite:

prepare as thoroughly as possible for rare, high-impact risk events in the tail.

There are two key reasons for this. First, because their impact can be enormous. And second, because in our highly interconnected world, a shock in one area can have knock-on repercussions. This raises the spectre of contagion – where a negative event in one domain triggers a non-linear chain reaction, spreading like a virus across interconnected systems.

This process, when run linearly, is further complicated by the fact that when you stress-test individual variables and assume they are bell-shaped, you can mislead yourself into thinking you are robust – when, in fact, in an interconnected Pareto world, a single risk factor can create a cascading contagion. That means you must model for single risk factors becoming multiple risk factors in a recursive Pareto tail.

Usually, regulatory requirements do not provide a model for running a business, but the solvency requirements and methodologies in banking and insurance do offer excellent guidance for testing risk in the tail. As is standard, they require sophisticated mathematical and statistical models to predict and mitigate, among other things, contagion effects. They stress-test the business to calibrate the scale of disaster a system can withstand before it breaks.

As part of risk and solvency assessments, a regulatory requirement is to ask questions which assess preparedness for events in the Pareto tail: can a business withstand a 1-in-100-year tail-risk event? A 1-in-200-year event? What can be changed to make the business more resilient to those shocks? They also run reverse stress tests that start with a predefined adverse outcome – such as, what three things could break the business? – and then work backwards to identify the scenarios or circumstances that could lead to that outcome.

Sometimes, as a result of an unexpected external event, one part of the business suffers while another thrives, creating a natural buffer. In our experience, while Covid was a powerful tail event causing our life insurance claims to rise, our health and motor insurance claims fell because non-Covid-related healthcare services were dramatically reduced, and people largely stayed at home. It is critical to try to model what is offsetting and what is reinforcing, and how the features interrelate, so as not to be lulled into a false sense of comfort. Tail events can multiply the effect – channelling the recursive nature of Pareto – or they could offset one another.

These practices that are commonplace in banking and insurance may be instructive for other businesses – using Pareto thinking to consider what can break the business. The issue is that risk, by definition, is in the tail, and deep thought, modelling and rigour are required to try to understand this and prepare for it.

In some cases, the hardest risk to withstand isn't an external shock – it is reputational damage. For Oxfam, the sexual exploitation allegations relating to their aid workers' behaviour in Haiti after the 2010 earthquake nearly sank the organization, posing a material risk to their funding and viability. They lost 7,000 regular donors in the immediate aftermath of the scandal and suffered severe reputational damage and erosion of public trust, which had to be rebuilt over several years. For Silicon Valley Bank, it was a combination of over-exposure to failed tech start-ups and a liquidity crisis that caused depositors to lose confidence – triggering a run on the bank and leading to its collapse. Ultimately, every business should want to know: what sort of event would break us? How robust are we?

In this context, business leaders often worry about black swan events – unpredictable, rare occurrences that have extreme and transformative consequences. The concept was first popularized by mathematical statistician Nassim Nicholas Taleb in his 2007 book *The Black Swan: The Impact of the Highly Improbable.* The term 'black swan' comes from the once widespread belief that all swans were white – an assumption shattered by the discovery of black swans in seventeenth-century Australia.

Some examples of black swan events often cited include:

- The First World War, where the assassination of Archduke Franz Ferdinand triggered an unforeseen global conflict.
- The 1918 Spanish Flu, which killed 50 million people worldwide.
- The 1929 Wall Street Crash and the Great Depression, the scale of which was unexpected.
- The 9/11 terrorist attacks on the US in 2001.
- The 2008 global financial crisis.

Over time, 'black swan' has become shorthand for unexpected, far-reaching disaster.

Taleb's theory, like Pareto, can be used to argue that, when conducting risk assessments, we must prepare for unpredictable, high-impact events that can't be foreseen – rather than relying on probabilistic models that assume business as usual. Both theories powerfully expose the limitations of human forecasting when it is based on conventional risk management using bell-shaped distributions.

The way I tend to distinguish between black swan and Pareto is that a black swan event could be seen as an occurrence at the extreme end in the tail of the tail of a Pareto distribution – but not all events in the tail carry the weight of being a black swan. Also, black swan events tend, with some exceptions, to be negative shocks, whereas Pareto events in the tail can be either positive or negative.

Positive examples of black swan events include unexpected medical breakthroughs, such as the accidental discovery of penicillin by Alexander Fleming in 1928, and the chance discovery of X-rays by physicist Wilhelm Röntgen in 1895, both of which revolutionized medicine. The viral explosion of YouTube in 2005, initially built as a dating site and which transformed media and entertainment, is another.

By contrast, many technological shifts that feel sudden are not true black swans if they emerged from clear, observable trends; for example, the rise of social media platforms such as WhatsApp and TikTok was rapid and impactful, but not fundamentally unpredictable. The invention of the steam engine, similarly, was transformative, yet not a black swan event, because it developed gradually from a long line of scientific and engineering advances. In this sense, it is better seen as a classic case of long-tail innovation – the product of many small steps and incremental improvements culminating in a breakthrough.

There are also links between the black swan theory and surprise theory, in that both focus on plausible yet unpredictable events and the failure of probability-based forecasting. However, Shackle placed more emphasis than Taleb on the power of positive surprises – not just negative shocks.

There is a case to be made that while individual black swan events remain rare, the collective likelihood of impactful rare events affecting the world in any given year is significantly higher, and rising, due to the increased interconnectedness of global markets and systems. As mentioned earlier, a trade disruption in one region (such as the Suez Canal blockage), or a climate disaster in another (such as drought or flooding in a key food-producing region of Africa), can have ripple effects far beyond their point of origin. Likewise, the chance of an epidemic escalating into a global pandemic is far greater in today's hyperconnected world of jumbo jets than it was in the early twentieth-century era of biplanes – especially when positive feedback loops amplify and accelerate cascading impacts.

So, while the nature of any individual shock event remains rare, the collective frequency of globally impactful surprises is increasing. From a risk management perspective, the Pareto distribution gives us a way to model the idea that rare, high-impact events are an inherent feature of complex systems. In the context of an insurance business and beyond, Pareto modelling provides a visual and mathematical framework to assess and price the risk of such events, and to build greater resilience into the system.

From an individual's perspective, it is a curious paradox that we tend to be neurotic about low-probability events that we perceive to be high-risk and in the tail – like dying in a plane crash (as rare as 1 in 13.7 million passengers globally) – while remaining largely indifferent to the statistically far more dangerous aspects of daily life, such as slipping in the shower or having an accident while driving.

This reminds me of an opinion piece I read, the author of which was turning 80.[18] In considering how to maximize his health and life expectancy, his research showed that a major cause of death was slipping in the bath in advanced age. His remedy was to be extra cautious when stepping in and out of the bath, and he calculated that this would reduce the chance of a fall to one in a thousand baths. He soon, however, realized the cognitive error here – because he bathed every day – and therefore 365 times a year. The effect of this is that within three years, he will have had over 1,000 baths, meaning that he would be expected to face a fatal fall within just three years.

This reveals a behavioural inconsistency: in our personal lives, we overreact to rare, dramatic risks and under-react to mundane, cumulative ones. Yet in business, we often do the reverse – we focus on the average case, ignoring extreme tail risks, despite being systemically exposed to uncertainty.

In this context, Pareto thinking offers a useful corrective. It helps sharpen decision-making and improves how we model and prepare for complexity, volatility and the truly consequential.

In Innovation – Achieve Disruption in the Pareto Tail

If contagion is the danger that can bring you down with exponential impact, then innovation is the rocket fuel that can propel you forward with the same multiplicative Pareto-like effect.

Research consistently demonstrates a strong correlation between innovation and superior business performance. Research by management consultants Bain & Company shows that companies in the top quartile of innovation performance exhibit significantly faster growth compared to their peers, with average annual growth rates of 13 per cent versus 5 per cent. Over five years, this ratchets up, with top performers growing 84 per cent compared to 28 per cent for lower performers, a difference of more than 50 percentage points.[19]

While we get this intuitively, many business leaders tend to focus on incremental improvements in the head of the Pareto distribution – flexing existing parameters and building on what already works – instead of on true breakthrough innovation in the Pareto tail. This approach is not surprising – it is less risky and less costly to implement, but it also leads to suboptimal results – for example, too many products which don't get traction.

Innovation in the Pareto tail (as shown in the graph below), however, is truly disruptive and transformative, and leads to products or business models with disproportionate impact.

Shackle's potential surprise theory, with its emphasis on what might be, encourages us to think more creatively about opportunities that could deliver disproportionate impact – sometimes delivering what customers didn't even know they needed.

Pareto and Innovation

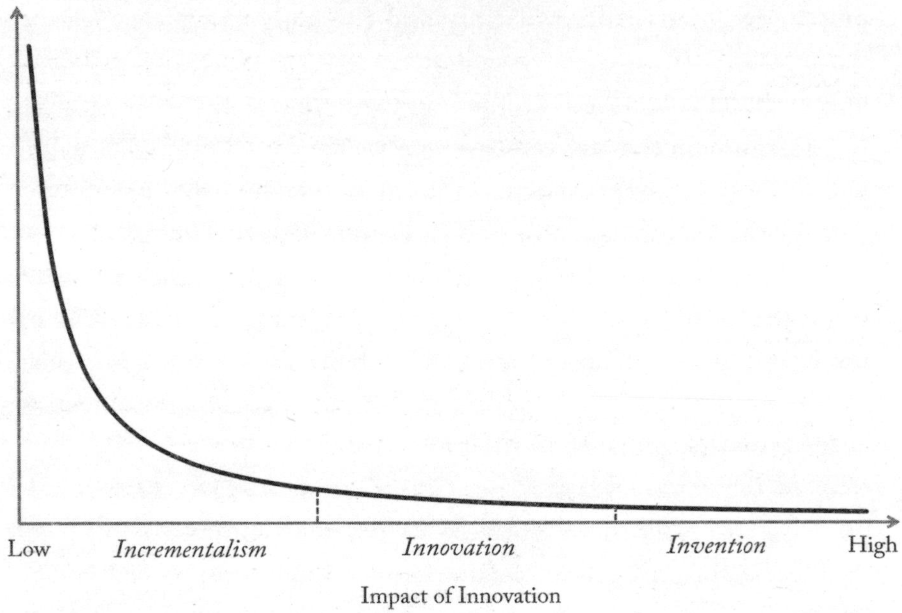

The question is how to deliver Pareto-style innovation. It is an elusive problem, but in our experience, the most important step is to be led by purpose and start with the end in mind, as we did with the 'make gyms free' or the 'get your Apple Watch for free' approaches. Starting with purpose, vision and the end in mind differs dramatically in approach and effect from incrementalism, which starts with what has been developed and works bottom up to improve it. The results of this bottom-up approach are often mundane and outdated by the time they are launched.

BYD (Build Your Dreams), a prominent Chinese electric vehicle manufacturer, is doing this in the hopes of revolutionizing the EV charging experience and hence the entire EV market. They have a clear end in mind, with the ambition of '5 minutes, 500 kilometres' – aiming to develop technology that allows for a 5-minute charge to provide a 500 km range. If they achieve this ambitious goal, they will likely redefine competition in their industry.

When intended R&D is rooted in purpose (say 'to make people healthier') and when it starts with the end in mind (say 'to make gyms free'), it is more likely to be in the tail, a benefit of which is its expansive nature – the very opposite of competing in a constrained way on price or gradual improvement. One door opens and leads to another. It is the recursive nature of Pareto – where a small shift in one part of a system can produce further dramatic, unpredictable changes.

In our case, what began with a simple end in mind – of making the gyms free – developed into a multidimensional Shared-Value business model. The recursive nature of Pareto keeps it developing and evolving, given the scale of our data – 60 million life years of longitudinal, clinical, wellness and behavioural data (the largest data set of its kind globally), and the emerging power of AI. At the time of writing, we launched a partnership with Google, VitalityAI, that uses our data and emerging AI to hyper-personalize next best health actions based on an individual's specific risk factors, provide accurate context and guides for why these actions are necessary, communicate using LLMs in ways that a specific member would respond to, and – crucially – offer retail or financial incentives and rewards that our data shows the specific member would value.

This journey from the bath to VitalityAI illustrates the power of innovation in the tail. It points out an important principle that applies to innovation – it is not finite: we don't run out of ideas, quite the opposite, innovation in the tail is recursive with one idea leading to another, and so on. The end in mind keeps developing as you reach the previous end in mind, so to speak.

Research by management consultants McKinsey & Company

finds that a relatively small number of firms making bold strategic moves generate the majority of productivity growth – and in powerful sporadic bursts rather than a smooth trickle of gradual change.[20] Their 2025 report, 'The Power of One: How Standout Firms Grow National Productivity', revealed that fewer than a hundred firms in their sample of 8,300 accounted for two-thirds of the productivity gains in the three country samples they analysed – Germany, the UK and the US. This, they said, was a more concentrated, dynamic and sporadic pattern than existing literature tends to highlight, with progress on productivity being defined by a few firms moving a mile rather than many firms moving an inch.

When firms become more productive, they concluded, so do economies. At the extreme – or in the long tail – a single firm can move the productivity needle for entire economies. Consider the remarkable story of Novo Nordisk.

How the Innovation of a Single Company Changed an Entire Country

The impact of innovating in the tail is powerfully illustrated by the extraordinary rise of Danish pharmaceutical business Novo Nordisk – a business that, until late 2024, few outside of diabetes care had even heard of, but which has since become one of the largest companies in the world by market capitalization.

How did they do it? Through relentless investment in research and development. But their success wasn't just about product innovation – it came from thinking laterally and applying that innovation to new, unexpected markets.

Founded in 1923, Novo Nordisk began as a niche business focused on diabetes care. The business invested heavily in R&D and, in 1982, entered the emerging market for recombinant human insulin, following a breakthrough by scientists at a biotechnology business called Genentech. The result was Novolet, a pre-filled insulin delivery pen that replaced animal-derived insulin and traditional syringes – transforming the safety, ease of use and effectiveness of diabetes treatment.

They soon became a global leader in diabetes care, with a reputation for being outstanding within their field. For decades, their leadership team stayed focused on this specialized market.

Then came the pivot that catapulted Novo Nordisk onto the global stage.

They realized that the drugs they had developed to treat diabetes could also address a far larger and rapidly growing issue: obesity. Compared to the diabetes market, the obesity market was expanding at a much faster rate, driven by rising awareness of the associated health risks.

In 2017, Novo Nordisk launched Ozempic, primarily for diabetes. But a side effect of Ozempic was weight loss, making it appealing for patients dealing with both diabetes and obesity. Then in 2021, they launched Wegovy – this time directly targeting the obesity market. Unlike Ozempic, which was originally approved only for diabetes, Wegovy was approved for weight management in people with obesity or those overweight with weight-related conditions.

These two drugs turned out, as we now know, to be game-changers. Delivered via weekly injections, both contain semaglutide, a compound that mimics the body's natural GLP-1 hormone released during eating. It helps regulate insulin, blood sugar and appetite. Both drugs would achieve booming sales and massive commercial success. As David Wallace-Wells wrote in *The New York Times* at the end of 2024: 'They called 2023 the "year of Ozempic", but now it seems GLP-1 drugs might define an entire decade – or an even longer era.'[21]

The potential is staggering. Around 40 per cent of American adults – over 100 million people – are classified as obese, compared with 38 million with diabetes. Globally, more than a billion people are affected by obesity.

Furthermore, the drugs are now widely claimed to offer significant benefits beyond diabetes and weight management. Evidence is emerging that GLP-1 receptor agonists like semaglutide may have therapeutic potential beyond diabetes and weight loss, including benefits for heart, kidney and liver disease, as well as neurological conditions like Alzheimer's, dementia and Parkinson's disease. Early clinical trials also suggest they can reduce alcohol consumption, significantly, lowering cravings in people with alcohol use disorder.[22]

Wegovy is now available in the UK on the NHS for adults meeting specific criteria: a Body Mass Index of 35 or more and at least one obesity-related condition, such as cardiovascular disease or hypertension. Privately, it remains costly – ranging from £139 to £269 for a month's supply, depending on the dose. In the UK, our business, Vitality, became the first health insurer to offer up to 20 per cent discounts on Wegovy and other GLP-1 drugs.[23] Competitors will likely follow, enabling Wegovy's use even more.

What caused Novo Nordisk to pivot? Was it careful planning or a lucky break? It appears it was both. The 'lucky' break came during clinical trials when it was discovered that semaglutide significantly suppressed appetite and promoted weight loss. The hard work lay in decades of scientific investment in biotechnology and rigorous trials. The genius was in how they responded to their own accidental breakthrough – quickly recognizing the opportunity and moving with agility.

Not all companies did. Pfizer, for example, identified GLP-1's potential for tackling obesity thirty-five years ago, but shelved the research, citing uncertainty about the drug's future and market potential. As former Harvard Medical School dean Jeffrey Flier noted in a 2024 paper, the first commercial effort to progress this class of drug was abandoned by Pfizer, despite remarkable early advances, back in 1990.[24]

In contrast, Novo Nordisk's success has been remarkable.

Alongside Eli Lilly, they now dominate a weight loss drug market that ballooned seven-fold in three years – to $24 billion in 2023 and is projected to exceed $100 billion by 2030.

Their success has not just been a boon for its shareholders – it has reshaped the entire Danish economy. In 2022, two-thirds of Denmark's economic growth could be attributed to a single industry – pharmaceuticals – according to the country's national statistics agency. By early 2023, the impact was even more dramatic, with 90 per cent of Denmark's 1.9 per cent GDP growth coming from Novo Nordisk alone.[25] Without the business's contribution, the country's economy would have flatlined.

Its two blockbuster drugs accounted for the lion's share of Denmark's 13.4 per cent export growth that year. Meanwhile, surging tax payments from Novo Nordisk – totalling more than $3 billion – helped fund national priorities, including green initiatives and defence. Even after the share price dropped in 2025, Novo Nordisk's value ranged from 45 per cent to 85 per cent of Denmark's entire GDP, estimated at between $404 billion and $460 billion.

What is interesting is that at the time of writing, Novo Nordisk is under considerable pressure because its innovation was so powerful that it cannot meet the demand created, enabling competitive and other market forces to fill the gap and undermine its success.

The influence of a single business on a country of six million people is not something that fits within a neat, bell curve distribution. This is a Pareto story – an innovation in the tail that created disproportionate national impact. A classic case of the tail wagging the dog.

Managing Talent – In the Tail

Every business leader knows the importance of attracting and developing the best people. I keep relearning the power of people, and as I have said, our business has been built on their talent.

Time and again, I have seen individuals achieve things they never imagined. That is one of the core reasons I am writing this book: it stems from a deep conviction about human potential.

I have also seen first-hand the transformative impact of good leadership. No matter how strong a product idea or business plan may be, weak leadership can sink it. Conversely, great leadership can elevate it – and build something extraordinary.

One of the key tasks of leadership is to establish a clear framework for identifying and nurturing top talent. Many traditional performance rating systems – across both the private and public sectors – evaluate staff using the statistical model of the bell curve. This model assumes that most employees fall within the average range, with a small number of very high and very low performers.

As I mentioned in the First Principle, Jack Welch, former CEO of General Electric, popularized a performance model sometimes called 'rank and yank' – or the '20–70–10' model, which is really a forced distribution that resembles a bell curve. At GE, he implemented it by ranking employees according to performance: the top 20 per cent were seen as the most productive, the middle 70 per cent as adequate, and the bottom 10 per cent as underperforming – often leading to dismissal. This approach, while seemingly radical, reflects a classic traditional bell curve mindset.

One reason the bell curve still endures is its simplicity: it allows HR departments to calculate a straightforward arithmetic 'average' and design compensation schemes accordingly – rewarding those who are above average and penalizing those below.

But in a networked, Pareto-like system, the average becomes a meaningless concept. In a Pareto distribution, a small number of hyper-performers drastically distort the curve, and most individuals fall below the mean.

A landmark 2011 study by American organizational psychologists Ernest O'Boyle Jr and Herman Aguinis analysed the performance of more than 630,000 individuals across fields including business, sports, entertainment and science. Their conclusion: individual performance follows a Pareto-style power-law distribution far more closely than a bell curve.[26]

This research prompted some companies – such as Microsoft – to fundamentally rethink how they attract and retain talent. It led to a renewed focus on identifying and hiring top performers – and paying them top rates to keep them. In doing so, they moved away from traditional pay bands and adopted more flexible compensation models. Bill Gates once remarked that a handful of individuals at Microsoft 'made' the company, and that without them, 'there would be no Microsoft'.[27] Other companies that have adjusted their HR strategies in light of these findings include Google, Netflix, Apple, Salesforce, Amazon and Meta.

In an increasingly networked world, the issue of talent in the tail is more and more crucial because networks massively amplify the impact of rare, unconventional talent, making it essential to identify exceptional individuals who are often missed by traditional measures of ability.[28]

The question every business leader must ask is: how do we identify, attract and develop the best possible talent pool? What they should also ask is: what does Pareto teach us about doing it effectively?

Intuitively, we know that a few people in a large organization can make a disproportionately large difference. Any seasoned leader can cite anecdotes of their own. I once heard the CEO of a multinational company, when asked how many people worked for his organization, quip, 'about half'.

But the reality of the exceptional power of a small number of people may lead to the simple conclusion that we should only focus on talent in the tail in both the recruiting process and in terms of talent development – just hire a few brilliant people and assume the rest will follow. Yet this is incorrect because it undermines the reality that every single person in an organization contributes to its performance and the formation of the tail. A business is a complex, interconnected system of talent. This has profound implications for how human resource leaders should think about hiring, empowering, evaluating and compensating staff.

Let me explain. When an organization hires, it is building its own network from the ground up. The dynamics of that network will naturally produce a tail of top performers. But the quality of the tail depends on the quality of the whole. The implication is clear: the better every individual is, the better the tail will be.

In other words, being deliberate, precise and meticulous about every hire ensures that the resulting tail – out of which the superstars will emerge – is stronger than it would have been otherwise. The talent that falls in the head of your distribution is the talent in the tail of your competitors. Crucially and consequentially, your tail of talent is more skewed than theirs. Every person matters – not just because they might be in the tail, but because they are part of the system that forms it.

The correct conclusion from the fact that Pareto applies to talent is both simple and powerful: great organizations are obsessive about hiring – because every single individual who joins helps shape the tail.

The Vexing Problem of Remuneration

Pareto has important implications for how organizations remunerate people. This is a complicated and sensitive area, as pay has become a central concern of corporate governance. Most governance frameworks are designed to ensure that remuneration sits within accepted norms – and those norms are implicitly bell-shaped. Outliers raise red flags precisely because they sit outside the ordinary. Yet in a Pareto world, the people who create disproportionate value are, by definition, outliers.

In public companies, executive remuneration is subject to intense governance scrutiny, regulatory oversight and shifting public expectations. In many countries, shareholders vote on executive pay, with real consequences if those votes fail. This creates conservatism, rigour and caution from boards – much of which is necessary. The complexity here cannot be overstated – boards must ensure that key executives are paid appropriately and pay-for-performance is properly and equitably applied, so that shareholders' interests are protected. At the same time, organizations must attract and retain top talent, often competing across jurisdictions or with private firms not subject to the same constraints. Getting remuneration right is therefore critical.

Difficulties arise because boards rely heavily on formal external benchmarking to determine 'appropriate' pay. These benchmarks are built on the assumption that performance – and therefore remuneration – is bell-shaped. But executive performance is not normally distributed; it follows a Pareto distribution with a long tail. Applying bell curve benchmarks to Pareto outcomes leads to predictable distortions.

These forces are accelerating. The growing power of global proxy voting agencies such as Institutional Shareholder Services, known as the ISS, and Glass Lewis, which issue guidance on the AGM resolutions of listed companies all over the world, also leads to the enforcement of a set of principles and norms for remuneration that discourages practices outside the norm. This guidance is often a tick-box exercise, without application of mind to the specific context and motivations for different approaches by specific companies.

It is important, I want to stress, that careful governance is needed, but the unintended effects of this governance come in two forms.

Problem 1: Paying too little for the tail

First, exceptional performance is under-rewarded. If a small number of individuals contribute disproportionately to organizational success, their remuneration should reflect that. Bell-shaped benchmarks compress differences at the top, failing to allow sufficient flexibility for tail performance. The gap between the mean and 90th percentile in a normal distribution vastly understates the difference in value creation that a Pareto distribution implies, as depicted in the graph below.

Pareto Impact versus Normal Remuneration

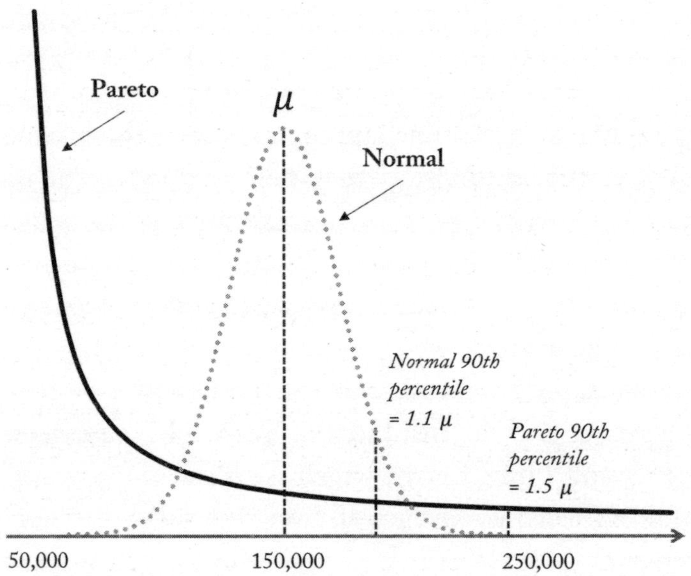

Pareto thinking demands less equality and more differentiation. When tail performers are paid as if they are merely 'above average', organizations risk losing their most valuable people.

Problem 2: Paying too much for the middle

Second, boards almost universally believe their executives are above average and therefore target pay above the median – often the 70th percentile. While that belief may be reasonable for any single firm, it cannot be true for all firms simultaneously.

When many companies target above-median pay, a ratchet effect emerges. Each round of benchmarking pushes remuneration higher, regardless of whether productivity or value creation has increased. This leads to systemic inflation in executive pay – particularly for average performers.

The problem is real and well documented. A 2023 study by the Economic Policy Institute found that CEO pay in the US rose by 1,085 per cent between 1978 and 2023 – compared to just 24 per cent for typical workers.[29] In 2023, American CEOs earned 290 times the pay of the average employee, up from just 21 times in 1965.

The consequences of ignoring the Pareto tail in remuneration therefore lead to two distorting outcomes, both of which hobble a company's competitive position: paying exceptional performers too little, which risks losing them, and paying average performers too much, which inflates costs and creates poor incentives.

Fixing this begins with introducing Pareto thinking into debates on remuneration. Elon Musk's proposal of extremely skewed, performance-linked rewards may, at the time of writing, go too far, but it makes the underlying point well: value creation is not evenly distributed, and pay structures should reflect that reality.

Fixing Unemployment – Support Start-Ups in the Pareto Tail to Create Jobs at Scale

Unemployment is a cause of suffering in many countries. In South Africa, close to 8 million people are unemployed and a further 3.7 million are willing and able to work but have stopped searching due to a lack of opportunities – bringing the expanded unemployment rate to over 40 per cent, one of the highest in the world.

In every country, this is a tragedy: for the individuals affected, for the families who depend on them, and for the country. So much hardship. So much wasted potential.

The structural impacts of unemployment are far-reaching: economically, it reduces output and slows growth; socially, it deepens poverty, inequality, crime and social exclusion; and personally, it leads to mental health struggles, family stress and a loss of identity.

Reducing unemployment is an incredibly complex multidimensional challenge.

Keynesian approaches focus on boosting demand in the economy, typically through major infrastructure projects, social programmes and large-scale hiring of public sector workers – funded through substantial government spending. In contrast, classical or neoclassical approaches – rooted in the thinking of Adam Smith and Milton Friedman – emphasize minimal state intervention. They advocate for supply-side measures such as fostering business-friendly environments: promoting labour flexibility, improving education, offering tax incentives, reducing red tape and lowering barriers to entry.

A widely held belief is that big business creates jobs. This often leads governments to apply pressure – through incentives or regulations – on big business to help generate employment, or to centre policy reforms on large enterprises. Policymakers often relegate entrepreneurs to the 'nice-to-have category', viewing their effect on employment as marginal.

But this belief is an error of logic – large businesses do not create jobs. In fact, they usually work hard to destroy them. There is typically no malice in this; it is simply a structural reality.

For large companies – particularly those listed on public capital markets – shareholders typically expect profits to grow faster than the Consumer Price Index (CPI) before executives become eligible for bonus payments. Research shows that standard shareholder expectations for growth are between CPI plus 5 to 10 per cent. But at the same time, economic growth in advanced economies has ranged between CPI and CPI plus 2.5 per cent over the past five-, ten- and twenty-year periods. So, to meet shareholder expectations, large businesses must grow their profits at rates significantly above the rate of growth of the economies in which they operate.

The question is: how? Consider that profit is, very simply, revenue minus expenses. A business can increase its profits by raising revenue, cutting expenses, or both.

Logically, large businesses cannot sustainably grow their revenue – their top line – at rates significantly above the rate of growth of the country's economy in which they operate, because collectively they make up a substantial share of a country's economy – in a sense, together with government, they are most of the economy. In the US, for example, large businesses – those with 500 or more employees – account for close to 50 per cent of private sector employment. The rate of growth of their collective revenue cannot be much higher than the national economic growth.

The central way big business can outperform national economic growth and meet shareholder expectations is by focusing on efficiencies and reducing expenses – which typically involves cutting jobs or capping job growth.

The reality, therefore, is that big business, structurally, does not drive job creation. The broader data bears this out: both big business and government tend to grow employment slowly – typically by just a few percentage points per year. For example, according to the Office for National Statistics, UK public sector employment grew by 0.6 per cent in the year to March 2025.[30] Total workforce jobs increased by only 0.8 per cent, highlighting the sluggish pace of employment growth across established institutions.[31]

So, what must be done if governments want to create jobs at scale?

This is where the Pareto tail can offer a solution.

It turns out that in many economies, job creation comes primarily from small businesses – not the thousands of small 'mom and pop' stores, but rather start-ups and small businesses that start small and scale significantly.

The data tells us that approximately 70–80 per cent of start-ups fail within their first ten years – and that of the small number of companies that do succeed, few scale dramatically. As a result, job creation depends disproportionately on the success of a modest number of start-ups in the tail of the tail of the Pareto distribution.

For example, Endeavor, an organization supporting a global community of high-impact entrepreneurs, has data showing that these entrepreneurs have a 20-times job creation multiplier within their ecosystems.[32]

The impact can be extraordinary – as our journey at Discovery illustrates.

When Discovery began in 1992, we had just one employee. Over the past thirty-four years, we have grown to employ more than 15,000 people directly and sustained a further 25,000 jobs indirectly through our global partner networks that have licensed our Vitality model. That is 40,000 jobs in total – representing an average annual growth rate of 37 per cent, far outstripping the typical 2–5 per cent growth rates targeted by large businesses.

But that's not the whole story. There is significant research on the second- and third-order effects of creating a single job. These refer to the indirect consequences that ripple out from the initial action. If the first-order effects are the people directly employed and indirectly employed in our partner and agent networks, the second-order effects refer to the ripple effects of jobs created in service suppliers in the supply chain (such as transport, office supplies, real estate) with third-order effects being jobs created from the increased spending of workers in the first- and second-order jobs. Second-order effects typically come from business-to-business spending; third order from household spending.

Studies quantifying these multipliers suggest a range: 1.6 for manufacturing jobs to 5.9 for high-tech jobs.[33] Applying, then, an average multiplier of 3.75 to our 40,000 jobs, it means Discovery has created – directly and indirectly – around 150,000 jobs in just over thirty years.

If one business can create 150,000 jobs in thirty years, then simple maths would mean 6.66 start-ups like Discovery would create one million jobs. To do it over ten years would require three times that number – twenty super high-impact entrepreneurs.

South Africa has a working-age population of approximately 40 million. This means that just twenty super-entrepreneurs out of 40 million people could create one million jobs. That's just one person in two million – a powerful example of the Pareto tail in action.

So how does one create the right conditions for this to happen?

Crucially, it requires national leadership with the vision and will to place entrepreneurship at the centre of economic policy. A clear signal from government that it supports and values entrepreneurial endeavour can shape the direction of the economy.

There are numerous practical government strategies to foster entrepreneurship, but here are just a few that I believe could make a material impact:

- Providing government-backed first-loss guarantees to private sector debt funds for entrepreneurs who struggle to access capital.

- Offering tax incentives for investors in scale-ups and introducing targeted start-up tax breaks.

- Creating a supportive regulatory environment – removing unnecessary regulations and reducing red tape.

- Embedding entrepreneurial thinking into schools and universities to nurture the next generation of innovators.

The goal should be to create an ecosystem in which entrepreneurship is valued and can thrive.

Some developing countries are already leading the way. In South America, Start-up Chile was launched in 2010 by the Chilean Economic Development Agency, offering funding (without requiring entrepreneurs to give up equity), visas, co-working space and mentorship to attract global entrepreneurs. The aim was to position Chile as a global innovation hub by attracting entrepreneurs, both locally and internationally. In 2016, the Indian government launched Start-up India to promote entrepreneurship nationally – offering tax exemptions, mentorship, regulatory relief and funding.

These programmes have been very successful. Start-up Chile has supported over 3,000 start-ups from eighty-five countries. Collectively, these ventures – with a notably high survival rate – have raised more than $1 billion in capital and contributed significantly to job creation and economic growth. The programme is regarded as one of the most successful government-led start-up accelerators globally and has inspired similar initiatives in Brazil, Mexico and Peru.

Start-up India operates at a much larger scale. Within its first nine years, nearly 159,000 start-ups were officially recognized, with more than 1.66 million direct jobs created. Today India ranks as the third largest start-up ecosystem in the world, behind only the US and China.

Among those 159,000 start-ups in India and 2,200 in Chile, a few will likely succeed at scale. And when they do, the employment impact could be Pareto-like – with a handful creating a massive number of jobs.

In these countries, and others, like Singapore, which strongly promotes entrepreneurship through low taxes, streamlined regulations, start-up grants and tax exemptions, entrepreneurs are not a 'nice-to-have' – they are essential. By creating fertile ground for entrepreneurship, these governments are creating the environment for a long Pareto tail to form, while also increasing the chances that ventures in the Pareto tail will break through and scale disproportionally.

As I described in the First Principle, it is attitude that shifts fundamentals – not the other way around.

Indeed, the policies and mindset that governments adopt toward entrepreneurship go a long way to addressing unemployment.

Pareto thinking reminds us that even a few super high-impact entrepreneurs in the tail of the tail can deliver a transformative boost to employment.

Postscript – A Dog Called Stanley

'Mark my words, that dog will be a failure.'

That is what I told Neville Koopowitz, then head of our UK business, when he shared his vision regarding a new advertising concept that involved a talking dog called Stanley. The idea had come from VCCP, our ad agency in the UK, to advertise the Vitality brand, but I was having none of it.

It was 2015 and we had just acquired Prudential's 50 per cent stake in our UK Vitality business the year before, thereby gaining full ownership of our UK operations. We had complete confidence in our products and believed in the business model – but our biggest worry was the loss of the Prudential brand, one of the oldest and strongest in the market. Could we manage without it? Our UK team had been tasked with building the Vitality brand from the ground up. Our survival in the UK would depend on it.

Now I was being told that our entire brand-building strategy was to rest on the back of a miniature black dachshund with a dry, ironic sense of humour that liked to take the mickey and was a reluctant participant in anything remotely involving exercise. Stanley, I was told, was apparently meant to be channelling the sharp wit of Ian Hislop, a staple of the popular BBC panel show *Have I Got News for You* and long-time editor of satirical magazine *Private Eye*. But to me, like the sausage dog itself, the concept barely had legs, and I told Neville this in no uncertain terms.

'It is a bad idea, it won't work, don't do it,' I said.

Neville disagreed and pushed back. He believed it was fresh, funny and memorable. He thought the wry humour would resonate with the British public, especially as we were trying to promote fitness, and we didn't want to come across as too worthy or finger-wagging.

At the time, our market share in the UK health and life insurance markets was under 5 per cent, and our brand recognition hovered just above zero. You could mention Vitality to the average Londoner, and they would have no idea what we did. So, choosing the advertising campaign that was going to project us onto the consciousness of the great British public was a big deal and would involve a substantial investment.

We just needed the right advertising concept.

VCCP had also presented an attractive alternative campaign – a pink thread moving through a black-and-white world, touching people and bringing them to life. It was elegant, it was on-message, and it visually captured how life expectancy could be improved through healthy behaviours. I liked it. I preferred it. I wanted it.

My leadership style is to try to build a consensus because that takes people along with you. I am sometimes criticized for being a slow decision maker, but that is because I like an argument to be won on its merits and then for us all to agree. I don't believe in pulling rank because I am the boss. So, we debated it. And Neville won. Thus began our journey with Stanley.

Ten years later, prompted brand awareness of Vitality in the UK has risen to 64 per cent, surpassing the average of our competitors for the first time. We have gone from near invisibility to being more recognizable than many market leaders, despite our smaller size and the fact that some of those competitors have been operating for over a century. That's huge inroads in a very short time. In private medical insurance, we are now the third largest provider, just ahead of Aviva, with the major players being Bupa and AXA Health. While we remain smaller, we are growing rapidly – and our brand recognition is through the roof for a business of our size.

All thanks to Stanley.

Every dog has its day – and I am told that, following our campaign, this short-legged hound became the 'hot' dog of Britain. Official Kennel Club registrations of the diminutive dachshund rose by 40 per cent between 2015 and 2018.[34]

Our Vitality ambassadors also became part of the story. Their charming interactions with Stanley became a hallmark of the adverts. We had runners Dame Jessica Ennis-Hill and Lord Sebastian Coe, cricketers Heather Knight, Joe Root and Jos Buttler, swimmer Ellie Simmonds and rugby players Jonny Wilkinson and Maro Itoje – all regularly upstaged by Stanley, who would typically have the last word.

Looking back, that moment when the ad concept hung in the balance – when Neville came to me with Stanley and I said no, and he pushed back – was a true Pareto tail moment.

Key Takeaway: Work in the Pareto Tail

We see the world around us as being normally distributed, but in truth, the new normal is non-normal.

The fact that Pareto is so ubiquitous in every aspect of our modern, networked world means that we should learn to anticipate it, rather than be surprised when it shows up. The fact that Pareto is stubborn and resilient – that it can't easily be flattened or ignored – adds another layer to its stickiness and pervasiveness.

But it is the fact that Pareto is recursive that should give us real pause for thought. Because if there is a Pareto tail inside a Pareto tail inside a Pareto tail – then the tail becomes an extraordinarily powerful lever to intervene in a system and to create exponential change at speed.

The mathematics of Pareto suggest that even our most daunting challenges – whether personal, organizational or national – are not insurmountable. Positive outcomes are possible that are orders of magnitude bigger than we would expect.

In our increasingly networked world, the upside of the sometimes-overwhelming complexity and unpredictability we face is this: outliers – individuals, choices, actions and interventions of exceptional calibre – can set entirely new trajectories, and in rapid time.

It also reminds us that it is never too late to create the progress we want to see. That should give us a sense of inspiration, hope and boundless possibility.

But to leverage the power of the Pareto tail, we need to draw on the first three Principles as they get us into the tail.

Work in the tail – let the tail wag the dog – and you'll be on your way to doing something remarkable.

The multiplier effect of the Fourth Principle, Pareto, is approximately 24 times. This is because it is the culmination of the other three Principles and is the multiplication of the impact of each of the first three Principles. I argue it is multiplicative, because each Principle operates on a different axis – opportunity (Optimism), availability (Urgency) and drive (Goals) – and their effects compound rather than overlap. Doubling your effective time (Urgency) allows you to pursue twice as many opportunities, and if you do it with Optimism, you are six times more likely to find and leverage value from them, the total impact is 2 × 6 = 12. Then, if your motivation to act on those opportunities is also doubled (Goals), the final impact becomes 12 × 2 = 24.

Does this 24-times multiplier sound incredible? It is not because that is precisely the power of the long tail of Pareto, and acting in the tail has considerable power, putting us in a prime position to reap the benefits of rapid and transformational change, and impact.

Consider my epiphany in the bath – I got to that point applying the other three Principles, and the effect on my own life was certainly greater than the 24 times it would have been without that moment in time, and the decisions based on it.

The 24-times multiplier also explains why raw talent and ability are less important than consistently applying the Four Principles – a 24-times multiplier is a greater difference than the difference between people of exceptional versus mundane ability. It explains why we often witness brilliant people with unique abilities making very little impact in life, while people deemed ordinary often make huge impacts. The difference is the Four Principles. The difference is a multiple of 24.

CONCLUSION

It may seem ironic that a journey through insurance and banking could offer wisdom about making our lives more meaningful and impactful. It turns out that in order to reveal our almost limitless potential, we need to understand what drives impact and how these factors are optimized, as well as how our miscoding corrupts this optimization process, and how we might remedy it.

The optimization challenge is clear. If time were infinite, we could achieve almost anything we aimed for – at some point. If we knew exactly how to leverage the potential of networks of people and structures towards realizing identified opportunities, we wouldn't need much time to make an impact. And if we had infinite drive to reach our lofty ambitions, we would achieve them come what may. But we have none of these and so impact is an optimization problem across these three dimensions. Critically, Disciplined Optimism, Focused Urgency and Declared Goals are interlinked. Optimizing each of them has a multiplicative effect that leads to decisions and actions that are life-changing in terms of their impact.

Through the warp and weft of stories, supported by data and mathematical analysis, I have tried to show how the Four Principles are transformational and can unleash powerful dynamics and forces within our lives – leading to non-linear outcomes. These Principles transformed the trajectory of my own life and enabled us at Discovery to make an impact far beyond anything we could have imagined.

My fervent hope is that you will grasp the power of these Four Principles and apply them to your life, and make whatever you deem important and dream about, possible and achievable.

As I have said, the Four Principles are counter-intuitive. They challenge how we've been coded and taught to think, and how we view the world. They're not as easy to internalize as they might first appear and are more complex than you may think. They require effort, reflection and repetition to embed. But once you adopt them and embrace the non-linearity of the networked world we live in, I challenge you not to feel exhilarated by the possibility and momentum they unlock.

I wrote this book to give voice to something I sensed intuitively early in my career but could not yet articulate – insights that I've come to express more clearly through building Discovery, engaging with broader social challenges, and working with some remarkable people.

I have wanted to share these Four Principles with you, so that you can use them to make the kind of impact that matters most to you. If you apply the Four Principles and they make a difference in your life, I would love to hear from you. Please feel free to write to me at adriang@discovery.co.za.

So here they are again:

- *Disciplined Optimism* – because attitude drives fundamentals.

- *Focused Urgency* – because your time is more limited than you think.

- *Declared Goals* – because creating a line in the sand activates loss aversion, motivation and real action.

- *The Pareto Tail* – because a few key decisions determine our trajectory.

Just don't say no one told you when to run.
This book is your starting gun.

APPENDICES

The intention of these technical appendices is to illustrate the Four Principles in mathematical terms, to demonstrate how and why they work. While scientific, the appendices are not intended to be academic but draw on and connect a range of theories from statistics and behavioural economics.

The impact of our actions is a function of many things, among which opportunity, time and effort are important:

Impact = f (Opportunity, Time, Effort, Other Factors)

To increase impact, we can apply the first three Principles:

- Positivity reveals opportunities and magnifies their impact in a network.
- Our time is subjective and can effectively be expanded.
- Reframing goals scales their motivational power to drive our efforts.

Each appendix demonstrates mathematically a possible impact multiplier obtainable from the manifestation of the first three Principles:

- *Optimism:* seek out positive signals and opportunities, and build coalitions.
- *Time:* acquire health and knowledge, and foster a sense of urgency.
- *Goals:* capture the power of loss aversion to increase motivation.

These Principles can multiply and therefore build on top of one another. There is more time for an optimist to seek opportunities, to influence networks to scale them, and to use goals to magnify their effort throughout.

According to the Fourth Principle, our life decisions are distributed in such a way that just a few have enormous impact. So, the result of applying the first three Principles is not just incremental but constitutes operating far into the long tail of this distribution.

Appendix 1

A multiplier for the effect of optimism on impact can be factorized as follows:

Impactful pursuit and realization of opportunities = *Effect of optimism on opportunity seeking* × *Scaling effect of optimism through networks*

The following sections aim to quantify what a value may be for such a multiplier.

Appendix 1.1 – Prospect Theory and Loss Aversion

The S-curve of value captures the asymmetry of value with respect to losses and equivalent gains.

Prospect theory is a behavioural economic theory developed by Daniel Kahneman and Amos Tversky in 1979. Compared to classical, idealized economic theories (like expected utility theory) it describes how people make decisions involving risk and uncertainty, especially when the outcomes involve gains or losses. It entails three key concepts:

1. *Reference Dependence:* People evaluate outcomes relative to a reference point (as a change from the status quo), rather than in absolute terms.

2. *Loss Aversion:* Losses feel more painful than equivalent gains feel pleasurable. This is because of the 'endowment effect' whereby people attach more value to what they already possess.

3. *Diminishing Sensitivity:* The psychological impact of changes diminishes as you move further from the reference point.

These concepts can be represented by a value function which maps objective outcomes in terms of losses and gains, against what decision-making agents perceive as their value. They can be summarized graphically:

Kahneman & Tversky's Depiction of Loss Aversion

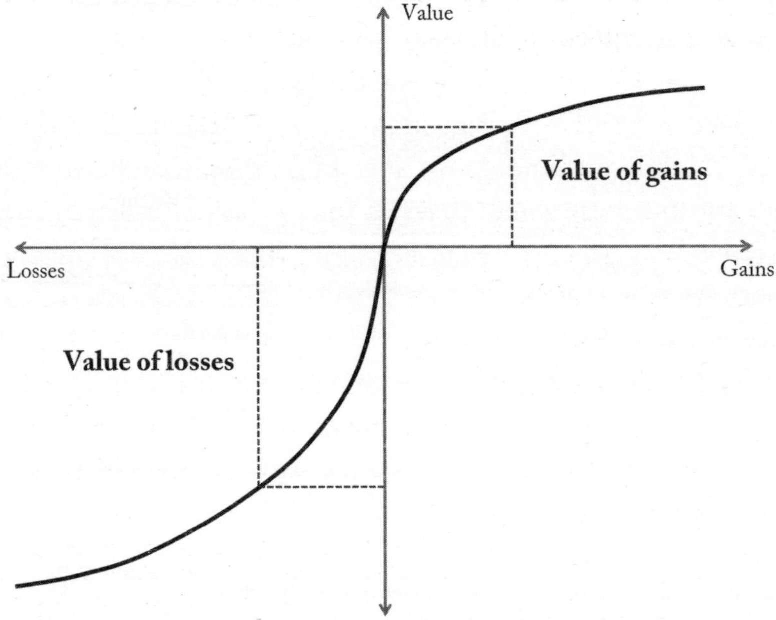

The graph of the value curve function illustrates the concepts of prospect theory as follows:

Observed decision-making phenomenon	Example	Loss value curve	Gain value curve
Reference dependence	If someone has $100, they will value an extra $10 not as a function of the state of having $110, but as the change of gaining $10	Represents amount of loss to the left of the origin	Represents amount of gain to the right of the origin
Loss aversion	A loss of $100 hurts more than a gain of $100	Steeper	Flatter
Diminishing sensitivity	The difference between $10 and $20 is felt more acutely than between $100 and $110	Convex	Concave

A function of this form, with parameters α, β and λ fits the features of the shape well, where x is the outcome, either a gain >0, or loss <0, and $v(x)$ represents an agent's value:

$$v(x) = \begin{cases} x^{\alpha} & \text{where } x \geq 0 \\ (-\lambda)(-x)^{\beta} & \text{where } x < 0 \end{cases}$$

Appendix 1.2 - Calculation of Loss Aversion

Losses tend to hurt twice as much as the utility derived from equivalent gains.

The degree of loss aversion implied for an agent with such a value function, is the ratio of the gradient of the loss curve to the gradient of the gain curve. The first derivative of the function with respect to x is given by:

	Loss value curve	Gain value curve
Derivative function	$v_{loss}'(x_{<0}) = \lambda\alpha(-x)^{\alpha-1}$	$v_{gain}'(x_{\geq 0}) = \alpha x^{\alpha-1}$

The slope of the loss curve divided by that of the gain curve is:

$$\frac{v_{loss}'(x_{<0})}{v_{gain}'(x_{\geq 0})} = \lambda\left(\frac{x_{<0}}{x_{\geq 0}}\right)^{\alpha-1}$$

$x_{<0}$ is a negative quantity, while $-x_{<0}$ is positive, therefore $\frac{x_{<0}}{x_{\geq 0}}$ equates to 1, and so the expression evaluates to λ. Thus, the agent's degree of loss aversion is determined by this parameter, and they will find losses hurt λ times more than equivalent gains feel good.

Kahneman and Tversky (1992) estimated a value for λ of 2.25, from empirical studies which asked surveyed populations to choose between different loss and gain scenarios.[1]

1 They also estimated α and β to both equal 0.88, parameters which respectively govern attitude to risk regarding gains (a concave curve, for risk aversion) and losses (a convex curve, for risk seeking).

A 2021 meta-study of 607 empirical results from 150 articles across economics, psychology and neuroscience, estimated the mean loss aversion coefficient to lie between 1.8 and 2.1 (Brown et al., 2024).

Appendix 1.3 – Negativity Bias

Negative attitudes are twice as prevalent and resistant to change as positive attitudes.

The principle of loss aversion, that losses loom larger than gains, can be generalized to domains other than the monetary. Deteriorations in relationship harmony, social approval, state of health and harm to self-esteem can all be felt as losses (assuming a consistent way of measuring these states). The hypotheses would be that hurtful actions can undo the effects of many kind acts, that one piece of criticism has a greater effect than several of praise, and the impact of stress and loneliness has a greater effect than the presence of the opposites. The evolutionary mechanisms would be the survival benefits of detecting threats to our health or maintaining our place in a supportive social community. In effect, we are conditioned to learn faster from punishment than from reward. This would be evidenced in greater salience, that is, we detect the negative more promptly than we take notice of the typical norm of the equivalent positive situation. It would also reflect in greater diagnosticity of the negative, that is, negativity is more informative in that it readily flags a threat, say of an anti-social act, by comparing it to the expectation of pro-social behaviour in general.

There is evidence in support of these hypotheses. An important meta-study by Baumeister (2001) consolidated many examples from various studies of the extent of negative biases, some of them with quantitative results. These are summarized in the graph below

Summary of Quantitative Results from Baumeister Meta-study

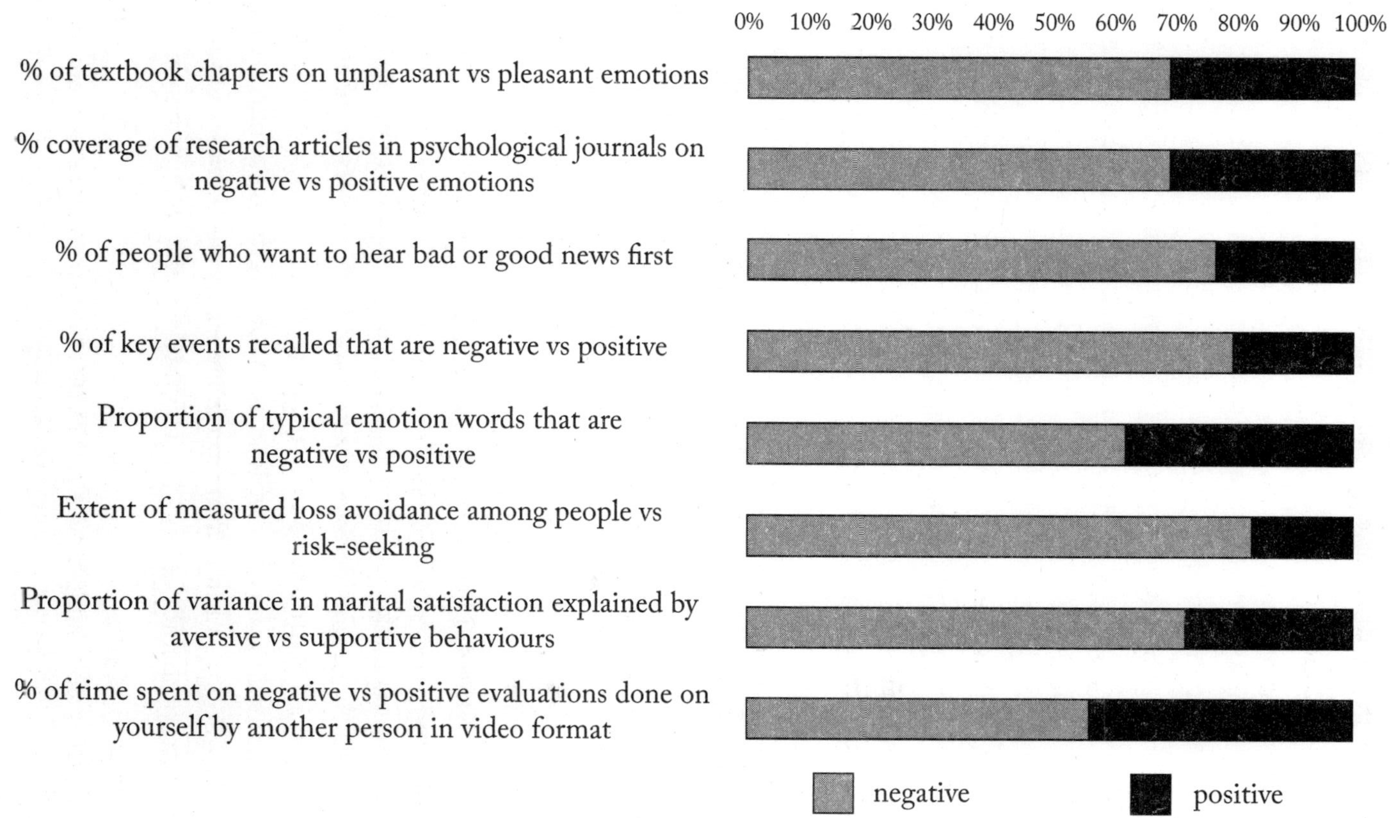

where the metrics of each study have been grouped into themes like prevalence of underlying psychological features, how people process information, what language emphasizes, et cetera. Each bar expresses the percentage split between negative and positive results on each metric.

Among the studies the negative proportions outweigh the positive by a factor of between 1.3 and 4.9, with a crude average of over two, indicating that the overall bias is near-universal and differs mainly in its magnitude rather than its presence.[1]

As well as being shown, as above, in terms of static attitudes to issues, the bias is also strongly seen in situations into which new information arrives. Other studies collected by Baumeister measured how much harder it can be to shift or offset an existing belief for the better with positive information, than it is to change it for the worse with negative information, with empirical studies over a range of domains indicating a ratio of relative impact of 2.3 to 5.

Heuristics drawn from these results are therefore that negative attitudes may be about twice as prevalent as positive attitudes, and that new positive information needs to outweigh new negative information also by a factor of two, to change attitudes. The theory of loss aversion from prospect theory provides a useful mathematical framework within which to understand this.

In some instances, loss aversion is of course adaptive, with respect to health and immediate danger, and with respect to relationship and social harmony. But in many respects, it can be maladaptive. In financial terms, it can lead to poorer outcomes than a rational risk-taking strategy that considers expected values of outcomes where probabilities can be accurately estimated. It can manifest

1 Of course estimates of these effects, where measurable in some way, will vary between people, cultures and domains.

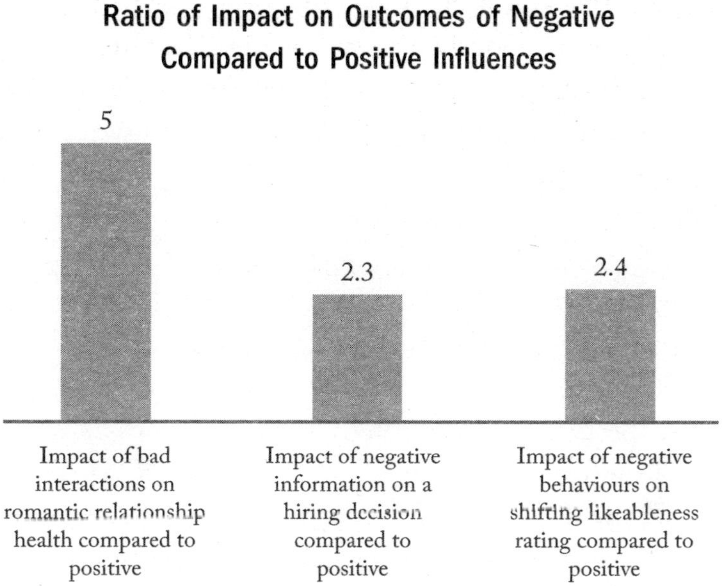

in terms of longer-term threats to health, for instance, where daily exercise represents a clear and immediate loss set against a vague and uncertain future state of health. It undermines trust and cooperation where a fear of betrayal can undermine the potential gains from open and collaborative action. In respect of career decisions, it can hold us back in a comfort zone rather than taking a calculated risk to take on an elevation in responsibility. And in general, in high opportunity settings, it can actively work against rational evaluation of potential upsides.

Appendix 1.4 - Seeking Out Positive Signals as a Tactic to Change a System

A deliberate attitude of optimism can double our ability to recognize opportunities.

Barbara Fredrickson's (2001) broaden-and-build theory – as depicted below – proposes that positive emotions (joy, interest, contentment), which optimists experience more frequently, broaden an individual's thought-action patterns, leading to more exploratory, open and creative behaviours.

Pessimists, on the other hand, tend to show a narrower focus, centred on perceived threat. Optimists notice peripheral information that a pessimist would miss, reframe problems as opportunities and explore novel ideas with less fear of failure.

The Broaden-and-Build Theory

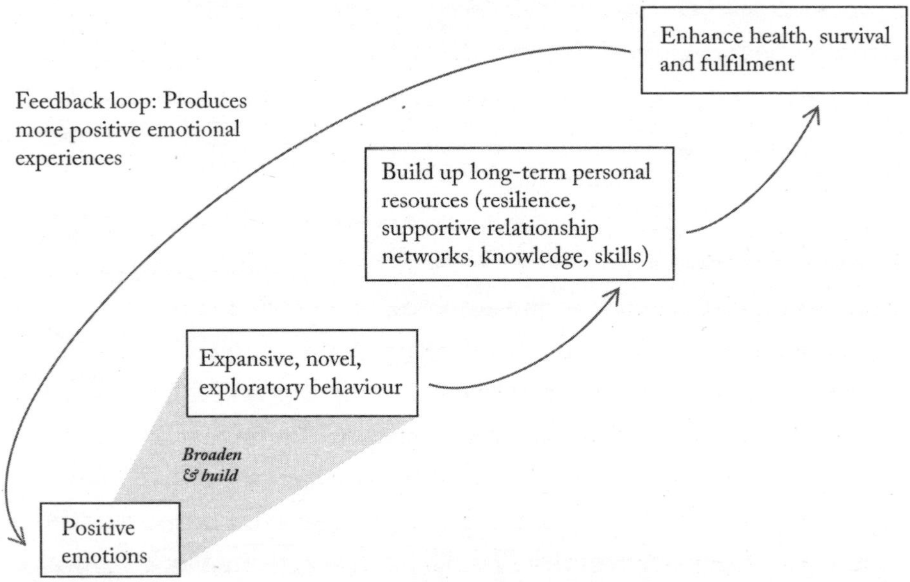

Researcher Alice Isen and colleagues (1987) found that deliberate priming of a test group in a laboratory experiment by showing a film with a positive tone, resulted in 75 per cent of these participants solving a problem involving imaginative use of materials they were given, compared to only 20 per cent finding the solution in the control group. The study showed that even a very mild positive feeling, induced just minutes before, dramatically increased creative insight. Isen argued that positive affect makes cognition more flexible and inclusive, allowing people to see unusual relationships between objects and concepts. Similar relationships have been found showing that positive affect leads to faster decision-making with no reduction in quality, better memory and higher likelihood of achieving win-win agreements in social tasks.

Therefore, a deliberately optimistic mindset can be applied to tune our loss aversion and reduce its maladaptive effects in respect of situations with high gain potential. It permits us to reframe these situations in terms of upside and, furthermore, learn more from success than from punishment or failure. In this way it can offset a general 2:1 pessimistic bias, and by triggering creativity, it can double our ability to recognize new opportunities, compared to the norm.

Appendix 1.5 – Amplification of Positive Behaviour Within a Network

Pro-social behaviour spreads within a network, diffusing knowledge and collaborative behaviour, at least tripling positive outcomes.

Fredrickson found furthermore that over time, a positive mindset and actions build durable personal resources. A key resource built through positivity is prosocial behaviour. A broadened mindset will make an individual more likely to initiate interactions, trust others and deepen relationships. In a network, this is a direct mechanism for link formation and strengthening, and utilization for the mutual benefit of those in the network.

This impact within a network can be thought of as a function of participation, diffusion and collaboration.

Participation and diffusion

Empirical evidence shows that positivity actively spreads from node to node, and the clustering effects it has in the network enable faster diffusion of information. Fowler and Christakis (2008) studied a network of 4,739 individuals followed from 1983 to 2003 in the Framingham study dataset, which among many other variables measured happiness according to the Center for Epidemiological Studies depression scale, including statements put to them relating to positivity such as: 'I felt hopeful about the future.' They found firstly that happiness clusters within the network.

But they also found that increased happiness in a node makes its connections happier – so an increase in the probability of a node becoming happy if another node related to it (called an alter) becomes happy. As per the graph below, it found significant effects on probability of individual happiness from spouses becoming happy (8 per cent effect on the individual), friends (25 per cent) and neighbours (34 per cent).

Happiness is Contagious

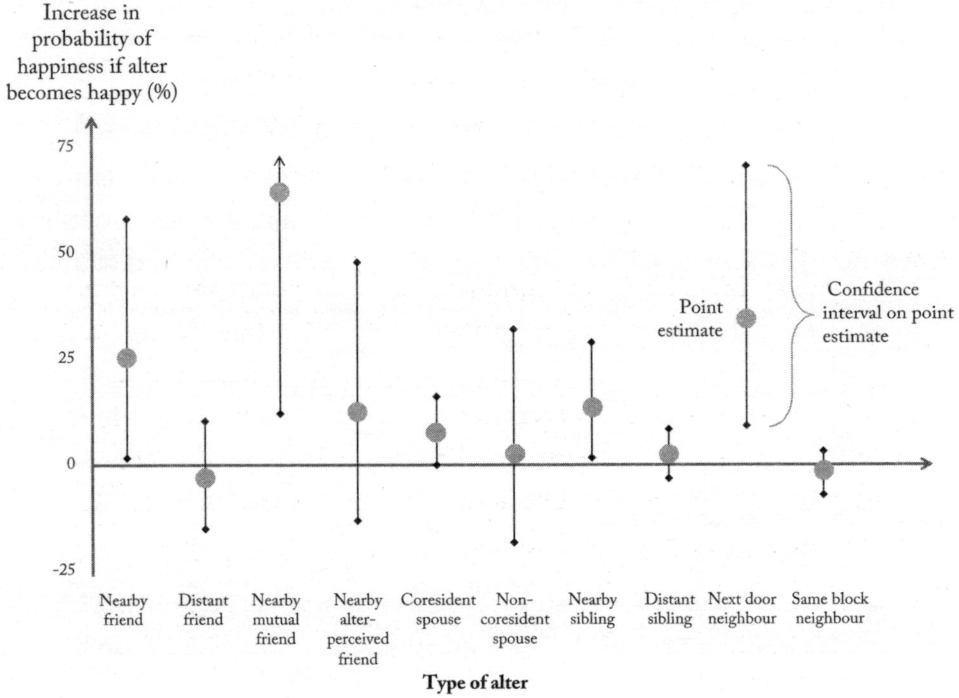

Therefore, one's positivity will tend to increase the positivity of others within one's immediate network, forming these dense clusters of positivity.

In general, stronger, more trusting relationships lower the barrier to sharing information, especially complex or valuable information. This can be modelled within network simulations using a higher probability of successful transmission of information across links characterized by high positivity/trust. This has been shown empirically by Levin and Cross (2004). Then, when information is introduced, it spreads faster and more completely through the more densely connected network, fostered by relational positivity. The average path length between any two nodes is lower, making the network more efficient.

But Centola (2010) showed empirically that behaviour also spreads, analysing the transmission of a health behaviour between two different types of networks in an experiment: (1) clustered networks and (2) random networks between people. Across six independent trials, the behaviour spread more quickly (four times faster) and reached a higher level of diffusion as measured by the fraction adopting the behaviour (42 per cent higher) in the clustered network compared to random networks.

Collaboration

Fowler and Christakis (2010) conducted a public goods game experiment in which participants in groups could contribute money for the benefit of their group. Critically, subjects were randomly reassigned to new groups of strangers in each round, allowing researchers to causally track how one person's behaviour influenced others.

They found that cooperative actions were contagious: a person's contribution was directly influenced by the generosity of their group members from the previous round. This influence then created a 'cascade', spreading across up to three degrees of separation through the network (from person A to B to C to D). By calculating the total cumulative impact of a single cooperative act – summing both the direct influence on immediate partners and the indirect, downstream influence on others over several rounds – the researchers demonstrated that for every one monetary unit a person initially contributed, it caused a ripple effect that led others in the network to collectively contribute an additional three units, effectively tripling the initial cooperative investment.

Cooperative Actions are Contagious

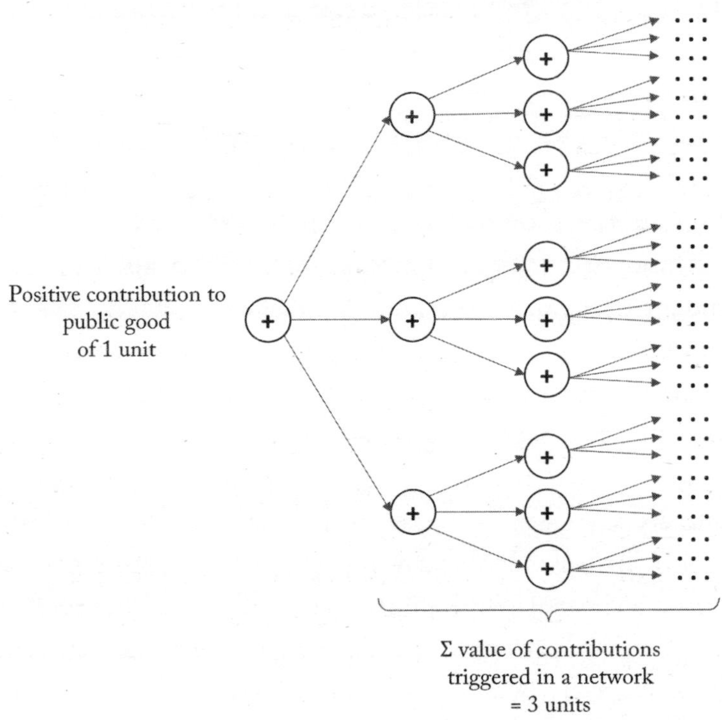

So, we argue that the multiplicative impact of optimism in a network is the cumulative effect of multipliers for participation, diffusion and collaboration, and therefore at least three times. Putting together the power of optimism to help the individual discover and correctly value opportunities, with its further power to generate network effects:

More impactful pursuit of opportunities = *Increased ability to see opportunities* × *Enhanced outcomes within a network*

$$= 2 \times 3 = 6$$

Therefore, in an interconnected world optimism has demonstrably superior adaptive value, contributes to collective flourishing, and indicatively, can multiply our impact six-fold.

Appendix 1 References

Roy F. Baumeister et al., 'Bad Is Stronger Than Good', *Review of General Psychology* 5, no. 4 (2001): 323–70, https://doi.org/10.1037/1089–2680.5.4.323.

Alexander L. Brown, Taisuke Imai, Ferdinand M. Vieider and Colin F. Camerer, 'Meta-analysis of empirical estimates of loss aversion', *Journal of Economic Literature* 62, no. 2 (2024): 485–516, https://doi.org/10.1257/jel.20221698.

Damon Centola, 'The Spread of Behavior in an Online Social Network', *Science* 329, no. 5996 (2010): 1194, https://doi.org/10.1126/science.1185231.

James H. Fowler and Nicholas A. Christakis, 'Cooperative Behavior Cascades in Human Social Networks', *Proceedings of the National Academy of Sciences* 107, no. 12 (2010): 5334–38, doi:10.1073/pnas.0913149107.

James H. Fowler and Nicholas A. Christakis, 'Dynamic Spread of Happiness in a Large Social Network: Longitudinal Analysis over 20 Years in the Framingham Heart Study', *British Medical Journal* 337 (2008): a2338, https://doi.org/10.1136/bmj.a2338.

Barbara L. Fredrickson, 'The Role of Positive Emotions in Positive

Psychology: The Broaden-and-Build Theory of Positive Emotions', *American Psychologist* 56, no. 3 (2001): 218–26, https://doi.org/10.1037/0003-066X.56.3.218.
Alice M. Isen, Kimberly A. Daubman, and Gary P. Nowicki, 'Positive Affect Facilitates Creative Problem Solving', *Journal of Personality and Social Psychology* 52, no. 6 (1987): 1122–31, https://doi.org/10.1037/0022-3514.52.6.1122.
Daniel Z. Levin and Rob Cross, 'The Strength of Weak Ties You Can Trust: The Mediating Role of Trust in Effective Knowledge Transfer', *Management Science* 50, no. 11 (2004): 1477–90, https://doi.org/10.1287/mnsc.1030.0136.
Amos Tversky and Daniel Kahneman, 'Advances in Prospect Theory: Cumulative Representation of Uncertainty', *Journal of Risk and Uncertainty* 5, no. 4 (1992): 297–323.

Appendix 2

The proposed multiplier for time is composed as follows:

$$\text{Increased effective time available} = \text{Effect of better health} \times \text{Effect of acquisition of knowledge} \times \text{Increased urgency}$$

The sections below provide a basis for estimating what the component effects may be.

Appendix 2.1 – The Log-Time Hypothesis and Time to Make an Impact

Time is subjective and there is less than you think.

Real time progresses linearly, so elapsed time at age R is simply R. Under logarithmic time the position is that, psychologically, the experience of the progression of time means that elapsed time is a non-linear function of the years already lived. The hypothesis is that the rate of change in perceived time at time R, $S(R)$, relative to real time can be expressed, for some constant k, as:

$$\frac{dS(R)}{dR} = \frac{k}{R}$$

So total perceived time from R_0 to R is:

$$\int_{R_0}^{R} \frac{1}{x}\,dx = \ln\left(\frac{R}{R_0}\right)$$

Often one sets R_0 to 1, measuring from end of the first year, producing:

$$S(R) = \ln(R)$$

So subjective time is a logarithmic function of real time, and perceived life up to an age x as a proportion of a total perceived lifespan of 80, is:

$$\frac{\ln(x)}{\ln(80)}$$

Allocating proportions of perceived life to distinct phases, this equation yields the '75:20:5' split:

Phase	Age	Elapsed perceived life	Effective proportion of life to have an impact	Linear proportion of life
Education	0–25	$\frac{\ln(25)}{\ln(80)} - 0 \approx 0.735$	75%	31%
Working life	25–65	$\frac{\ln(65)}{\ln(80)} - \frac{\ln(25)}{\ln(80)} \approx 0.218$	20%	50%
Retirement	65+	$\frac{\ln(80)}{\ln(80)} - \frac{\ln(65)}{\ln(80)} \approx 0.047$	5%	19%

Appendix 2.2 – The Effect of Health on Time

A healthy person has 25 per cent more time to make an impact than an unhealthy one.

One can focus on the experience of the passage of life in good health, which is the effective time to accomplish something. One has control of the relevant levers such as sufficient physical activity, good nutrition, rest and appropriate health screenings. The effect can be quantified using Disability-Adjusted Life Years (DALYs), which measure years lost to ill-health. Adjusting for DALYs makes a year of life for a healthy person worth substantially more than for an unhealthy one.

Assuming that from age eighteen, a healthy person begins to

DALY Value of a Year of Life

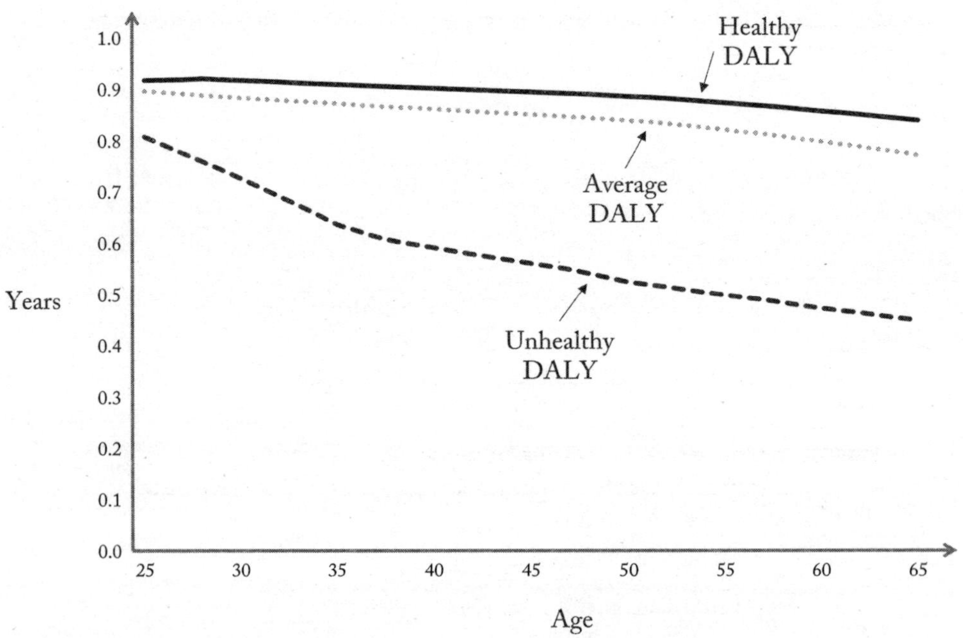

deviate from the average person over a period of ten years, until they are losing half the DALYs per year, and an unhealthy person is losing double the DALYs than average. Plotting what each year of life is worth shows that by age sixty-five, as per the graph below and adjusting for illness, a year of a healthy person's life is still worth about 85 per cent of a year, but for someone unhealthy, by this age a year is worth less than half.

Discounting the value of each year of life to represent its DALY, produces revised curves of actual versus perceived time for healthy and unhealthy people, initially shifting the split to 78:18:4, as perceived life becomes even more front-loaded due to health deterioration in later years.

But as shown in the curves below, good health shifts the passage of perceived time closer to linear, under which 50 per cent of lifespan is available. The result is that a healthy person gets to 19 per cent for the working years, while an unhealthy person is limited to 15 per cent. Maintaining health, therefore, increases the impact of time by approximately 25 per cent relative to an unhealthy person.[1]

1 Another option would be delaying retirement, extending the period of life in work after age sixty-five. But working longer actually buys less than 2 per cent in time to have an impact:

$$\left(\frac{\ln (70)}{\ln (80)}-\frac{\ln (25)}{\ln (80)}\right)-\left(\frac{\ln (65)}{\ln (80)}-\frac{\ln (25)}{\ln (80)}\right)=1.7\%$$

Impact of Health

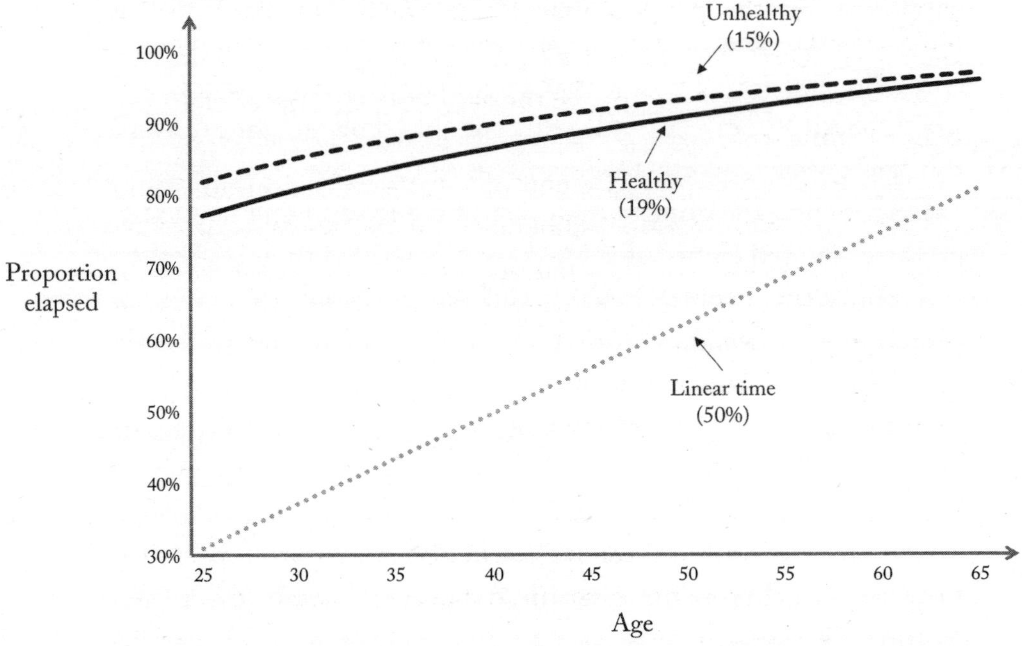

Appendix 2.3 – The Effect of Knowledge Acquisition on Time

Knowledge increases effective time to make an impact by a further 35 per cent.

Impact can be understood as a function of not only work rate and time, but also knowledge.

Knowledge increases capability and the density of output per unit of time. This can be modelled by weighting each year by an accumulating knowledge factor operating from age k_0 to R.

$$\sum_{x=k_0}^{R} \frac{1}{x} \, . \, Knowledge_x$$

Assume application of the Matthew Effect to the accumulation of knowledge, that change in knowledge over a lifetime is a proportion of the prior volume of knowledge in place, that is, $\Delta k = r.k_0$. This means: $k_1 = k_0 + r.k_0$, that is, $k_1 = k_0.(r+1)$

This we can generalize to give the accumulated impact of knowledge at time x: $k_x.(r+1)^x$

Now assume that after the end of formal education up to age twenty-five, training and deliberate cultivation of experience continue, resulting in an annual accumulation of knowledge of 3 per cent, giving the effective impact of time from age twenty-five to age R.

$$\sum_{x=25}^{R} \frac{1}{x} \cdot (1.03)^x$$

The compounding effect of knowledge acquisition offsets the logarithmic decay of perceived time, bending the life-curve back towards linearity.

Effective impact time increases as one gears it up with knowledge, to 26 per cent. This is approximately 35 per cent higher in relative terms than the 19 per cent of a healthy person.

Appendix 2.4 – Increasing Urgency

By imagining your older self, you can double your sense of urgency.

The experience of the passage of subjective time relative to objective time at two example ages is given by gradients on the logarithmic life curve:

Log Time

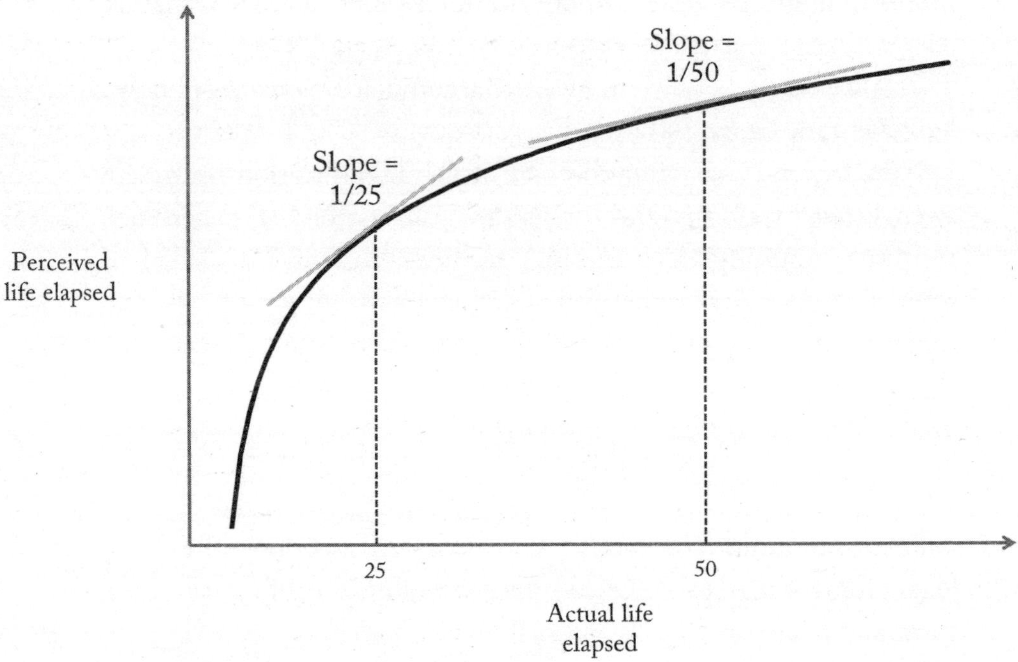

In tabular form:

Age	Slope on curve	First derivative	Interpretation	Sensation of time
25	Steeper	$\frac{dS}{dR}=\frac{1}{25}=0.040$	Long subjective time per unit real time	Seems to be passing more slowly
50	Flatter	$\frac{dS}{dR}=\frac{1}{50}=0.020$	Short subjective time per unit real time	Seems to be passing faster

An implication for young people is that to offset complacency about the passage of time, one needs to be deliberate in cultivating a sense of urgency. Someone aged twenty-five imagining themselves aged fifty could increase their urgency by the ratio of these two slopes, that is, two times. The magnitude of the effect will vary by age.

The implication of applying this urgency on top of the effects of health and knowledge is to further increase effective time to 32 per cent, an increase of 25 per cent on top of the impact of health and knowledge.

The cumulative result of changing one's approach to time can increase its effective quantity as follows:

$$\textit{Increased effective time available} = \textit{Effect of better health} \times \textit{Effect of acquisition of knowledge} \times \textit{Increased urgency}$$

$$= (1 + 25\%) \times (1 + 35\%) \times (1 + 25\%) - 1$$

$$\approx 2.1$$

This represents a more than doubling of effective time over an unhealthy person, and nearly double that of the average person. The results of the above sections can be summarized in this graph.

Proportion of Effective Lifetime Spent in Working Years

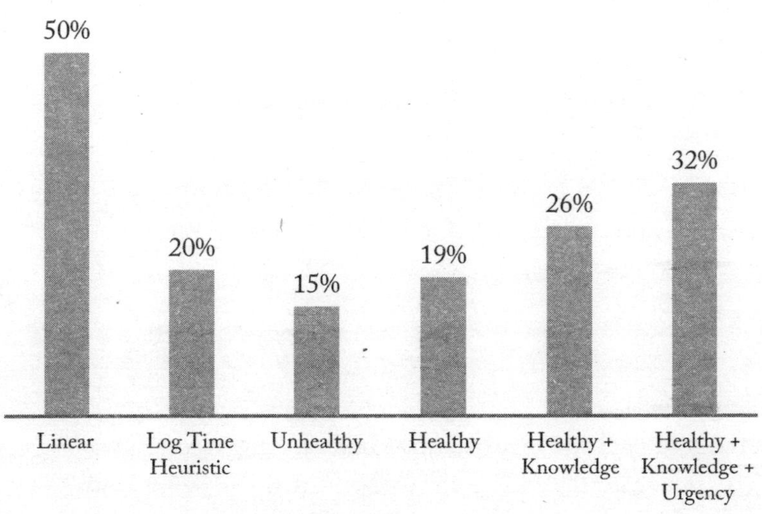

Appendix 3

Appendix 3.1 – The Effect of Framing on Motivation

Clearly defined, time-bound goals can double motivation by shifting attention implicitly from gains to losses.

In addition to the pessimism bias described above, prospect theory explains why framing effects, that is, how choices or goals are presented, influence decisions. Setting a goal can be considered in microeconomic terms to be equivalent to placing one's actions on the S-curve of value. Vague aims with no accountability will tend to situate on the gain side of the curve.

However, the same aims expressed very clearly, that is, as goals, with time-bounds, preferably shared or made public, will situate the intended actions on the loss side of the curve, since they become psychologically more like losses, with failure to achieve them now having a relatively higher price.

Under Tversky and Kahneman's estimate of λ, expressing objectives in terms of concrete goals can therefore double their motivational power.

$$\textit{Effort multiplier} = \textit{Increase in motivation} = \lambda \approx 2$$

Appendix 3.2 – How the First Three Principles Connect

Small gains across opportunity, time and effort compound to multiply overall impact.

$$\Delta\ \textit{Impact} = f\,(\Delta\ \textit{Opportunity},\ \Delta\ \textit{Time},\ \Delta\ \textit{Effort})$$

The effects of each of Optimism, Health, Knowledge and Urgency and Goal-setting, increase the impact of our actions, and conceptually can multiply, as shown in graph below:

- Application of deliberate positivity doubles the chances of finding opportunities, and with network effects, triples the value that can be generated from them.
- Doubling time doubles the effective period in which to exploit these opportunities in the network.
- Goal-setting enlists loss aversion to double motivation (both personally and within the network).

Multiplier Effects

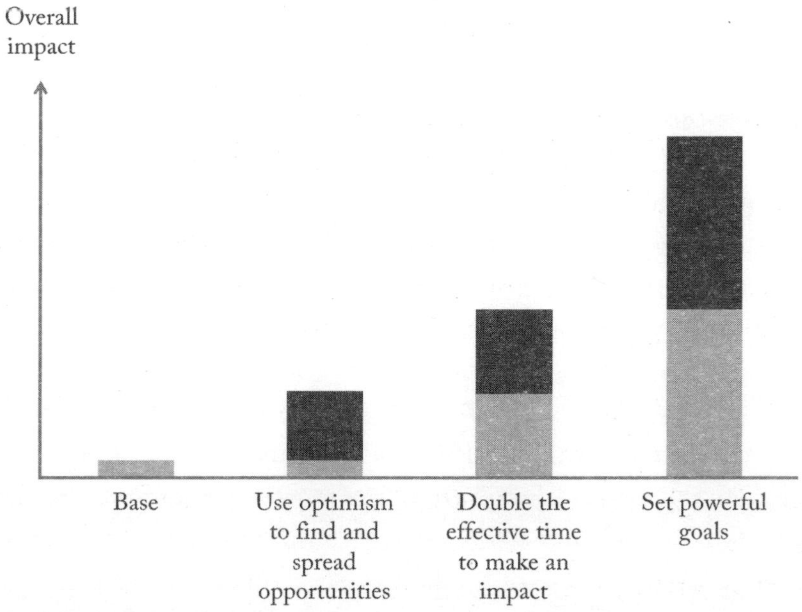

Appendix 3 References

Amos Tversky and Daniel Kahneman, 'Advances in Prospect Theory: Cumulative Representation of Uncertainty', *Journal of Risk and Uncertainty* 5, no. 4 (1992): 297–323.

Appendix 4

Appendix 4.1 - How the Pareto Principle Differs from the Pareto Distribution

The Pareto principle is a heuristic; the Pareto distribution is a function.

In everyday usage, the terms 'Pareto principle' and 'Pareto distribution' are often used interchangeably, but this is not strictly correct. For mathematicians and purists, the distinction is significant – especially when we graph the two or analyse events 'in the tail' of the distribution. While the nuances may not be critical for every reader, those interested in precision may find the explanation in this appendix helpful.

The Pareto principle, also known as the 80/20 rule, says that roughly 80 per cent of outcomes result from around 20 per cent of causes. This is a rule of thumb that is widely used in business and society. For example, Microsoft reported that fixing the top 20 per cent of bugs would eliminate 80 per cent of crashes, and in criminology, a small number of repeat offenders are said to be responsible for a large proportion of crime. The Pareto principle is an approximation, a heuristic meant to highlight the skewed distribution of cause and effect in various real-world scenarios.

On the other hand, the Pareto distribution, sometimes called the Pareto power-law distribution, is a mathematical function that describes a situation where a small number of extreme events dominate the system. Unlike the loosely defined Pareto principle, a Pareto distribution follows a precise power-law relationship (as described in the following appendices). It describes phenomena where a small number of occurrences exert a disproportionate influence – such as with stock market crashes, natural disasters or pandemics – where rare, extreme events cause massive disruption.

While both concepts capture the essential Pareto idea of disproportionate impact from a few causes, the Pareto distribution is a formal statistical model, whereas the Pareto principle is a generalized empirical observation. The key difference between them becomes especially important when depicted on a graph.

When the Pareto principle is plotted, the typical convention is to represent it as a bar graph with categories arranged in descending order of impact. The X-axis represents causes, the Y-axis outcomes. Highest impact causes appear first, with lower-impact causes stretching to the right and forming a tail. In the bar graph, low impact events are in the tail and so the tail is of little significance.

In contrast, when the Pareto distribution is plotted, the convention is to draw it as a line graph showing a steep drop followed by a long tail stretching along the X-axis. The X-axis typically represents a variable (such as magnitude of earthquakes) arranged in ascending order, from low values on the left to high values on the right. The Y-axis represents the probability/likelihood of the event. In the line graph, high impact, low probability events are in the tail – so the tail is very important.

Apart from the graphs, why does this distinction matter? The truth is they both capture the same type of disproportionate relationship. However, the Pareto principle tends to be used when talking more generally about decision-making or prioritizing effort, whereas the Pareto distribution – with its warning to focus on events in the tail – is the more accurate term for analysing extreme system-altering events.

These two Pareto terms differ furthermore from the concept of 'Pareto optimality', which in the disciplines of economics and game theory describes a situation in which resources are allocated in the most efficient possible way, meaning that no individual can be made better off without making someone else worse off. A situation where a Pareto improvement is possible is, for example, when A has a book about history and B a book about science but

A prefers science to history, and B vice versa. Pareto optimality can be obtained if they swap. But if A has a pizza and B has none, then while the situation is unfair, it is also Pareto-optimal, in that B cannot be made better off without A becoming worse off.

Appendix 4.2 – The Prevalence of Normal Distributions versus Power-Law Dynamics

Most outcomes are not evenly distributed – a few dominate the rest.

It is often implicitly or explicitly assumed that outcomes of phenomena and opportunities follow a normal distribution, with probability density function:

$$f_X(x) = \frac{1}{\sigma\sqrt{2\pi}} e^{-\frac{1}{2}\left(\frac{x-\mu}{\sigma}\right)^2}, \text{ with mean } \mu, \text{ and standard deviation (or sigma) } \sigma$$

But many phenomena in nature and human affairs follow a power-law distribution. These are characterized generally by a mathematical relationship where one quantity varies as a power of another, that is, takes the form:

$$f(x) = k.x^{-\alpha}$$

where k and α are constants. The exponent α determines the shape of the curve, in particular a lower α produces a heavier tail, as below (assuming $k = 1$), for instance in the graphs below.

Power-Law Curves

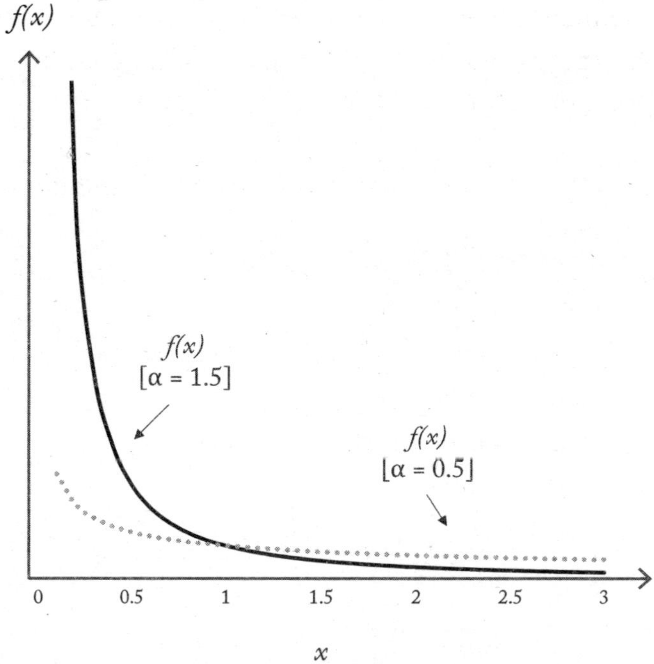

Based on this type of structure, it has been possible to estimate the values of α from empirical data.

Phenomenon[1]	Alpha value or range
Land ownership in Italy (Pareto's original study)	1.16
River basin areas	1.5
Species abundance	1.5
Frequency of use of words	1-2.2
Population of US cities	1-2.3

1 Examples from M. E. J. Newman, 'Power laws, Pareto distributions and Zipf's law', 2005.

Intensity of solar flares	1.8
Asteroid size	1.85
Intensity of wars	1.8–2
Frequency of family names	1.94
Size of forest fires	2
Website links	2
Social network followers, connections	2
File sizes on computer	2
Net worth of Americans	2.09
Telephone calls received	2.22
Number of hits on websites	2.40
Magnitude of earthquakes	2–3.04
Diameter of moon craters	2–3.14
Copies of books sold in the US	1.75–3.51
Number of citations to papers	3.04

The α corresponding to these example phenomena typically ranges from 2 to 3, with a lower α corresponding to greater inequality.

Power-law distributions, like Pareto, are ubiquitous in natural and human systems and frequently arise from their network dynamics. The mechanism of 'preferential attachment' provides a model for this process. In a growing network, new nodes connect to existing nodes with a probability proportional to the number of links those existing nodes already have. The Barabási–Albert model (Barabási & Albert, 1999) generates such networks. This example illustrates the evolution of such network structures, and the corresponding distribution of node degree.[1]

1 'Degree' of a node refers to the number of connections it has to other nodes.

Stage 1

Network Graph – 5 Nodes

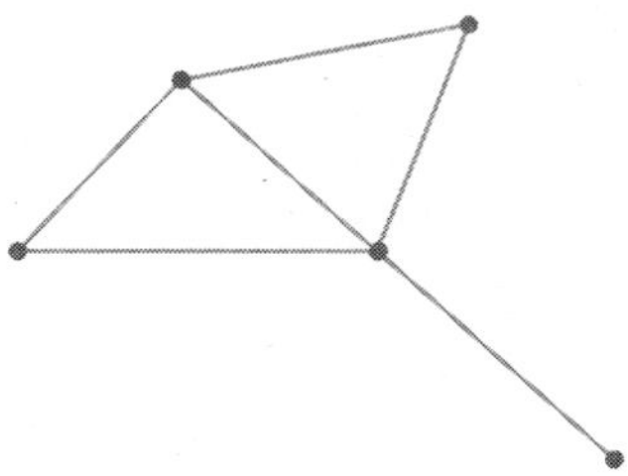

Degree Distribution – 5 Nodes

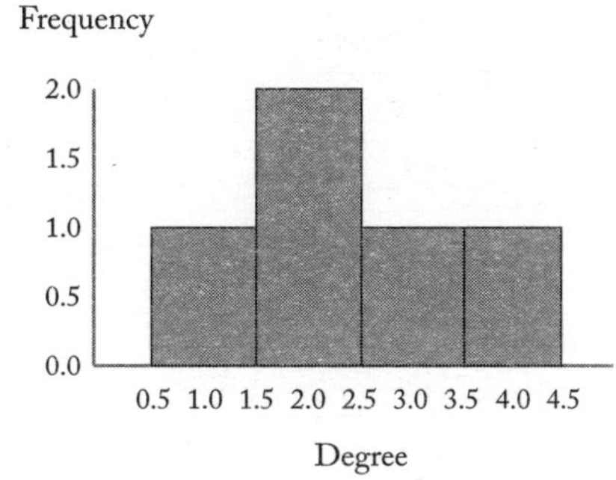

Stage 2

Network Graph – 10 Nodes

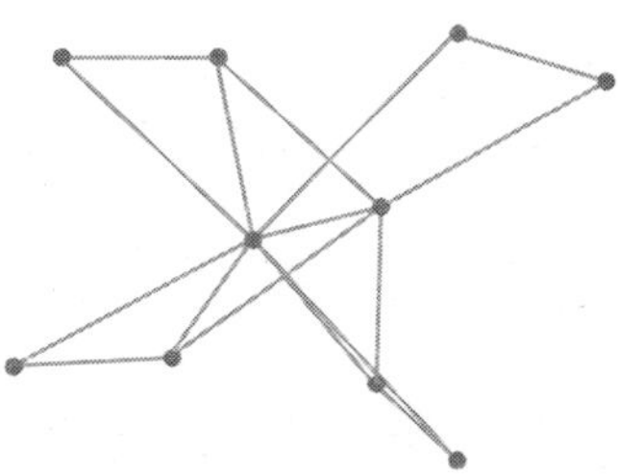

Degree Distribution – 10 Nodes

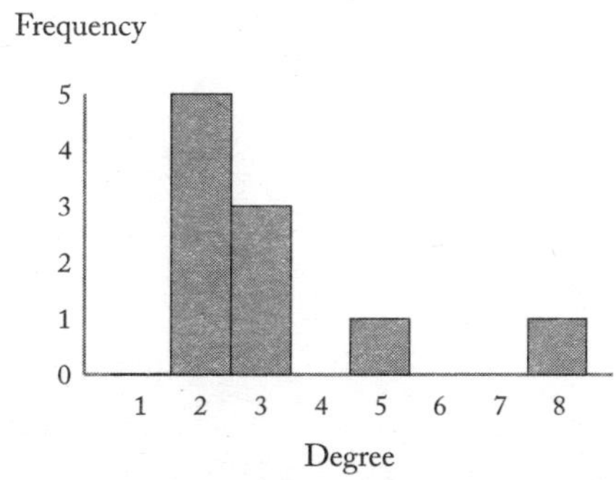

Stage 1 shows 5 nodes with few connections and little structure. Stage 2 shows 10 nodes, with a broader spread in node degree beginning to emerge.

At stage 3, with 20 nodes, the degree distribution spreads out further. It starts to become clear that some nodes are more connected than others. It is at Stage 4, with 50 nodes, that central nodes with many connections become apparent, and the distribution of node degree is becoming clearer.

Stage 3

Network Graph – 20 Nodes

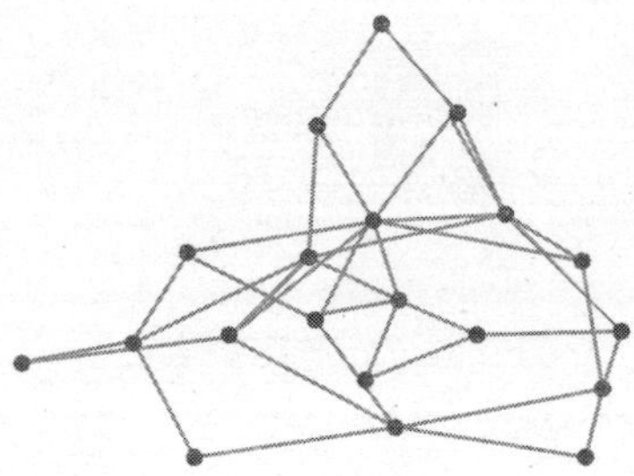

Degree Distribution – 20 Nodes

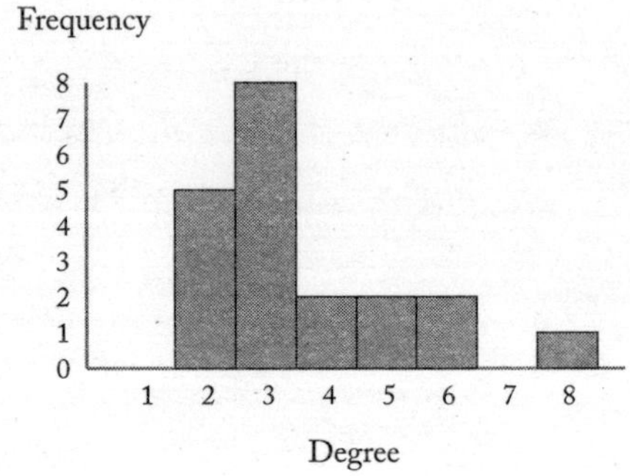

Stage 4

Network Graph – 50 Nodes

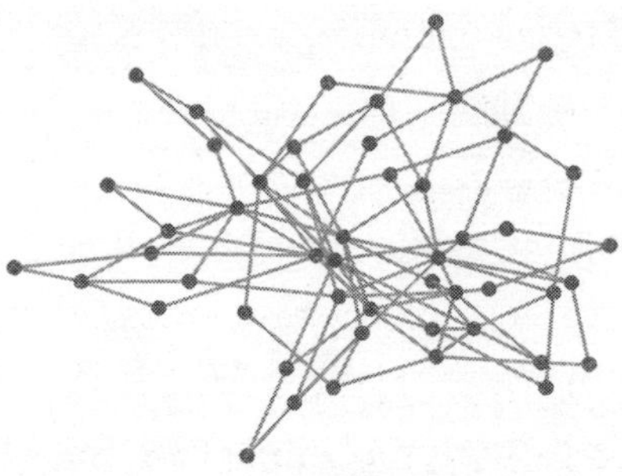

Degree Distribution – 50 Nodes

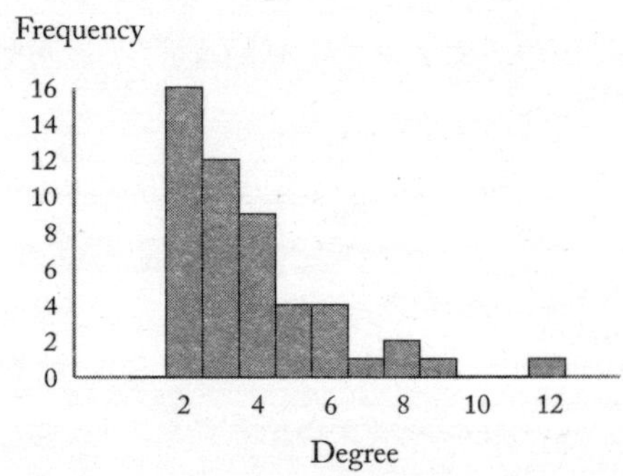

Continuing growth of this classic BA model, the resulting node degree distribution *P(x)*, can be seen to follow a power-law distribution proportional to x^{-3}. This simple mechanism of growth and preferential attachment explains the structure of many real-world networks, where a feedback loop causes popular hubs to attract new links at an accelerating rate.

Hechtlinger et al. (2024) offer a framework for understanding why big decisions – like emigration, marriage or career changes

– have a greater impact on subsequent decisions than smaller, everyday choices. Among their five main dimensions in which transformative life decisions differ from small, routine decisions, are two in particular:

- *Change of self – big decisions like emigration or leaving a religion can shift one's identity, beliefs and life trajectory.*
- *Irreversibility – many big decisions are difficult or impossible to undo, which leads to cascading consequences from the point at which they are decided, for example, the decision to have children.*

These dimensions mean that big decisions are not isolated – they reconfigure the context in which future decisions are made, whether defining what subsequent choices will be available, or defining one's future emotional states and evolving beliefs.

Applying the network model to life in general, one assumes that transformative decisions function as major nodes. Their high degree of influence on subsequent choices means they operate under a preferential attachment dynamic with respect to the addition of subsequent nodes. As a result, it is likely that the impact of the actions one takes in life follows some kind of power-law shape.

Appendix 4.3 – The Pareto Distribution

The Pareto distribution models outcomes where a small number of events account for a disproportionately large share of value.

The Pareto distribution is a continuous probability distribution following a power law. It is defined such that a random variable X has the following probability density function:

$$f_X(x) = \begin{cases} \dfrac{\alpha x_m^a}{x^{\alpha+1}} & \text{for } x \geq x_m \\ 0 & \text{for } x < x_m \end{cases}$$

where x_m is the minimum value of X for which the distribution is defined. This minimum is necessary to ensure that the distribution is properly normalized and reflects the natural lower bounds observed in the real world with respect to phenomena that follow a Pareto distribution.

α still governs the heaviness of the tail of the distribution, so a low α produces a heavier tail, as below (assuming $x_m = 1$). This means relatively more of the instances of X sampled from the distribution will take a higher value.

Pareto Probability Density Functions

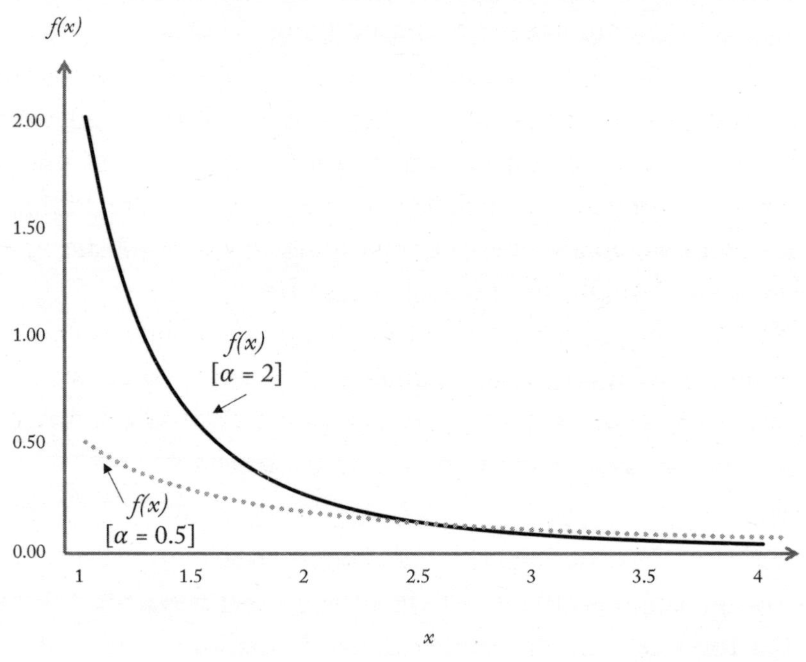

The expected value of a random variable following a Pareto distribution is:

$$E(X) = \begin{cases} \infty & \text{for } \alpha \leq 1 \\ \dfrac{\alpha x_m}{\alpha - 1} & \text{for } \alpha > 1 \end{cases}$$

The cumulative density function gives the probability that the random variable X is less than a value x:

$$F_X(x) = \begin{cases} 1 - \left(\dfrac{x_m}{x}\right)^{\alpha} & \text{for } x \leq x_m \\ 0 & \text{for } x > x_m \end{cases}$$

Appendix 4.4 – How Pareto Moves the Mean

Unlike normal distributions, Pareto systems allow small shifts to produce outsized changes in the mean.

The overall result of a system which follows a statistical distribution is a function of the mean of that distribution.

Assume a phenomenon like the scale of an opportunity, X (in arbitrary units), follows a Pareto distribution with $\alpha = 2$ and $x_m = 1$. Its mean is then 2, and variance is undefined.

Now assume also a belief that this phenomenon follows a normal distribution with the same mean, and a variance of 0.08, therefore standard deviation of 0.28. These can be graphed as follows.

Pareto – Normal Comparison

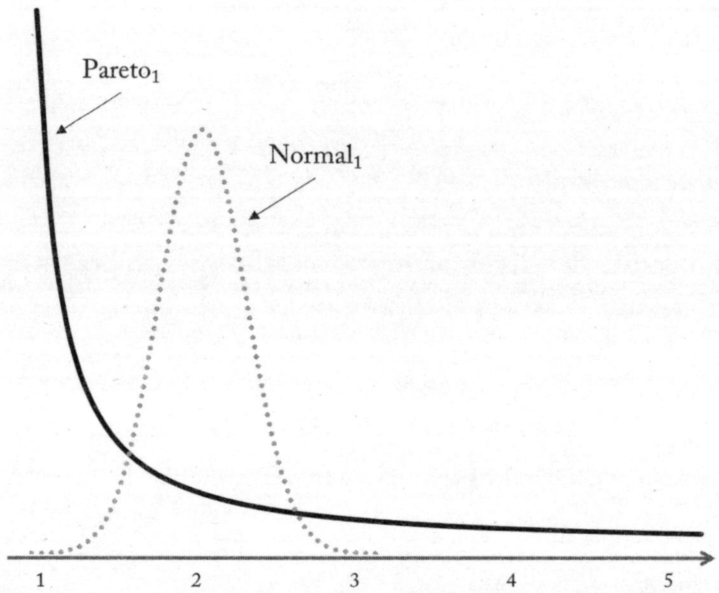

We want to compare how much one must shift each distribution to obtain a doubling of the mean.

For the Normal distribution, this involves doubling the mean parameter, to 4, producing the following, leaving the variance constant:

Normal Comparison

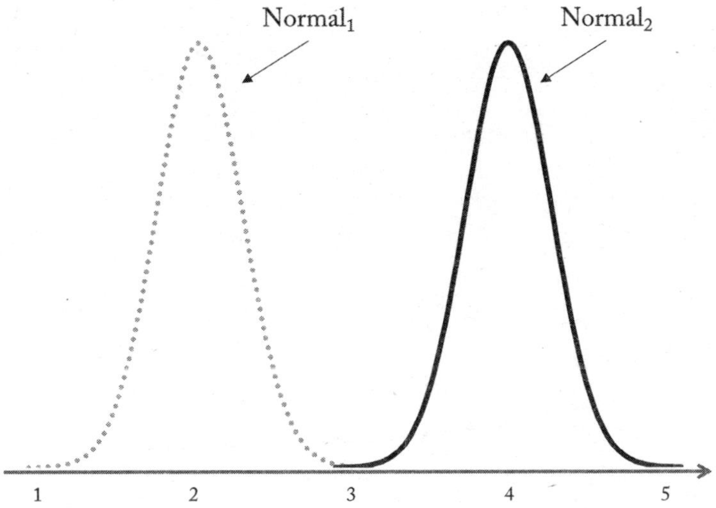

This requires shifting an amount of the distribution equivalent to more than 99 per cent:

$$F_{Normal_1}(x) - F_{Normal_2}(x)$$

where x is the crossing point of the two distributions.

To shift the Pareto mean, there is far less to move. To achieve a mean of 4, the alpha parameter needs to be 1.33, giving the following new distribution.

Pareto Comparison

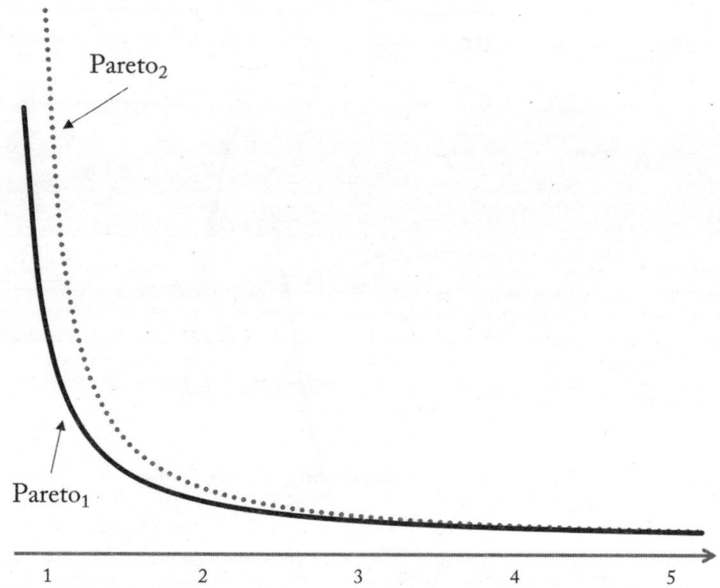

The amount of distribution shifted is far less, equivalent at the crossing point to about 15 per cent:

$$F_{Pareto_1}(x) - F_{Pareto_2}(x)$$

So, a small relative shift in the distribution can have an outsized influence on the mean.

Appendix 4.5 – How the Four Principles Connect

Applying the four principles together compounds impact, shifting ordinary actions into the extreme tail of outcomes.

Assume a Pareto distribution for the impact of our actions, and a multiplicative effect from each of the first three Principles on impact:

Scaled Up Impact in a Pareto World

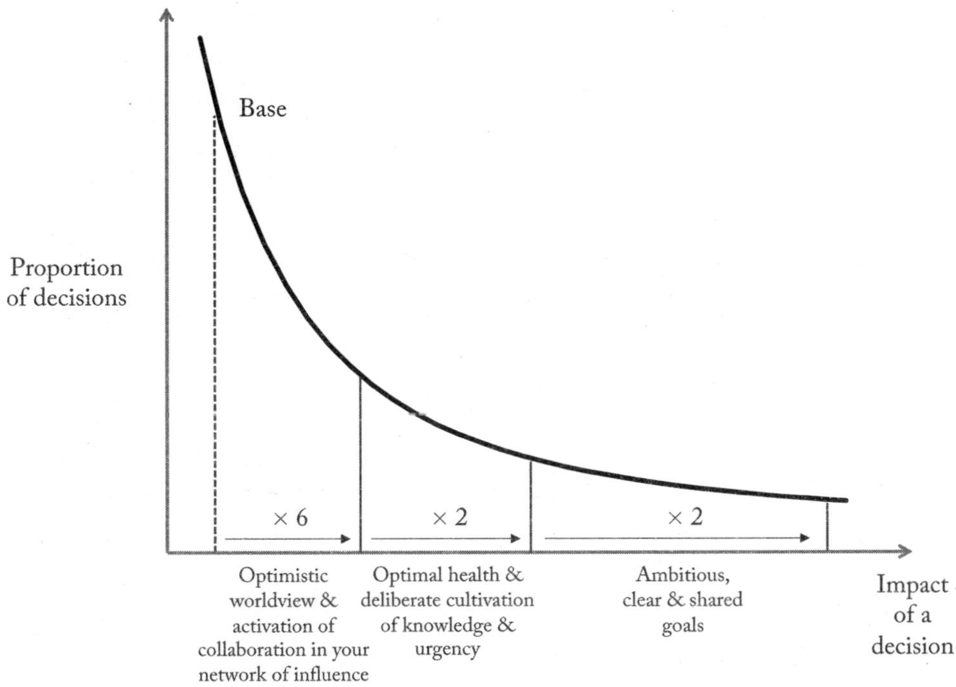

Now, assuming for a Pareto distribution of life decisions a parameter of 2 (in the range described in Appendix 5.2), and $x_m = 1$, corresponding to one's minimally important decisions, we get a mean impact of 2. Take as a base, decisions with an impact of 1.1, corresponding illustratively to those made by someone with default levels of pessimism, poor health and knowledge, low urgency and no goals. Then applying each Principle in turn, we multiply up the impact, and for each result use the cumulative density function of the distribution to compute how much of the distribution exceeds that result.

So as per the table below, to start with, 83 per cent of the distribution exceeds the value of 1.1. Multiplying that value by six, we get that already only 2.3 per cent of the distribution exceeds 6.6. And after all three Principles apply in succession, getting to a cumulative multiplier of 24, the impact of an action is 26.4, which will fall in the top 0.14 per cent of all actions. This is to say that the result is that an ordinary decision can become approximately a one-in-700 impact decision.

	Multiplier	Impact	$1 - F_X(x)$
Base	-	1.1	82.64%
x Optimism	6	6.6	2.30%
x Time	2	13.2	0.57%
x Goals	2	26.4	0.14%

Systematic application of Optimism, Time and Goal-setting will therefore generate the kind of actions that lie far into the Pareto tail, where they will have a significantly multiplied impact.

Appendix 4 References

Albert-László Barabási and Réka Albert, 'Emergence of Scaling in Random Networks', *Science* 286, no. 5439 (1999): 509–12.

Sean Hechtlinger et al., 'The Psychology of Life's Most Important Decisions', *American Psychologist* (2024), https://doi.org/10.1037/amp0001439.

Mark E. J. Newman, 'Power Laws, Pareto Distributions and Zipf's Law', *Contemporary Physics* 46, no. 5 (2005): 323–51, https://doi.org/10.1080/00107510500052444.

ACKNOWLEDGEMENTS

This book holds decades of learning, input, guidance and more from so many people. I am indebted to many but can only mention a few.

I must first and foremost thank my wife, Lauren, and our children, Sarah, Rebecca, Jake and Gabriel. They have been my inspiration and my motivation, and they have shared in the long and demanding journey of building Discovery with me. My journey started with them and has been for them – I started Discovery precisely at the time of the birth of Sarah, our first child.

My wife has been unconditionally supportive – she is my most honest critic and always cuts through ambiguity and nonsense. She has kept me true to myself, and her clarity of thought has been so important throughout my journey, and in the honesty and intent of this book. I am so grateful to her.

It is so important to me that I thank my parents who taught me that knowledge, truth and doing good must be pursued above all. They also instilled in me a deep-seated need to question what others take as dogma in order to make an impact, which has been a powerful gift in my journey. I hope this book makes a broad impact – it is their legacy.

I am further grateful to three exceptional colleagues and friends.

Barry Swartzberg and I started our journey together as university students and close friends. Working with Barry in my first job lit a fire in me. Despite our youth, we had deep conviction that we could build a business of considerable impact. We shared both values and vision, and Barry has been a major source of inspiration and support for me personally, and for this I am hugely grateful. *The Four Principles* is a manifestation of our journey. I have tried my best to reflect what we have built and pursued in this book.

Neville Koopowitz and I have had the privilege of working together for over three decades in building Discovery, and now in globalizing our Vitality Shared-Value model. We have a unique bond. Neville is a remarkable leader and central figure in the stories and anecdotes in the book and is an architect of a lot of what we have achieved. He embodies the Four Principles, and his impact is evidence of their power – and has given me deeper conviction of the need to share them with a broader audience.

Hylton Kallner, uniquely brilliant and driven, has been a force behind our success. We have worked closely together. He has deeply influenced me and supported me across multiple dimensions. We have spent many years debating what makes people successful and impactful, and how to bring out the best in the people we lead. Much of this thinking has made its way into the formulation of the Principles, and into the book.

Barry, Neville and Hylton have been incredibly generous in allowing me to tell their story. Every story, anecdote and lesson is theirs too.

Then, I am deeply grateful to Mark Tucker, my friend and mentor. His counsel – always rigorous, always humane – has helped guide me, and his support has been invaluable. We share a common vision and set of values. He is the embodiment of the Four Principles – his drive for urgency, the scale of his goals, and his actions in the tail are unique and remarkable. He has truly lived these Principles and has achieved global impact on a scale few have. Working with him is a privilege and his close friendship a rare gift.

Furthermore, I give substantial credit for my entire journey to Laurie Dippenaar, the source of our start-up capital, a founder and chair of RMB, the investment bank that was our major shareholder, and our first chairman – but he was and is much more than that. From the start he lit a fire in me about leadership, strength of character, doing the right thing and the power of careful thought and wisdom. He started me on this journey and all these years later he remains a close friend, confidant and mentor. I remain in awe of him.

Without my brilliant colleague Lisa Mondschein, this book would not have been written. She has been my collaborator in thinking, researching, communicating and writing. It was her determination to author a book that captured decades of this thinking and research. We both shared a passion to bring *The Four Principles* to life for a broader audience, and we set out to create a book of significant depth that would transcend our story and which we hoped would make a substantial impact. It was also her drive, hard work and obsession with detail and quality that enabled the writing of this book. This is as much her book as it is mine.

I have also leaned heavily on my two exceptional colleagues and friends, Jonny Broomberg and Lisa Klein. They have both been fundamental in my success, and in the success of Discovery. They are uniquely talented and have shared my vision and determination. I am so grateful for their advice and for their long hours in reading, checking and adding to the book.

The mathematical rigour is the incredible work of Simon Hendrie, one of our team's smartest actuaries and mathematicians. He eagerly collaborated and worked with me on the mathematical logic. We both felt the book required a rigorous mathematical underpinning to elevate it beyond just a few ideas, making it demonstrable and quantifiable.

I am very grateful to have David Cohen as my writer-collaborator.

He is a hugely accomplished author and journalist, and working with him was a privilege – and a lot of fun. We spent long hours talking, discovering and debating. I originally had the idea of a formal book laying out principles, logic and formulae. It was his brilliance and experience that convinced me not to do this, but to use my own story of Discovery and Vitality in order to bring the Principles to life. He managed to capture these stories in a way that is instructive, accessible and – we both hope – not self-indulgent. This is not the Discovery story but rather a book about the Four Principles for impact in life and leadership, with the Discovery journey as the main use case. A story on Discovery is for another book – perhaps.

I would also like to thank my agent Jim Levine and the Abner Stein team for their wise counsel and dedicated support throughout the process. Similarly, I would like to express my deep gratitude to publishers Pan Macmillan who have been a real pleasure to work with, and who have shown creativity, dedication and patience, particularly Kate Walsh in the UK and Terry Morris in South Africa.

In conclusion, I want to thank the incredible people who make up Discovery wherever they are globally. I have learned so much from them. We have shared an obsession enshrined in our core values to 'liberate the best in our people'. This is what this book is about.

NOTES

Introduction

1 George E. P. Box and Norman R. Draper, *Empirical Model-Building and Response Surfaces* (New York: Wiley, 1987).

The First Principle

1 Asphalt Industry Alliance, *ALARM Survey 2025: Annual Local Authority Road Maintenance Survey* (London: Asphalt Industry Alliance, March 2025), https://www.asphaltuk.org/wp-content/uploads/ALARM-survey-2025.pdf.
2 'Council Pothole Compensation Claims Double in a Year', RAC Media, 21 November 2024, https://media.rac.co.uk/council-pothole-compensation-claims-double-in-a-year-3355825.
3 Freda Lewis-Stempel, 'Chancellor's £500m Pledge for Potholes Is Slammed as a "Drop in the Ocean" Compared to £16bn Needed', *This Is Money*, 31 October 2024, https://www.thisismoney.co.uk/money/cars/article-14024297/chancellors-500m-potholes-slammed-drop-ocean-compared-16bn-needed.html.
4 Martin Z. Braun, 'N. Y. Governor Hochul Declares $1 billion "War on Potholes"', *Bloomberg News*, 18 January 2022, https://www.bloomberg.com/news/articles/2022–01–18/n-y-governor-kathy-hochul-declares-1-billion-war-on-potholes.
5 Daniel Kahneman and Amos Tversky, 'Prospect Theory: An Analysis of Decision under Risk', *Econometrica* 47, no. 2 (1979): 263–91, https://doi.org/10.2307/1914185.
6 Roy F. Baumeister, Ellen Bratslavsky, Catrin Finkenauer and Kathleen D. Vohs, 'Bad Is Stronger than Good', *Review of General Psychology* 5, no. 4 (2001): 323–70, https://doi.org/10.1037/1089–2680.5.4.323.
7 Roy F. Baumeister and Mark R. Leary, 'The Need to Belong: Desire for

Interpersonal Attachments as a Fundamental Human Motivation', *Psychological Bulletin* 117, no. 3 (1995): 497–529, https://doi.org/10.1037/0033-2909.117.3.497.

8 John T. Cacioppo and Gary G. Berntson, 'Relationship between Attitudes and Evaluative Space: A Critical Review, with Emphasis on the Separability of Positive and Negative Substrates', *Psychological Bulletin* 115, no. 3 (1994): 401–23, https://doi.org/10.1037/0033-2909.115.3.401.

9 Elaine Fox, Victoria Lester, Andrew Russo and Kevin Bowles, 'Facial Expressions of Emotion: Are Angry Faces Detected More Efficiently?', *Cognition & Emotion* 14, no. 1 (2000): 61–92, https://doi.org/10.1080/026999300378996.

10 Elizabeth A. Kensinger and Suzanne Corkin, 'Memory Enhancement for Emotional Words: Are Emotional Words More Vividly Remembered than Neutral Words?', *Memory & Cognition* 31, no. 8 (2003): 1169–80, https://doi.org/10.3758/BF03195800.

11 M. M. Bradley, M. Codispoti, B. N. Cuthbert and P. J. Lang, 'Emotion and Motivation I: Defensive and Appetitive Reactions in Picture Processing', *Emotion* 1, no. 3 (2001): 276–98, https://doi.org/10.1037/1528-3542.1.3.276.

12 Matt Ridley, *The Rational Optimist: How Prosperity Evolves* (New York: HarperCollins, 2010).

13 James Clear, '40 Years of Stanford Research Found That People with This One Quality Are More Likely to Succeed', *James Clear*, accessed 19 August 2025, https://jamesclear.com/delayed-gratification.

14 Roy F. Baumeister, Ellen Bratslavsky, Catrin Finkenauer and Kathleen D. Vohs, 'Bad Is Stronger than Good', *Review of General Psychology* 5, no. 4 (2001): 323–70, https://doi.org/10.1037/1089-2680.5.4.323.

15 Barbara L. Fredrickson, 'The Role of Positive Emotions in Positive Psychology: The Broaden-and-Build Theory of Positive Emotions', *American Psychologist* 56, no. 3 (2001): 218–26, https://doi.org/10.1037/0003-066X.56.3.218.

16 Alice M. Isen, Kimberly A. Daubman and Gary P. Nowicki, 'Positive Affect Facilitates Creative Problem Solving', *Journal of Personality and Social Psychology* 52, no. 6 (1987): 1122–31, https://doi.org/10.1037/0022-3514.52.6.1122.

17 Edwin Cameron, Rebecca Gore, and Sohela Surajpal, *Behind Prison Walls: Unlocking a Safer South Africa* (Cape Town: Tafelberg, 2025), ISBN 9780624092698.

18 Damon Centola, 'The Spread of Behavior in an Online Social Network Experiment', *Science* 329, no. 5996 (2010): 1194–97, https://doi.org/10.1126/science.1185231.

19 James H. Fowler and Nicholas A. Christakis, 'Dynamic Spread of Happiness in a Large Social Network', *BMJ* 337 (2008): a2338, https://doi.org/10.1136/bmj.a2338.

20 Daniel Z. Levin and Rob Cross, 'The Strength of Weak Ties You Can Trust',

Management Science 50, no. 11 (2004): 1477–90, https://doi.org/10.1287/mnsc.1030.0136.

21 James H. Fowler and Nicholas A. Christakis, 'Cooperative Behavior Cascades in Human Social Networks', *Proceedings of the National Academy of Sciences* 107, no. 12 (2010): 5334–38, https://doi.org/10.1073/pnas.0913149107.

22 Donella H. Meadows, 'Leverage Points: Places to Intervene in a System' (Hartland, VT: Sustainability Institute, 1999), https://donellameadows.org/archives/leverage-points-places-to-intervene-in-a-system/.

23 'Electricity Production by Country 2025', *World Population Review*, accessed 19 August 2025, https://worldpopulationreview.com/country-rankings/electricity-production-by-country.

24 Rob Rose and David Pilling, 'South Africa's Blackouts Crisis Is "Fixed", Says Eskom', *Financial Times*, 22 May 2024, https://www.ft.com/content/d6cc1482–4c28–4566–9902-db9d05436058.

25 Adrian Gore, 'My View on SA Remains Unchanged: We Need Action, Not Despair', *News24*, 30 March 2023, https://www.news24.com/opinions/friday-briefing/adrian-gore-my-view-on-sa-remains-unchanged-we-need-action-not-despair-20230330.

26 Nedbank Group, '2023 Results Media Release: Interim Results', 8 August 2023, https://group.nedbank.co.za/content/dam/group/pdf/20_financial-results/2023/interim-results/2023-results-media-release-nedbank.pdf.

27 Hartmut Winkler, 'South Africa's Power Crisis Will Continue until 2025 – and Blackouts Will Take Five Years to Phase Out', *The Conversation*, 7 June 2023, https://theconversation.com/south-africas-power-crisis-will-continue-until-2025-and-blackouts-will-take-5-years-to-phase-out-206343.

28 Rob Rose and David Pilling, 'South Africa's Blackouts Crisis Is "Fixed", Says Eskom', *Financial Times*, 22 May 2024, https://www.ft.com/content/d6cc1482–4c28–4566–9902-db9d05436058.

29 Tim Cohen, 'Why Is South Africa's Economy Not Growing?', *Daily Maverick*, 4 December 2024, https://www.dailymaverick.co.za/article/2024–12–04-why-is-south-africas-economy-not-growing/.

30 Martin Seligman, 'Learned Helplessness', *Annual Review of Medicine* 23 (1972): 407–12, https://doi.org/10.1146/annurev.me.23.020172.002203.

31 Martin Seligman, *Learned Optimism: How to Change Your Mind and Your Life* (New York: Vintage Books, 2006; originally published 1991).

32 Oswald Spengler, *The Decline of the West*, vols. 1 and 2, trans. Charles Francis Atkinson (New York: Alfred A. Knopf, 1926–28).

33 Ipsos MORI, 'What Worries the World', accessed 20 August 2025, https://www.ipsos.com/en/what-worries-world.

34 'Our World in Data, The World as 100 People Over the Last Two Centuries', *Voronoi*, accessed 20 August 2025, https://www.voronoiapp.com/other/The-World-as-100-People-Over-the-Last-Two-Centuries-785.

35 David Edgerton, 'Yes, We're in a Bad Way. But to Wallow in Myths of British "Declinism" Won't Help Us Thrive', *The Observer*, 12 June 2022, https://www.theguardian.com/commentisfree/2022/jun/12/yes-were-in-a-bad-way-but-to-wallow-in-myths-of-british-declinism-wont-help-us-thrive.

36 Ziva Kunda, 'The Case for Motivated Reasoning', *Psychological Bulletin* 108, no. 3 (1990): 480–98, https://doi.org/10.1037/0033–2909.108.3.480.

37 Hans Rosling, with Ola Rosling and Anna Rosling Rönnlund, *Factfulness: Ten Reasons We're Wrong About the World – and Why Things Are Better Than You Think* (New York: Flatiron Books, 2018).

38 Katy Milkman, 'How Does Information's Repetition Affect Its Believability?', *Milkman Delivers*, 26 November 2024, https://katymilkman.substack.com/p/how-does-informations-repetition.

39 Robert Ralston, 'Make Us Great Again: The Causes of Declinism in Major Powers', *Security Studies* 31, no. 4 (2022): 667–702, https://doi.org/10.1080/09636412.2022.2133626.

40 Jonathan Wolfe and Emmett Lindner, 'Trump Took Office, Vowing "America's Decline Is Over"', *The New York Times*, 21 January 2025, https://www.nytimes.com/2025/01/21/briefing/trump-gaza-climate.html.

41 George M. Constantinides, Maurizio Montone, Valerio Potì and Stella Spilioti, 'Sentiment, Productivity, and Economic Growth', NBER Working Paper no. 31031 (Cambridge, MA: National Bureau of Economic Research, 2023).

42 Laura Young, '10 Unicorns That Were Founded During Recessions', *Republic*, 27 May 2022, https://www.republic.co/blog/10-unicorns-founded-during-recessions/.

43 Harvard Business Review, 'Should You Launch Products During a Recession?', September–October 2023.

44 Jonathan M. Ellen, Nancy S. Hessol, Willi McCright, Susan F. Kohn and Willi McFarland, 'Socioeconomic Differences in HIV Testing and Return for Test Results among Young Men', *Journal of Adolescent Health* 34, no. 2 (2004): 97–104.

45 Lauren Eskreis-Winkler and Ayelet Fishbach, 'Not Learning from Failure – The Greatest Failure of All', *Psychological Science* 30, no. 12 (2019): 1733–44, https://doi.org/10.1177/0956797619881133.

46 K. C. Diwas, Bradley R. Staats and Francesca Gino, 'Learning from My Success and from Others' Failure: Evidence from Minimally Invasive Cardiac Surgery', *Harvard Business School Working Knowledge*, Working Paper no. 12–065, 19 July 2012, https://www.hbs.edu/ris/Publication%20Files/12–065_424cf0f7-a97c-4eb4–867c-fe6198c31763.pdf.

47 David Rock, 'SCARF: A Brain-Based Model for Collaborating with and Influencing Others', *NeuroLeadership Journal*, no. 1 (2008): 44–52.

48 Gallup, 'How Employees' Strengths Make Your Company Stronger', 2016,

https://www.gallup.com/workplace/231605/employees-strengths-company-stronger.aspx.
49 Hal J. Whiting, Theresa Kline and Lorne Sulsky, 'The Performance Appraisal Congruency Scale: An Assessment of Person-Environment Fit', *International Journal of Productivity and Performance Management* 57, no. 3 (2008): 223–36.
50 Marcial Losada and Emily Heaphy, 'The Role of Positivity and Connectivity in the Performance of Business Teams: A Nonlinear Dynamics Model', *American Behavioral Scientist* 47, no. 6 (2004): 740–65, https://doi.org/10.1177/0002764203260208.

The Second Principle

1 Dr Seuss, *Oh, the Places You'll Go!* (New York: Random House, 1990).
2 J. H. Wearden, 'Paul Janet and Changes in the Apparent Speed of Passage of Time with Aging', *Timing & Time Perception* 10, no. 3 (2021): 279–89, https://doi.org/10.1163/22134468-bja10049.
3 Philip G. Zimbardo and John N. Boyd, 'Putting Time in Perspective: A Valid, Reliable Individual-Differences Metric', *Journal of Personality and Social Psychology* 77, no. 6 (1999): 1271–88, https://doi.org/10.1037/0022–3514.77.6.1271.
4 Pink Floyd, 'Time', track 5 on *The Dark Side of the Moon*, Harvest Records, 1973.
5 Stephen Hawking, *Black Holes and Baby Universes and Other Essays* (New York: Bantam Books, 1993).
6 Vitality, '10 Years of Britain's Healthiest Workplace: The Changing Face of the UK at Work', accessed 20 August 2025, https://adviser.vitality.co.uk/campaigns/britains-healthiest-workplace-10-year-insights/.
7 Timothy A. Salthouse, 'The Processing-Speed Theory of Adult Age Differences in Cognition', *Psychological Review* 103, no. 3 (1996): 403–28, https://doi.org/10.1037/0033–295x.103.3.403.
8 Vitality and the London School of Economics and Political Science, *The Vitality Habit Index: How to Create Habits for a Longer, Healthier Life* (London: Vitality, 2024).
9 John Hattie, *Visible Learning: A Synthesis of Over 800 Meta-Analyses Relating to Achievement* (London: Routledge, 2009).
10 John Sweller, 'Cognitive Load during Problem Solving: Effects on Learning', *Cognitive Science* 12, no. 2 (1988): 257–85, https://doi.org/10.1207/s15516709cog1202_4.
11 Robert K. Merton, 'The Matthew Effect in Science: The Reward and Communication Systems of Science Are Considered', *Science* 159, no. 3810 (1968): 56–83, https://doi.org/10.1126/science.159.3810.56.
12 Alan M. Collins and Elizabeth F. Loftus, 'A Spreading-Activation Theory

of Semantic Processing', *Psychological Review* 82, no. 6 (1975): 407–28, https://doi.org/10.1037/0033-295X.82.6.407.

13 Donald Hebb, *The Organization of Behaviour: A Neuropsychological Theory* (New York: Wiley, 1949).

14 Ewing Marion Kauffman Foundation, 'Who is the Entrepreneur? New Entrepreneurs in the United States, 1996–2021', *Trends in Entrepreneurship Series* (Kansas City, Missouri, October 2022).

15 Robert Roy Britt, 'Think You're Too Old to Start a Business? Research Says You're Wrong', *CO– by US Chamber of Commerce*, 14 December 2020, https://www.uschamber.com/co/grow/thrive/middle-aged-entrepreneurs-success.

16 Pierre Azoulay, Benjamin Jones, J. Daniel Kim and Javier Miranda, 'Research: The Average Age of a Successful Startup Founder is 45', *Harvard Business Review*, 11 July 2018, https://hbr.org/2018/07/research-the-average-age-of-a-successful-startup-founder-is-45.

17 Adrian Bejan, 'Why the Days Seem Shorter as We Get Older', *European Review* 27, no. 2 (2019): 187–94, https://doi.org/10.1017/S1062798718000741.

18 Aditi Subramaniam, 'Time Perception: How Our Brains Shape Our Sense of Reality', *Psychology Today*, 30 March 2023, https://www.psychologytoday.com/za/blog/parenting-from-a-neuroscience-perspective/202303/time-perception-how-our-brains-shape-our.

19 James Clear, 'The Downside of Work-Life Balance', *James Clear*, 10 February 2020, https://jamesclear.com/four-burners-theory.

20 Ray Dalio, *Principles: Life and Work* (New York: Simon & Schuster, 2017).

21 Jim Loehr and Tony Schwartz, *The Power of Full Engagement: Managing Energy, Not Time, Is the Key to High Performance and Personal Renewal* (New York: Free Press, 2003).

22 Robin Sharma, *The 5AM Club: Own Your Morning, Elevate Your Life* (Toronto: HarperCollins Canada, 2018).

23 Gallup, *State of the Global Workplace: 2024 Report* (Washington, DC: Gallup, 2024), https://www.ahtd.org/files/state-of-the-global-workplace-2024-key-insights.pdf.

24 Munich Re Automation Solutions Ltd, 'VitalityLife (UK)', accessed 20 August 2025, https://www.munichre.com/automation-solutions/en/resources/case-studies/vitalitylife-uk.html.

25 Vitality Group, 'AIA and Discovery Launch "AIA Vitality" in Asia-Pacific', 3 January 2014, https://www.vitalitygroup.com/insights/aia-and-discovery-launch-aia-vitality-in-asia-pacific/.

26 John Hancock, 'John Hancock Leaves Traditional Life Insurance Model Behind to Incentivize Longer, Healthier Lives', *PR Newswire*, 19 September 2018, https://www.prnewswire.com/news-releases/john-hancock-leaves-traditional-life-insurance-model-behind-to-incentivize-longer-healthier-lives-300715351.html.

27 Staff Writer, 'John Hancock Doubles Down on Wearable-Tech with Vitality Partnership', *Reinsurance News*, 20 September 2018, https://www.reinsurancene.ws/john-hancock-doubles-down-on-wearable-tech-with-vitality-partnership/.

28 Robert Cummings, 'How Shared Value Insurance Is Transforming People's Lives and The Industry', *Forbes*, 8 September 2021, https://www.forbes.com/sites/sap/2021/09/08/how-shared-value-insurance-is-transforming-peoples-lives-and-the-industry/.

29 Max Kleiber, 'Body Size and Metabolism', *Hilgardia* 6, no. 11 (1932): 315–53.

30 Geoffrey B. West, James H. Brown and Brian J. Enquist, 'A General Model for the Origin of Allometric Scaling Laws in Biology', *Science* 276, no. 5309 (1997): 122–26, https://doi.org/10.1126/science.276.5309.122.

31 Robert M. Metcalfe, 'Metcalfe's Law: A Network Becomes More Valuable as It Reaches More Users', *InfoWorld* 17, no. 40 (1995): 53.

32 Chris Zook and James Allen, *The Founder's Mentality: How to Overcome the Predictable Crises of Growth* (Boston: Harvard Business Review Press, 2016).

33 Ronald Coase, 'The Nature of the Firm', *Economica* 4, no. 16 (1937): 386–405.

The Third Principle

1 Hersh Shefrin and Meir Statman, 'The Disposition to Sell Winners Too Early and Ride Losers Too Long: Theory and Evidence', *The Journal of Finance* 40, no. 3 (July 1985): 777–90, https://doi.org/10.1111/j.1540–6261.1985.tb05002.x.

2 Terrance Odean, 'Are Investors Reluctant to Realize Their Losses?', *The Journal of Finance* 53, no. 5 (1998): 1775–98, https://doi.org/10.1111/0022–1082.00072.

3 Beth E. Meyerowitz and Shelly Chaiken, 'The Effect of Message Framing on Breast Self-Examination Attitudes, Intentions, and Behavior', *Journal of Personality and Social Psychology* 52, no. 3 (1987): 500–10, https://doi.org/10.1037/0022–3514.52.3.500.

4 Praveen Aggarwal, Sung Youl Jun and Jong Ho Huh, 'Scarcity Messages: A Consumer Competition Perspective', *Journal of Advertising* 40, no. 3 (2011): 19–30, https://doi.org/10.2753/JOA0091–3367400302.

5 Devin G. Pope and Maurice E. Schweitzer, 'Is Tiger Woods Loss Averse? Persistent Bias in the Face of Experience, Competition, and High Stakes', *American Economic Review* 101, no. 1 (2011): 129–57, https://doi.org/10.1257/aer.101.1.129.

6 Michael Bar-Eli, Ofer H. Azar, Ilana Ritov, Yael Keidar-Levin and Galit Schein, 'Action Bias among Elite Soccer Goalkeepers: The Case of Penalty

Kicks', *Journal of Economic Psychology* 28, no. 5 (2007): 606–21, https://doi.org/10.1016/j.joep.2006.12.002.

7 Matt Goldman and Justin Rao, 'Loss Aversion Around a Fixed Reference Point in Highly Experienced Agents', *SSRN Working Paper*, June 2017, https://ssrn.com/abstract=2988575.

8 Marco Hafner, Jack Pollard and Christian Van Stolk, 'Incentives and Physical Activity: An Assessment of the Association Between Vitality's Active Rewards with Apple Watch Benefit and Sustained Physical Activity Improvements', *RAND Health Quarterly* 9, no. 1 (2020), https://www.rand.org/pubs/periodicals/health-quarterly/issues/v9/n1/04.html.

9 Edwin A. Locke and Gary P. Latham, *A Theory of Goal-Setting and Task Performance* (Englewood Cliffs, NJ: Prentice Hall, 1990).

10 Eric Klinger, 'Goal Commitments and the Content of Thoughts and Dreams: Basic Principles', *Frontiers in Psychology* 4 (2013), https://doi.org/10.3389/fpsyg.2013.00415.

11 Chip Heath, Richard P. Larrick and George Wu, 'Goals as Reference Points', *Cognitive Psychology* 38, no. 1 (1999): 79–109, https://doi.org/10.1006/cogp.1998.0708.

12 James Clear, *Atomic Habits: An Easy & Proven Way to Build Good Habits & Break Bad Ones* (New York: Avery, 2018).

13 Clark L. Hull, 'The Goal-Gradient Hypothesis and Maze Learning', *Psychological Review* 39, no. 1 (1932): 25–43, https://doi.org/10.1037/h0072640.

14 Ran Kivetz, Oleg Urminsky and Yuhuang Zheng, 'The Goal-Gradient Hypothesis Resurrected: Purchase Acceleration, Illusionary Goal Progress, and Customer Retention', *Journal of Marketing Research* 43, no. 1 (2006): 39–58, https://doi.org/10.1509/jmkr.43.1.39.

15 Reid Forgrave, '"All It Is Is Pain": The Olympian Testing the Limits of Endurance,' *The New York Times Magazine*, 5 February 2026, https://www.nytimes.com/2026/02/05/magazine/jessie-diggins-ski-winter-olympics-milan.html.

16 Daniel Duane, 'Opinion: El Capitan, My El Capitan', *The New York Times*, 9 June 2017, https://www.nytimes.com/2017/06/09/opinion/el-capitan-my-el-capitan.html.

17 Victoria Husted Medvec, Scott F. Madey and Thomas Gilovich, 'When Less Is More: Counterfactual Thinking and Satisfaction Among Olympic Medallists', *Journal of Personality and Social Psychology* 69, no. 4 (1995): 603–10, https://doi.org/10.1037/0022–3514.69.4.603.

18 William M. Hedgcock, Andrea W. Luangrath and Raelyn Webster, 'Counterfactual Thinking and Facial Expressions Among Olympic Medallists: A Conceptual Replication of Medvec, Madey, and Gilovich's (1995) Findings', *Journal of Experimental Psychology* 150, no. 6 (2021): e13–e21, https://doi.org/10.1037/xge0000992.

19 Christian Ehrlich, 'Evaluation of the Happiness Through Goal-Setting Training', *Psychological Reports* 126, no. 4 (2022): 1910–32, https://doi.org/10.1177/00332941211071007.
20 Arthur C. Brooks, 'The Success-Then-Happiness Fallacy', *Harvard Business Review*, 12 August 2025.
21 Arthur C. Brooks, *The Happiness Files: Insights on Work and Life* (Boston: Harvard Business Review Press, 2025).
22 Charles R. Snyder, *The Psychology of Hope: You Can Get There from Here* (New York: Free Press, 1994).
23 Kelly McMasters, 'Why I Write My Own Obituary Every Year', *The New York Times*, 29 September 2024, https://www.nytimes.com/2024/09/29/opinion/write-your-own-obituary.html.
24 Letters page, 'I Write My Obituary, So I Can Live a Better Life', *The New York Times*, 13 October 2024, https://www.nytimes.com/2024/10/13/opinion/letters/writing-own-obituary.html.
25 Dan Ariely, *The Upside of Irrationality: The Unexpected Benefits of Defying Logic at Work and at Home* (New York: Harper, 2010).
26 Dan Ariely, *Painful Lessons* (Duke University, 2008).
27 Scott D. Anthony, Alasdair Trotter and Evan I. Schwartz, 'The Top 20 Business Transformations of the Last Decade', *Harvard Business Review*, 24 September 2019.
28 Simon Sinek, *Start with Why: How Great Leaders Inspire Everyone to Take Action* (New York: Portfolio/Penguin, 2011).
29 Deborah Wetzel, 'Bolsa Família: Brazil's Quiet Revolution', World Bank, 4 November 2013, https://www.worldbank.org/en/news/opinion/2013/11/04/bolsa-familia-Brazil-quiet-revolution.
30 Amie Shei, 'Brazil's Conditional Cash Transfer Program Associated With Declines in Infant Mortality Rates', *Health Affairs* 32, no. 7 (2013): 1274–81, https://doi.org/10.1377/hlthaff.2012.0827.
31 Lucia Bosone and Frederic Martinez, 'When, How and Why Is Loss-Framing More Effective than Gain-and Non-Gain-Framing in the Promotion of Detection Behaviours', *International Review of Social Psychology* 30, no. 1 (2017): 184–92, https://doi.org/10.5334/irsp.15.
32 'Growth Could Triple if SA Government Reform Accelerates, Says Think-Tank', *Marketwatch*, 7 October 2024, https://marketwatch.com.na/government/growth-could-triple-if-sa-government-reform-accelerates-says-think-tank2024-10-07135837. Also, Carol Paton, 'Growth Could Triple if Government Reform Accelerates, Says Think-Tank', *News24*, 4 October 2024.

The Fourth Principle

1 Michael E. Porter, Mark R. Kramer and Aldo Sesia, 'Discovery Limited', Harvard Business School Case 715–423 (December 2014; revised July 2021).

2 Albert-László Barabási and Réka Albert, 'Emergence of Scaling in Random Networks', *Science* 286, no. 5439 (1999): 509–12, https://doi.org/10.1126/science.286.5439.509.

3 Sean Hechtlinger et al., 'The Psychology of Life's Most Important Decisions', *American Psychologist* (2024), https://doi.org/10.1037/amp0001439.

4 Benoit B. Mandelbrot, *Fractals: Form, Chance, and Dimension* (San Francisco: W. H. Freeman, 1977).

5 Philip W. Anderson, 'Some Thoughts about Distribution in Economics', in *The Economy as an Evolving Complex System II*, ed. W. Brian Arthur (Boca Raton, FL: CRC Press, 1997).

6 Michael E. Porter and Mark R. Kramer, 'Creating Shared Value: How to Reinvent Capitalism – and Unleash a Wave of Innovation and Growth', *Harvard Business Review* 89, no. 1/2 (January–February 2011): 62–77.

7 Vitality and London School of Economics and Political Science, *The Vitality Habit Index: How to Create Habits for a Longer, Healthier Life* (March 2024).

8 Gareth van Zyl, 'Discovery Launches Free Apple Watch Initiative', *News24*, 1 December 2015, https://www.news24.com/business/discovery-launches-free-apple-watch-initiative-20151201.

9 'Discovery to Give Away a Free Apple Watch to Vitality Members', *BusinessTech*, 1 December 2015, https://businesstech.co.za/news/banking/105801/discovery-to-give-away-a-free-apple-watch-to-vitality-members/.

10 Toby Shapshak, 'How Incentives – And a Free Apple Watch – Make People Healthier', *Forbes*, 29 November 2018, https://www.forbes.com/sites/tobyshapshak/2018/11/29/how-incentives-and-a-free-apple-watch-make-people-healthier/.

11 Marco Hafner, Jack Pollard and Christian Van Stolk, 'Incentives and Physical Activity: An Assessment of the Association Between Vitality's Active Rewards with Apple Watch Benefit and Sustained Physical Activity Improvements' (Santa Monica, CA: RAND Corporation, 2018).

12 Jodi Wishnia, Dave Strugnell, Anja Smith and Shivani Ranchod, 'The Supply of and Need for Medical Specialists in South Africa' (Cape Town: Percept, 2019).

13 National Department of Health, *2030 Human Resources for Health Strategy: Investing in the Health Workforce for Universal Health Coverage*, final ed. (Pretoria: National Department of Health, 2022), https://www.health.gov.za/wp-content/uploads/2022/03/HRH-Strategy-Final.pdf.

14 World Health Organization, 'Global Strategy on Human Resources for Health: Workforce 2030' (Geneva: World Health Organization, 2016).
15 Peter E. Earl, 'G. L. S. Shackle's Introspective Behavioral Economics', *Journal of Behavioral Economics for Policy* 2, no. 1 (2018): 19–23.
16 Shell, 'What Are Shell Scenarios?' *Shell Global*, accessed 20 August 2025, https://www.shell.com/news-and-insights/scenarios/what-are-shell-scenarios.html.
17 Adam Kahane, 'Learning from Experience: The Mont Fleur Scenario Exercise', *Reos Partners*, March 2010, https://reospartners.com/blog/learnings-mont-fleur-scenarios.
18 Jared Diamond, 'That Daily Shower Can Be a Killer', *The New York Times*, 28 January 2013.
19 Eric Almquist, Mitchell Leiman, Darrell Rigby and Alex Roth, 'Taking the Measure of Your Innovation Performance', Bain & Company, accessed 20 August 2025, https://www.bain.com/insights/taking-the-measure-of-your-innovation-performance.
20 Jan Mischke et al., 'The Power of One: How Standout Firms Grow National Productivity', McKinsey Global Institute, 6 May 2025, https://www.mckinsey.com/mgi/our-research/the-power-of-one-how-standout-firms-grow-national-productivity.
21 David Wallace-Wells, 'Researchers Identified the Key Breakthrough for GLP-1 Drugs in the 1980s, but Pfizer Walked Away', *The New York Times*, 25 December 2024, https://www.nytimes.com/2024/12/25/health/glp-1-drugs-pfizer.html.
22 Christian S. Hendershot et al., 'Once-Weekly Semaglutide in Adults with Alcohol Use Disorder: A Randomized Clinical Trial', *JAMA Psychiatry*, published online 12 February 2025, https://doi.org/10.1001/jamapsychiatry.2024.4789.
23 Julia Kollewe, 'Vitality Is First to Offer Weight-Loss Jabs', *The Guardian*, 15 February 2025, https://www.theguardian.com/society/2025/feb/12/uk-health-insurer-vitality-to-offer-members-discounted-anti-obesity-drugs.
24 Jeffrey S. Flier, 'Drug Development Failure: How GLP-1 Development Was Abandoned in 1990', *Perspectives in Biology and Medicine* 67, no. 3 (2024): 325–36, https://doi.org/10.1353/pbm.2024.a936213.
25 Eshe Nelson, 'How Ozempic and Weight Loss Drugs Are Reshaping Denmark's Economy', *The New York Times*, 28 August 2023, https://www.nytimes.com/2023/08/28/business/ozempic-denmark-economy.html.
26 Ernest O'Boyle Jr and Herman Aguinis, 'The Best and the Rest: Revisiting the Norm of Normality of Individual Performance', *Personnel Psychology* 65, no. 1 (2012): 79–119, https://doi.org/10.1111/j.1744–6570.2011.01247.x.
27 Josh Bersin, 'The Myth of the Bell Curve: Look for the Hyper-Performers', *Forbes*, 19 February 2014, https://www.forbes.com/sites/joshbersin/2014/02/19/the-myth-of-the-bell-curve-look-for-the-hyper-performers/.

28 'How to Spot a Genius', *The Economist*, accessed 20 December 2025, https://www.economist.com/finance-and-economics/2025/09/23/how-to-spot-a-genius.

29 Josh Bivens, Elise Gould and Jori Kandra, 'CEO Pay Declined in 2023: But It Has Soared 1,085% Since 1978 Compared with a 24% Rise in Typical Workers' Pay', *Economic Policy Institute*, 19 September 2024, https://www.epi.org/publication/ceo-pay-in-2023/.

30 Office for National Statistics, 'Public Sector Employment, March 2025', UK Government, accessed 20 August 2025, https://www.ons.gov.uk/employmentandlabourmarket/peopleinwork/publicsectorpersonnel/bulletins/publicsectoremployment/march2025.

31 Office for National Statistics, 'UK Labour Market: June 2025', UK Government, accessed 20 August 2025, https://www.ons.gov.uk/employmentandlabourmarket/peopleinwork/employmentandemployeetypes/bulletins/uklabourmarket/june2025.

32 Endeavor South Africa, 'Did You Know, Endeavor Has Research That Shows That High Growth Entrepreneurs Have a 20 Times Multiplier in Their Ecosystems!', *Medium*, 16 July 2022, https://endeavorsouthafrica.medium.com/did-you-know-endeavor-has-research-that-shows-that-high-growth-entrepreneurs-have-a-20-times-dcbb7bf32d94.

33 Timothy J. Bartik and Nathan Sotherland, 'Local Job Multipliers in the United States: Variation with Local Characteristics and with High-Tech Shocks', *Upjohn Institute Working Paper* 19–301 (Kalamazoo, MI: W. E. Upjohn Institute for Employment Research, April 2019), https://doi.org/10.17848/wp19–301.

34 Gillian Crawley, 'How the Sausage Dog Became a Hot Dog: Popularity for the Short-Legged Puppy', *Daily Express*, 2 April 2018, https://www.express.co.uk/life-style/life/944019/dachshund-popularity-trend-why-are-dachshunds-so-popular.

INDEX

Page references in *italics* indicate images.